Black Women in Politics

Black Women in Politics

Identity, Power, and Justice in the New Millennium

National Political Science Review, Volume 16

Michael Mitchell
David Covin, editors

With Nikol Alexander-Floyd and Julia S. Jordan-Zachery, guest editors

A Publication of the National Conference of Black Political Scientists

Transaction Publishers
New Brunswick (U.S.A.) and London (U.K.)

Library of Congress Catalog Number: 2014009852
ISBN: 978-1-4128-5469-6
Printed in the United States of America

Library of Congress Cataloging-in-Publication Data

Black women in politics : identity, power, and justice in the new millennium / Michael Mitchell and David Covin, editors ; with Nikol Alexander-Floyd and Julia Jordan-Zachery, guest editors.
     pages cm
  "National Political Science Review Volume 16 (2014)."
  Includes bibliographical references.
  ISBN 978-1-4128-5469-6
  1. African American women—Political activity. 2. African American women politicians. 3. Women political scientists—United States. 4. African Americans—Politics and government—21st century. I. Mitchell, Michael, 1944- II. Covin, David, 1940- III. National political science review.
  E185.86.B5424 2014
  320.082—dc23

2014009852

Contents

Editors' Note

Volume 16 of the *National Political Science Review (NPSR)* is a special issue devoted to Black women in politics. Under the leadership of our guest editors, Volume 16 contains a collection of well-researched and tightly argued articles that examine the political experiences of African descended women in the United States, the diaspora, and the African continent from Black feminist perspectives.

African American women have continuously played a decisive role in the struggle for justice and equality in America. This role stretches across the expanse of the Black political experience and includes such figures as Harriet Tubman, Ida B. Wells, Ella Baker, and Fannie Lou Hamer. In more contemporary times, African American women have continued the tradition of struggle as demonstrated by their institutional presence in American politics, serving as Members of Congress and in state legislatures. They have also made their way as elected officials and policy makers at all levels and as strategic voting constituencies in national elections. Their counterparts in Africa and throughout the diaspora have undertaken similar efforts. In other words, Black women have carved out a presence whose dynamism deserves close scrutiny and attention.

Notwithstanding their more visible roles in the conventional institutions of politics, Black women experience cross pressures that constrain their capacities to exercise power in a variety of domains. Our guest editors focus on this point. They have selected, through peer review, research articles that take as their starting point the concept of intersectionality. Intersectionality is examined throughout these articles in analyzing the cross pressures felt by African descended women as political agents in the domains of elections, public policy, and social activism. Their challenges and initiatives are explored in public spaces, institutional behaviors, and public policy. In the end, Volume 16 of the *NPSR* makes its contribution to the work of Black feminist scholars whose efforts have expanded our understanding about the dynamics of power in the study of politics writ large. We thank our guest editors, Nikol Alexander-Floyd of Rutgers University and Julia Jordan-Zachery of Providence College, in assembling this *NPSR* special issue on *Black Women in Politics*.

This volume also contains other works that complement the major articles in this issue. They include an essay on Black leadership, radical versus moderate, in the city of New Orleans and one on the contours of the *Shelby v. Holder* Supreme Court decision. The editors also introduce a new series comprising tabular representations on selected trends in Black politics. The book review section provides a lively and fully critical discussion on selected recent works related to Black women in politics.

This issue also notes the passing of two pioneers in the study of Black politics, namely William (Nick) Nelson and Hanes Walton, Jr.

Guest Editors' Note

In recent years, we have witnessed increased attention being paid to the concept of intersectionality in the social sciences. As conceived by Black women and other women of color, intersectionality, as an approach to politics and research, accounts for and addresses the mutually constitutive forces of race, class, and gender. Much of the research produced under the rubric of "intersectionality," however, fails to take into account the extensive literature on the topic, particularly the research and theories produced by Black women or other women of color. Moreover, despite the new-found popularity of intersectionality, there is still a relative dearth of literature on Black women as political subjects and the role of gender in Black politics. Given the role that Black women play in politics—as voters, as social movement and community activists, as elected officials, and as subjects of public policy discourse—it is imperative that we expend greater energy and attention on investigating Black political women. This special issue on Black women in politics—the first to appear in any political science journal—provides a much-needed context for exploring recent developments in Black women in politics as a subfield of political science in its own right. It highlights three dimensions—identity, power, and justice—that are foundational to intersectionality theory and politics as developed by Black women and other women of color.

Centering Black women as subjects of research has been a fundamental component of Black feminist theory and politics. As the Combahee River Collective's classic statement of Black feminist ideology puts it: "This focusing on our own oppression is embodied in the concept of identity politics. We believe that the most profound and potentially the most radical politics come directly out of our own identity . . ." (The Combahee River Collective 1995, 234). Significantly, while mainstream feminist theory views identity politics as a limited, monovocal definition of women's experiences and politics, one that attempts to speak for women as an essentialized category of difference, radical Black feminists operate from a complex and variegated framework that captures the differences among Black women's lives and looks at a range of important factors related to oppression, as opposed to attempting to foreground one single dimension of identity. This form of identity politics, as Duchess Harris states, is "polyvocal" (Harris 2001, 300). Furthermore, according to one of the Combahee River Collective's founders, Barbara Smith, the term identity politics was first promulgated by their Black feminist organization; as she remarks, "'We [the Combahee River Collective] came up with the term 'identity politics'" (Smith, quoted in Harris 2001, 300). The idea of identity politics, first espoused by Black feminists in the Combahee River Collective, has been lost in the ruins of academic debate. It needs to be recovered so that we can understand identity in a sophisticated way in order to inform our political assessments, priorities, and actions.

One might suggest that Black women have reached a level of success such that their needs are secondary to other political concerns in Black communities, and/or that we live in a postracial, postfeminist moment. To be sure, one can point to markers of formal equality for Black women in terms of appointed officials, greater educational access, and greater voter participation. Such indicators, however, have to be viewed in a much broader context. Black women are still disproportionately represented among the poor, are the fastest growing segment of the population being incarcerated, are relegated to the lowest paid jobs in the economy, and face serious barriers for advancement and a "concrete wall" (Bell and Nkomo 2001) in terms of promotion, even in the professions. Focusing on models of success obscures the more mundane realities of oppression that Black women confront daily.

Indeed, there is a need, now, more than ever, to center Black women in our research. In so doing, we can better trace the operation of power as it is manifest in this historical moment when individuals and groups cling to postcivil rights, postfeminist fantasies, as opposed to the realities that people actually have to live. Given that Black women are collectively impacted by a range of structural forms of oppression, investigating their lives and the politics in which they are embedded, and that they develop, provides a window into a multitude of contemporary political issues, from crime and punishment, public health issues, such as the HIV/AIDS crisis; labor market segregation/segmentation to discrimination in the workplace; educational access, hate crimes; geopolitical concerns; sex trafficking; and violence in intimate partner relationships and in war.

A radical Black feminist understanding of identity politics that centers Black women as political subjects, moreover, not only best exposes the operation of power, but also places a priority on justice as the goal of academic inquiry. In the midst of advanced corporatization and neoliberalization of the academy, scholars are rewarded for research focusing on apolitical aims, individual subjectivity, or questions of representation outside of any connection to macro-institutional concerns, such as public policy or legal change. Research on Black women in politics, from a radical Black feminist perspective, demonstrates how a scholarly focus on Black political women and the forces that impact their lives illuminates and helps address a range of political phenomena, including, but not limited to, the production of founding narratives and political and social arrangements of the United States; the rationalizing ideologies that legitimate and sustain colonial and neocolonial relationships; the politics of cultural production and representation, and their relationship to material conditions of inequality; the sedimentation of structural inequality; and the creation of social and economic policy. This type of Black feminist research is not merely aimed at describing phenomena and outlining political happenings as ends in themselves, but is ultimately motivated by a desire to challenge and transform existing inequitable relationships and conditions in Black communities. This special issue on Black women in politics, thus, seeks to advance an examination of identity, politics, and justice in the best tradition of radical theorizing and politics in Black communities. Each piece makes a substantive contribution to the subfield of Black women in politics and serves as a model, methodologically and otherwise, upon which future work can be based.

How do we begin to theorize Black women's political activity? How do we begin to explain how Black women are treated in political science research? In this special edition, the contributing authors take up these general questions. The articles contribute to cutting-edge research that pushes our understanding of Black women's politics across a wide spectrum of issues. We have organized the articles into three general groups. The first group concentrates on the "state" of the discipline. Alexander-Floyd and Jordan-Zachery's articles interrogate Black women's treatment by the discipline of political science, in general, and in political science intersectionality research, specifically. In "Why Political Scientists Don't Study Black Women, But Historians and Sociologists Do: On Intersectionality and the Remapping of the Study of Black Political Women," Alexander-Floyd, comparing political science to sister disciplines, considers the extent to which political scientists investigate the lives of Black women and issues of race, class, and gender more broadly. Utilizing insights from Black feminist geography, she compares the production of research on Black women across four fields–political science, sociology, history, and economics. Her analysis shows the "absented presence" of Black women in political science research and how garreting can provide a means of responding to such treatment of Black women. Alexander-Floyd concludes that re-creation of the intellectual geography of political science into a space that intellectually and profession-ally addresses the presence of Black women would require a Perestroika-like effort to restructure the discipline. Jordan-Zachery takes up the question of how the politics of research, specifically intersectionality research, result in the further marginalization of Black women. According to Jordan-Zachery, there is an omission project occurring in published political science research generally, and within intersectionality research specif-ically. To explore the politics of intersectionality research, she examines the relationship between the novel, *The Help*, and intersectionality research to show how these cultural and academic phenomena mirror each other and reinforce and normalize the treatment of Black women. She posits that the misappropriation of intersectionality as a theory and approach to research, wherein Black women's theories are invoked only to silence their voices through exclusion parallels the misappropriation of Black women's voices for the advancement of the White female main character in *The Help*. In both instances, Black women's voices are muted and their quest for social justice stymied.

In the second group, Ndubuizu's and Jordan-Zachery and Wilson's articles examine the relationship between discourse, cultural politics, and the policymaking process. Ndubuizu, via a critical discourse analysis from a Black feminist perspective, analyzes how gender and other identity markers shape and influence the formation of Black leadership. Her study examines how D.C. Councilmember Marion Barry promoted conservative welfare and public/rental housing reforms between 2007 and 2011 via his use of narratives of economic and social mobility, class-based notions of proper parenting practices, Black paternalism, and Black cultural pathology logic in order to increase his political visibility. She contends that race-first politicians, such as Marion Barry, are able to maintain their relevance in local politics, because their political agenda, coupled with their discursive posturing, works to reinforce "culturally accepted yet problematic gendered relations be-tween Black male officials and Black women." In "Talking about Gender while Ignoring Race and Class," Jordan-Zachery and Wilson in their critical policy analysis of The Fair Pay Act and the Paycheck Fairness Act, explore how differences between and within groups of women are employed in the framing of pay equity. They conduct a discourse analysis of the floor speeches of members of congress, analyzing if and how congress members recognize differences between and within groups of women. They maintain that utilizing a particular gender ideology in the framing and analysis of such policies serves to obscure and perpetuate inequalities both within and between various groups of women. Jordan-Zachery and Wilson suggest the use of a Black feminist critical policy analysis framework to allow for analyses that concentrate on the frames themselves and how power dynamics and hierarchies are employed in the frames. According to the authors, such work is important for recognizing women's differential experiences with labor force discrimination and can enhance the effectiveness of any pay equity policies.

Wallace, Brown, and Block and Haynes, in the third group, explore how Black women make space for their political engagement, whether in the role of civil society organizers, elected officials, or as the First (Black) Lady of the United States, and how we understand their politics in such spaces. These articles outline the politics of the intersection of raced-gendered identity, among other identity markers, and Black feminist praxis. As argued by Wallace, dominant understandings of women's political activities tend to exclude the varied experiences of marginalized women. Furthermore, extant research on indigenous civil society organizations in developing countries often concentrates on groups with closer ties to international donors. She posits that such a limited focus is problematic as the distinction between public and private spaces are reified thereby limiting our theorizing of "politics beyond distinct engagements through formalized advocacy." Wallace addresses this research void by bringing together intersectionality and syncre-nationalism to analyze the ways in which "Muslim women in Nigeria construct and deploy an inclusive politics." She relies on semi-structured interviews and participant observation to show how these women's organizational efforts simultaneously occupy public and domestic spheres, while utilizing different discursive approaches to addressing gender inequality. Brown's article, "Black Women's Pathways to the Statehouse: The Impact of Race/Gender Identities," provides a case study of Black women Maryland state legislators with the goal of illustrating how their race/gender identity influences the experiences and barriers they faced in their initial quest for legislative office. Using feminist life histories, gathered through in-depth interviews, Brown's investigation allows her to "fully uncover how a legislator's race/gender identities have been enacted and experienced over time rather than solely relying on a snapshot of a particular period in her life." This study advances our understanding of the functioning of race and gender in electoral politics.

Block and Haynes's contribution, "Taking to the Airwaves: Using Content Analyses of Survey Toplines and Filmographies to Test the 'Michelle Obama Image Transformation' (MOIT) Hypothesis," explores how Mrs. Obama's public image is transformed via her various media appearances. In their content analysis of over a hundred toplines (summary documents of survey results) from nearly a dozen commercial polls during the 2008 and 2012 presidential campaign cycles, combined with Michelle Obama's filmography, they show Mrs. Obama's polling numbers are "influenced by both the *frequency* and the *type* of TV appearances she makes." As they demonstrate, Mrs. Obama's image transformation seeks to reconcile "the sometimes-competing motives of racial uplift and feminine respectability." This research expands not only existing understandings of the implications of Mrs. Obama's image transformation, but also seeks to document the impact of symbols of Black womanhood on the public's perceptions of not only Mrs. Obama but Black women in general.

Collectively, these varied articles make an important contribution to our understanding of Black political women. They are diverse in their foci—from public policy, to political figures, to social movements, to meta-questions regarding the politics of research—and methodological approaches—featuring participant observation, life histories, critical discourse analyses, topline surveys, statistical analyses, and feminist theorizing. We trust that this collection will enliven academic discussion, inform future research, and provide a basis for facilitating liberatory politics for Black women and Black communities.

References

Bell, Ella, and Stella Nkomo. 2001. *Our Separate Ways: Black and White Women and the Struggle for Professional Identity*. Boston, MA: Harvard Business School Press.

Harris, Duchess. 2001. "From the Kennedy Commission to the Combahee Collective: Black Feminist Organizing, 1960–80." In *Sisters in the Struggle: African American Women in the Civil Rights-Black Power Movement*, ed. Bettye Collier-Thomas and V. P. Franklin, 280–301. New York: New York University Press.

The Combahee River Collective. 1995. "A Black Feminist Statement." In *Words of Fire: An Anthology of African-American Feminist Thought*, ed. Beverly Guy-Sheftall, 232–40. New York: The New Press.

Special Issue Articles

Why Political Scientists Don't Study Black Women, But Historians and Sociologists Do: On Intersectionality and the Remapping of the Study of Black Political Women

Nikol Alexander-Floyd
Rutgers University, New Brunswick

Recent discussions on intersectionality in political science have sparked increased attention in research to race, gender, and other identity categories, particularly in terms of "descriptive" statistical analysis (Jordan-Zachery 2007). Given that Black women and other women of color developed intersectionality as a means of assessing and confronting their own life circumstances, it behooves us to consider the extent to which political scientists investigate the lives of Black women and issues of race, class, and gender more broadly. More specifically, what do we know about the comparative progress of scholarship on Black women and Black gender politics in the academic field of political science as compared to other disciplines? What are some of the disciplinary challenges that beset the would-be Black feminist political scientist? How do the limits of research on Black political women point to deeper problems regarding political and epistemological orientations of political science?[1] In this essay, I offer not a comprehensive multidisciplinary analysis, but a broad snapshot of four sister disciplines: political science, sociology, history, and economics. I provide a general landscape of the research on Black women in these fields both to underscore the relative dearth of literature on Black women in political science, and to set the stage for a conversation about how best to influence the social production of political science as a disciplinary and intellectual "space" as well as the "place" of Black women within it.

An emphasis on space and place in this essay helps me to better conceptualize the politics at work in the knowledge production of the discipline, and I offer, here, a few clarifying definitions. "Space," as we know, "is regarded largely as a dimension within which matter is located or a grid within which substantive items are contained" (Agnew 2011, 316). However, following McKittrick (2006), I see both space, the general physical and metaphorical context, and place, the specific meanings and patterns of embodiment or social, political, or other forms of relating within a given location or context, as *socially* produced and contested. Indeed, as Dorthe Possing relates, the "politics of place": "relates to how places, such as regions, localities, nations, [or disciplines] are used to define groups of people in relation to other groups of people and is about constructing and defining the boundaries of a place, and involves negotiations about who and what is 'inside' and 'outside' that place" (Possing 2010, 2). I draw attention to the raced and gendered dimensions of political science as an academic space, and the place-making politics necessary to investigate Black political women.[2]

In addressing these issues of gender, race, space, and place as they relate to Black political women and research, I proceed along two fronts—the first is statistical, assessing the percentages of articles on Black women in political science, specifically as compared to history, sociology, and economics; the second part is interpretive/theoretical, reviewing the possible motivations for the paucity of research and suggesting how it can be counteracted. Significantly, although there are journals, such as *Politics & Gender* in political science and *Gender & Society* in sociology, that showcase work on women and gender politics, I focus on mainstream journals in these disciplines, as opposed to those connected to particular subfields, in order to highlight (as I further amplify below) the "absented presence" (Walcott 2001; McKittrick 2006) of Black political women as subjects of research in the space of mainstream political science. This allows us to account for the paradox of Black women's hypervisibility and centrality to politics, on the one hand, and Black women's invisibility or "absented presence," on the other. After surveying mainstream journals within each discipline, I utilize this survey to stage a conversation about the importance of centering Black political women in political science research and the place-making strategies or garreting used to illuminate Black women as subjects of research. Ultimately, I conclude that in order to re-create the intellectual geography of political science, a Perestroika-like effort to restructure the discipline as it relates to expanding research on Black women as political subjects and Black gender politics is required. By Perestroika, I refer to the decade-plus push in mainstream political science to "restructure" or redefine what constitutes knowledge and how to produce knowledge that is politically relevant (Monroe 2005). As it relates to Black political women and Black gender politics, we need to not only increase the amount of research, but also utilize a specifically Black feminist frame of reference (Alexander-Floyd 2007), one that embraces interdisciplinarity and utilizes a broader range of foci and post-positivist methodologies. I now turn to an examination of research on Black women to expose the raced and gendered spatial dimensions of political science relative to other disciplines.

Studying African American Women and Black Gender Politics across Disciplines: Overview and Research Design

Almost thirty years ago, political scientist Ernest Wilson III provoked discussion by highlighting the relative inattention given to studying Black issues in political science relative to other "sister disciplines" (Wilson 1985). Specifically, he asked:

> Does the study of Afro-American subjects occupy a different place in our discipline from that of other traditions of inquiry, and if so, why? Why does political science seem to address questions of black political behavior with less assiduity than her sister disciplines address questions of black history or black group behavior? (Wilson 1985, 601)

Wilson addressed these questions arguing that the "paradigmatic" approach of the discipline, its focus on elites and formal politics, mismatched the "empirical" reality of Black politics, which focused on "bottom up" politics and both formal *and* informal politics, such as social movement activity (604). His review of publications on Black issues in major journals between 1970 and 1985 across the disciplines of political science, history, sociology, and economics, showed political science to lag behind history and sociology in terms of publications. Subsequent examination by Wilson and Frasure (2007) revealed a consistent pattern of relative neglect from 1986 to 2003, concerning race and Black politics in political science compared to other disciplines.

For this study, I used the same approach utilized by Wilson and Frasure in terms of journal selection, the database used to survey research (i.e., JSTOR), and the search for key terms relevant to the subspecialty of Black women's studies. More specifically, I reviewed the same three top journals in each discipline, namely: *The American Political Science Review, American Journal of Political Science*, and *The Journal of Politics* in political science; *American Journal of Sociology, American Sociological Review*, and *Social Forces* in sociology; *The American Historical Review, American Quarterly*, and *Journal of American History* in history; and *American Economic Review, Journal of Political Economy*, and *The Quarterly Journal of Economics* in economics. Also, I used the same two time periods from this previous research, 1970–1985 and 1986–2003, and added a third, 2004–2008. The following terms were searched using JSTOR: "Black women," "African-American women," "Afro-American women," "Black feminism," or "womanism." Additionally, consistent with earlier work (Wilson 1985; Wilson and Frasure 2007), I examined totals for full-length articles for each period along three different axes—text only, title only, and abstract only. Each of the latter designations—text, title, and abstract only, yield related, but more or less detailed, levels of results. The full-length articles, as well as titles and abstracts, were determined using a search function in JSTOR, which allows terms to be searched throughout specific journals within particular time frames. In this way, the terms could be isolated across the three dimensions of inquiry (i.e., full-length articles, titles, and abstracts). Given the search terms' explicit focus on Black women, this study excludes those articles utilizing research on Black women, but framed under the rubric of "women of color." This approach promises to render those articles directly relevant to the area of study in question.

Some might suggest that the outcomes of this query will yield decidedly predictable results. After all, the relative inattention of political science compared to sociology and history is an anticipated outcome, given prior research on the study of race in political science compared to other fields. This study is important, however, because it provides one means of documenting—and throwing into sharp relief—the current treatment of Black women as subjects of research in mainstream journals across key traditional social science disciplines. My purpose is to let the journals serve as markers of current conditions, telling the story of political science's suppression of work on Black political women in its own valued idiom of quantitative metrics. The paucity of research on Black women in political science, moreover, can be usefully explained by joining political science's analysis of the circulation of power with geography's concerns with the politics of space and place. This conjoining can enable us to see how dominant norms construct intellectual and material space as well as one's sense of place within disciplines. Following geography scholars, such as Walcott (2001) and McKittrick (2006), I draw on the notion of an "absented presence" to explain the politics at work in the production of space in political science. For McKittrick and Walcott, Black women and Black communities, respectively, are actively elided in the production of narratives of nation, home, and belonging. Likewise, the data I assess highlight the absented presence of Black political subjects in political science research.

Findings: General Numeric and Statistical Profile

The results of this examination paint a very sobering picture regarding the state of research on Black women, particularly in political science. The data discussed below similarly bespeak the absented presence of Black women. Although Black women and Black gender politics are central to US political development, mainstream scholarship "disappears" (Alexander-Floyd 2012) them from the production of political science as an intellectual or disciplinary space.

The first-time period, 1970–1985, yielded only three, ninety-four, thirty-nine, and twenty-seven full-length articles with some mention of Black women, African-American women, Afro-American women, Black feminism, or womanism in political science, sociology, history, and economics, respectively (Table 1). Although sociology, history, and economics arguably produced more articles with the key terms related to Black women, they too marginalized the study of Black women in mainstream journals. From 1970 to 1985, the same political science journals published *no* articles with titles and abstracts indicating a relationship to Black women (Table 1).

In the second-time period reviewed, 1986–2003, all four disciplines showed progress, but political science still lagged behind sociology and history, continuing to reflect the absented presence of Black women as political subjects. Indeed, as Table 2 indicates, sociology and history were the two top performers in terms of full-length articles with some mention of research terms, with 283 and 234 full-length articles, respectively. A closer look at the results connected to title and abstract only searches, however, reveals a less optimistic picture all around. Between 1986 and 2003, for instance, political science published thirty-two full-length articles with some mention of the terms "black women," "African-American women," "Afro-American women," "Negro women," "Black feminism," or "womanism." None of the journals, however, showed titles or abstracts related to these terms. Also, although sociology had 283 full-length articles, it had only one article with the key search items, and twenty-one abstracts that contained these terms, suggesting a greater prominence of issues related to Black women in this field, compared to political science, but still a relatively small number.

A review of articles with the respective terms, published from 2004 to 2008 reveals little change in the general number and distribution of articles by discipline. Sociology continued to have the largest number of search terms with seventy-three full-length articles including at least one of the primary search terms, with history following at a close second at seventy-one, and political science and economics tied at thirteen articles a piece. None of the journals during the period had any of the key terms ("Black women," "African-American women," "Afro-American women," "negro women," "black feminism," or "womanism") as part of their titles. In terms of abstracts with key terms, sociology generated eight and political science generated two (Table 3).

The absented presence of Black women as political subjects reveals the inherently raced and gendered dimensions of political science as intellectual space. It undergirds a

Table 1,
Search Totals for Full-Length Articles (FLAs) by Titles and Abstracts, 1970–1985

	Total FLA[a]	Title Only[b]	Percentage of Total FLAs (%)	Abstract Only[c]	Percentage of Total FLAs (%)
Political Science					
The American Political Science Review	0	0	0	0	0
American Journal of Political Science	3	0	0	0	0
The Journal of Politics	3	0	0	0	0
Total	6	0	0	0	0
Sociology					
American Journal of Sociology	32	0	0	3	9
American Sociological Review	33	0	0	2	6
Social Forces	29	0	0	5	17
Total	94	0	0	10	11
History					
The American Historical Review	11	0	0	NA	NA
American Quarterly	10	0	0	NA	NA
Journal of American History	18	1	6	NA	NA
Total	39	1	3	NA	NA
Economics					
American Economic Review	19	1	5	0	0
Journal of Political Economy	8	0	0	0	0
The Quarterly Journal of Economics	0	0	0	0	0
Total	27	1	4	0	0

Source: Author's compilation of JSTOR computer-generated citations by discipline, with percentages rounded to whole numbers.

[a] Keyword search for "black women" or "African-American women" or "Afro-American women" or "negro women" or "black feminism" or "womanism" in FLAs, excluding reviews, opinion pieces, and other items. Note that the FLAs, as well as titles and abstracts, were determined using a search function in JSTOR, which allows terms to be searched throughout specific journals.

[b] Keyword search for "black women" or "African-American women" or "Afro-American women" or "negro women" or "black feminism" or "womanism" in titles only, excluding text, abstracts, author names, and captions.

[c] Keyword search for "black women" or "African-American women" or "Afro-American women" or "negro women" or "black feminism" or "womanism" in abstracts only, excluding text, titles, author names, and captions. Abstract information is not available for the history journals selected (except *American Quarterly* beginning in 2003).

dominant politics of place which suggests that political science as a discipline is inhabited by and/or is the proper "place" of White male political subjects. Oppositional political

Table 2.
Search Totals for Full-Length Articles (FLAs) by Titles and Abstracts, 1986–2003

	Total FLA[a]	Title Only[b]	Percentage of Total FLAs (%)	Abstract Only[c]	Percentage of Total FLAs (%)
Political Science					
The American Political Science Review	11	0	0	0	0
American Journal of Political Science	8	0	0	0	0
The Journal of Politics	15	0	0	0	0
Total	34	0	0	0	0
Sociology					
American Journal of Sociology	118	1	<1	5	4
American Sociological Review	72	0	0	10	14
Social Forces	93	0	0	6	6
Total	283	1	<0.5	21	7
History					
The American Historical Review	53	0	0	NA	NA
American Quarterly	81	0	0	NA	NA
Journal of American History	97	4	3	NA	NA
Total	231	4	2	NA	NA
Economics					
American Economic Review	45	7	16	0	0
Journal of Political Economy	8	0	0	0	0
The Quarterly Journal of Economics	11	0	0	0	0
Total	64	7	11	0	0

Source: Author's compilation of JSTOR computer-generated citations by discipline, with percentages rounded to whole numbers.

[a] Keyword search for "black women" or "African-American women" or "Afro-American women" or "negro women" or "black feminism" or "womanism" in FLAs, excluding reviews, opinion pieces, and other items. Note that the FLAs, as well as titles and abstracts, were determined using a search function in JSTOR, which allows terms to be searched throughout specific journals.

[b] Keyword search for "black women" or "African-American women" or "Afro-American women" or "negro women" or "black feminism" or "womanism" in titles only, excluding text, abstracts, author names, and captions.

[c] Keyword search for "black women" or "African-American women" or "Afro-American women" or "negro women" or "black feminism" or "womanism" in abstracts only, excluding text, titles, author names, and captions. Abstract information is not available for the history journals selected (except *American Quarterly* beginning in 2003).

geographies by subaltern subjects, however, have pushed back against this dominant geographic political configuration. As previously mentioned, in each of the disciplines examined, specialized journals, which address race and/or gender, arguably provide

Table 3.
Search Totals for Full-Length Articles (FLAs) by Titles and Abstracts, 2004–2008

	Total FLA[a]	Title Only[b]	Percentage of Total FLAs (%)	Abstract Only[c]	Percentage of Total FLAs (%)
Political Science					
The American Political Science Review	1	0	0	0	0
American Journal of Political Science	3	0	0	2	67
The Journal of Politics	9	0	0	2	31
Total	13	0	0	4	31
Sociology					
American Journal of Sociology	14	0	0	0	0
American Sociological Review	21	0	0	4	19
Social Forces	38	0	0	4	11
Total	73	0	0	8	11
History					
The American Historical Review	14	0	0	NA	NA
American Quarterly	33	0	0	NA	NA
Journal of American History	24	0	0	NA	NA
Total	71	0	0	NA	NA
Economics					
American Economic Review	6	0	0	0	0
Journal of Political Economy	2	0	0	0	0
The Quarterly Journal of Economics	5	0	0	0	0
Total	13	0	0	0	0

Source: Author's compilation of JSTOR computer-generated citations by discipline, with percentages rounded to whole numbers.

[a] Keyword search for "black women" or "African-American women" or "Afro-American women" or "negro women" or "black feminism" or "womanism" in FLAs, excluding reviews, opinion pieces, and other items. Note that the FLAs, as well as titles and abstracts, were determined using a search function in JSTOR, which allows terms to be searched throughout specific journals.

[b] Keyword search for "black women" or "African-American women" or "Afro-American women" or "negro women" or "black feminism" or "womanism" in titles only, excluding text, abstracts, author names, and captions.

[c] Keyword search for "black women" or "African-American women" or "Afro-American women" or "negro women" or "black feminism" or "womanism" in abstracts only, excluding text, titles, author names, and captions. Abstract information is not available for the history journals selected (except *American Quarterly* beginning in 2003).

greater exposure to work on Black women as subjects. Political science, for instance, has seen the emergence of the *Journal of Politics, Groups, and Identities*, and the journal in which this article, "Why Political Scientists Don't Study Black Women, But Historians and Sociologists Do," appears, namely, *The National Political Science Review*, that generally deals with United States and international racial politics, and *Journal of Women, Politics, and Policy* (formerly *Women and Politics*) and the newer *Politics & Gender*, which centers women's political experiences and gender politics. Sociology's *Gender & Society* and *Race, Class, and Gender*, History's *Journal of Women's History*, and Economics' *Feminist Economics* have served as similar outlets. However, even within these venues, conventional wisdom suggests that even greater attention needs to be accorded Black women and Black gender politics. The data here are offered to provide a view of mainstream journals in these disciplines.

Discussion

The results of this general survey of literature published about Black women in these four disciplines is consistent with the research and scholarship of intersectionality scholars, which details the special challenges associated with producing work about Black women as political, historical, social, and economic actors (see, e.g., Dill and Zambrana 2009), such as deeply entrenched masculinist methods, a failure to support research on Black women as legitimate, and access to publishing outlets, to name a few. The persistence of limitations on the amount of research on Black women, even amidst progress, parallels an equally persistent paradox in the treatment of Black women in the United States, namely their hypervisibility and political centrality, on the one hand, and invisibility, on the other.

Some might regard attention to Black women as a key point of emphasis to be misguided, either because it centers on identity or because it should be replaced by considerations of gender as a sole analytic category. But, a priority on research centering on Black women as political, social, historical, and economic subjects, especially from a specifically Black feminist frame of reference, is of central importance in countering the paradox of invisibility and hypervisibility. In some respects, Black women are hypervisble in terms of the dominant cultural symbols by which they are defined, a fact that accounts for the impact of stereotypes, for instance, in the development of social welfare and family-related policy (see, e.g., Hancock 2004). Yet, at the same time, Black women's needs are largely neglected in terms of social policy (e.g., in poverty, HIV/AIDS, reproductive health, employment, and education), discrimination (e.g., in the workplace), and abuse (e.g., in terms of rape, harassment, and coercive control in domestic spaces). Black feminist scholarship centering on Black women resists the hegemonic gaze invested in seeing Black women as the source of a range of difficulties, as opposed to addressing the range of problems that hamper their life chances and quality of life.

Political scientists' adoption of a Black feminist orientation is consistent with the best of feminist and Black studies approaches already at work in the discipline. One of the hallmarks of Black or Africana Studies research, for instance, is its emphasis on having a "centered" approach, which focuses on understanding and addressing the experiences of Blacks across the diaspora; in keeping with this approach, Black feminist research should center on Black women as subjects and the gender politics in and/or through which Black women operate. This emphasis on centering on the Black experience holds true, not only in terms of Afro-centric perspectives, but also in other liberal and progressive approaches to Black studies. This priority has been best represented in political science, moreover, by pioneering scholars in the subfield of Black politics, such as Jones (1972, 1977), Prestage

(1991), and Walters (2003), among others, many of whom ventured to develop a "Black political science," that is, a political science geared toward advancing social justice in the lives of people of African descent in the United States and elsewhere (Jones 1977).

Also, in a related vein, feminists have rightly stressed the need for more research on political women and feminist research on gender. Some feminist political scientists have rightly pointed out a need to go beyond scholarship that merely adopts a "great women" approach. Research on political women can include, but must ultimately reach further than, an effort to situate individual figures that are missing from historical or political narratives, and must abandon notions of a singular category marked "woman," for which we can make political claims (Carroll and Zerilli 1993). But poststructuralist and women of color critiques of the category "woman" ought not cause us to lose focus of an analysis of how Black women are oppressed or their efforts to resist such oppression. As the Caribbean Black feminist, Eudine Barriteau, reminds us, "Shifting to gender as an analytical frame certainly does not mean that the study of women is abandoned or that one cannot maintain an exclusive focus on women in research. Neither does it mean that gender studies must automatically include men" (Barriteau 2003, 43). All scholars concerned about Black gender politics must remain, as pioneering political scientist Jewell Prestage insists, "in quest of the African American [or Black] political woman" (Prestage 1991).

Notably, the disconnect between the critical importance of Black women and Black gender politics and the relative paucity of research on Black women in mainstream political science journals, represents no benign neglect, but mirrors and helps to facilitate the contentious nature of Black women's relationship to mainstream culture and politics. Although we are in a period of increased visibility for Blacks and other racial minorities in the profession (at least in terms of formal leadership roles in political science associations), the raison d'être of political science remains the same: political system maintenance, including the assertion of race, gender, and class hierarchies. As Mack Jones detailed decades ago, mainstream US political science serves first and foremost to undergird the dominant patterns and structures through which power circulates. He explains, ". . . [A]merican education and educators in general and as a consequence American political science and political scientists are essential cogs in the wheel of oppression, for they serve to legitimate its legal and philosophical foundations" (Jones 1977, 12). The task for progressive Black political scientists, in Jones's view, is to resist the operation of oppressive political systems.

Notably, Jones's point regarding the system maintenance role of political science is underscored by the role of racist thinking as reflected in the scholarship of luminaries that founded the field and in the framing of core foci in political science research. Political scientist Jessica Blatt, in her history of racial politics in the discipline, dispels the notion that political science has "evaded" race, pointing instead to how racial politics instrumentally shaped the discipline's origins. "Founders" of the field, such as John W. Burgess, who led the first PhD granting department in political science at Columbia, articulated central theories of political science within the racist logic of the time. Burgess, for instance, saw democracy as an important principle, but located its authority, not in government, but in the state, that is, "the gradual and continuous development of human society . . . the gradual realization . . . of the universal principles of human nature" (Burgess, quoted in Blatt 2012, 7).

According to Blatt, one of the principal goals of the state was to foster an "ethnically homogenous" populace and further inculcate Teutonic values within US law and politics. She also sheds a different light on conventional wisdom, which states that explicit racist ideology or race talk largely stopped after World War I. Although certain types of racial thinking, consistent with biologically based notions of race, dissipated post World War I, they were replaced by different, race-based discourses "such as eugenics and mental testing" (22). Blatt explains:

> [W]hen political scientists rejected "the state" and its racial basis—they still looked to "race" to provide intellectual purchase on political life. Of course, this research program was not a fruitful one . . . But it is significant in representing early attempts by prominent political scientists to orient political science toward the measurement and evaluation of the traits of populations. This latter program has of course been enormously fruitful, . . . in the fields of political psychology, opinion research, and political behavior research. Since the 1980s it has also been revived . . . in the form of attempts to link genetic traits to political attitudes. (Blatt 2012, 25)

Work on race, in others words, has left an indelible imprint on political science, particularly in terms of methods and definitions of knowledge production. The question of why political scientists do not study Black women, relative to other disciplines, is not one of simply methods or foci. The elements of methods and foci are critically important because they are the means through which political science "evades" Black women and politics, but they are not the reason for it. They are horses pulling a very big cart, namely: a societal neglect and oppression of Black women abetted by the production of academic knowledge.

The question is: what is to be done? How can the development of a new political science, one that adopts a Black feminist frame of reference, best be developed? The answer lies in the rescripting of the terrain of struggle, both institutionally and intellectually. Indeed, drawing on Black feminist geography, I suggest that Black feminist scholarship on Black political women will thrive with the assertion and strengthening of garrets of resistance in order to respacialize the disciplinary terrain and make a place for Black feminist work. As noted Black feminist geographer, McKittrick (2006) relates, the classic text by Harriet Jacobs (aka Linda Brent), *Incidents in the Life of a Slave Girl* (Jacobs 2009) provides critical insights for reorienting Black feminist thinking. Jacobs, McKittrick recalls, was able to eventually escape from slavery by holding up for seven years in a crawl space of her grandmother's attic (Jacobs 2009, 37). This space, which was "9' × 7' × 3'," allowed her to trick her owner into believing she had escaped and redirect his attention and resources to apprehend her and return her to bondage, while she was able to observe her family and effect her eventual permanent liberation from her condition of enslavement (Jacobs 2009, 37–44). Thus, although the garret for Jacobs was a place of confinement, it eventually secured her ultimate freedom in escaping from slavery in the South. She was positioned, in this "loophole of retreat" (Jacobs 2009, 37), in a way that gave her a special mode of insight in observing the slave community in which she was embedded (Jacobs 2009, 41–43). Even as she was located in the oppressive context of slavery, through her garreting of herself, she was able to resist it from within. So the garret points not only to the active resistance that Black women can mount politically in ways that can afford them a "loophole of retreat" by which they advance a liberating politics, but to the way in which Black women have, in fact, been central, not marginal, to political development in the United States and elsewhere in the African Diaspora. Jacobs's garreting demonstrates how Black women have produced oppositional geographies. This example of garreting, I contend, also provides us a powerful way to think about how to construct oppositional geographies in utilizing a Black feminist frame of reference for political science.

Specifically, there are two ways the concept of garrets or garreting can be important: materially, that is, in terms of the production of Black feminist scholarship on Black women, and metaphorically, that is, again, in terms of how we as Black feminist scholars analyze and assess the lives and political efforts of Black women, as constitutive of mainstream politics, as opposed to residing on the margins. As to the material issue of knowledge production, garreting occurs through creating mechanisms and spaces to authorize and facilitate work on Black women and Black gender politics. Producing journals and developing book series or other inroads at presses are, of course, important means of directly supporting publication. Importantly, these are just examples of a broader constellation of inroads that support research and publication. Black women have supported scholars and their research, for instance, through producing edited volumes, hosting conferences, giving publication prizes, and/or developing social networks that can provide mentoring and psychosocial support necessary to thrive in the academy. The Association of Black Women Historians (ABWH) is a case in point. The ABWH has been a key institutional location for mentoring Black women historians and for authorizing and supporting research about and by Black women. Through its annual meeting, held in tandem with The Association for the Study of African American Life and History (ASALH), and its awards, which recognize scholarship for Black women, it has helped both to institutionalize the specialty of Black women's history and support those intellectual laborers committed to such work. This has occurred alongside participation within other institutional locations. Still, the ABWH has served as a mode of garreting in the way McKittrick describes, that is, production of a social space that disrupts the dominant intellectual geographical terrain. A similar process of garreting has been important for other disciplines that are more productive in terms of their work on Black women. In sociology, for instance, the section on race, ethnicity and gender, as well as specialized journals, such as *Race and Ethnicity* and *Gender and Society* facilitate the respatialization of sociology. This does not marginalize or (re)segregate Black feminist scholars. Whether they gravitate toward what are considered mainstream circles of power or favor non-hegemonic locations, they continue to operate within disciplinary matrixes.

In political science, Black women and other women of color are working to develop similar forms of garreting. Preconference meetings at the American Political Science Association for women of color have been an important means of networking and of disseminating information about publication, particularly for emerging scholars. Most recently, scholars have worked to convene a meeting of women of color to do this, a meeting that is being developed by Black women, among others. The formation of the Association for the Study of Black Women in Politics is another effort. Modeled after the ABWH, the ASBWP has two missions: to facilitate the professionalization of Black women political scientists and to support progressive, Black feminist research on Black women in politics in the United States and throughout the African Diaspora. Originated in 2004 and formally incorporated in 2008, the ASBWP has begun annual awards to recognize important research on Black women in politics. Although it has been generally welcomed, particularly by Black women political scientists who research Black women in politics, the organizers (including the author), who were junior scholars when they began this effort, have faced challenges in terms of antifeminist sentiments within the discipline, as well as the daily pressures of managing institutional racism and sexism in academe, such as putatively higher standards for research productivity and challenges to professional authority. Future plans for the ASBWP include mentoring initiatives and partnering with established conferences to secure programming space at annual meetings. Efforts of organizations, such as the ABWH or ASBWP, help to rewrite or restructure the social production of disciplinary space.

Of course, not all Black women's geographies are inherently oppositional. Black women can produce geographies that *do* support hegemonic geographical arrangements, both materially and metaphorically. This is arguably the case in terms of how intersectionality is currently being discussed in political science. As Julia Jordan-Zachery's article in this same volume of the NPSR demonstrates, a focus on intersectionality does not necessarily provide research that illuminates Black political women and their political strivings. It just as easily gives way to descriptive research and, in some cases, research that does not focus on race, but general attributes of difference. Black women in particular and women of color more generally are "disappeared" (Alexander-Floyd 2012) as subjects and progenitors of intersectionality research.

Importantly, scholars who do seek to remap the intellectual terrain of their disciplines in oppositional ways typically do so through integrating insights from other fields and through challenging the received epistemological and methodological orientations of their disciplines. The personal accounts of some of the most noted pioneers of Black women's history demonstrate this latter point. In her contribution to her edited collection, *Telling Histories* (White 2008), a compilation of first-hand accounts of Black women historians' academic lives, historian Deborah Gray White powerfully records the challenges she faced in producing Black women's history. Her first book, *Ar'n't I a Woman* (White 1985) is universally regarded as a watershed moment in Black women's history and in the study of slavery. But, as an assistant professor, she faced seemingly insurmountable challenges, stemming in no small part from a lack of understanding about the relevance of scholarship on Black women in her discipline. She explains: "I had no reason to be optimistic about finding a publisher because publishers' critiques were . . . dismissive. 'It was not complete, there was not enough work, the proof wasn't there.' And, then almost universally, publishers added, 'There is no audience for this book'" (White 2008, 96). But for a chance reading by Anne Firor Scott of the dissertation on which the book was based and Scott's subsequent offer to speak to a publisher, this pathbreaking work might not have been published. Similarly, Darlene Clark Hine (2008), eminent scholar of Black women's history, received a very traditional graduate education, generally devoid of any treatment of Black women as historical subjects. When community members prevailed upon her to do a history of Black club women in Indiana, she embarked on a journey that would help to rewrite Black women's history and reshape her own trajectory as a scholar. Although earlier scholars producing groundbreaking works generally have challenges initiating new fields of study, the resistance to doing work on Black women is persistent. Historian Mia Bay, hailing from a younger generation of scholars, notes that there was little discussion of Black women as historical subjects in graduate school and that her own entrée into this area of scholarly concern was occasioned by women's studies scholars within and outside of history circles post graduate school (Bay 2008, 192–93). Interdisciplinary interventions proved pivotal to the production of scholarship on Black women as historical actors, as these examples illustrate.

The same interdisciplinary push can be seen in political science. Beginning in the 1960s, scholars, particularly from Atlanta University and Howard University, led a concerted effort to integrate Black studies approaches vis-à-vis the development of scholarship focused on Blacks and their political experiences. Indeed, the formation of the National Conference of Black Political Scientists in 1968 was birthed in this moment of intellectual commitment to producing knowledge that could effectively respond to the needs of Blacks in the United States and globally (McCormick 2009). This push for the development of a Black political science was buoyed by the activist climate of the time and the push for Black studies in the academy. One can recall *Death of White Sociology* (Ladner 1973) as a volume that marked a similar thrust in the field of sociology. Women's studies had a similar effect across disciplines, the creation of the Women and Politics subfield at Rutgers University, being perhaps the most prominent example in political science. As the aforementioned text suggests, increased attention needs to be paid to interdisciplinarity and the politics of methodology in order to expand scholarship on Black women and Black gender politics in political science. To be sure, there has been progress. Further advancement, however, requires attention to the material means of scholarly production.

In addition to place making as it relates to knowledge production, garreting is equally important in terms of the approach we take to studying Black political women. More specifically, we typically think of Black women and Black feminist politics in terms of being located at the margins. McKittrick (2006, 56–59), building on the insights of Patricia Hill Collins, who also questions the utility of situating Black women as marginal, provocatively suggests that such a framing actually reproduces the militaristic and binary formulations associated with conquest and colonization. The notion of the garret suggests Black women's struggle against domination occurs, not from the location of the margins, but from within the center or midst of geographic and political landscapes. In the case of Harriet Jacobs (Linda Brent), her experience of surviving in the garret of her grandmother's attic for seven years demonstrates the complicated paradox of struggle amidst racial-sexual terror. Drawing on McKittrick's formulations regarding Black feminist geography for our understanding of politics yields potentially powerful results. We would find that Black women's experiences and politics might still be found in "the last place they thought of" (McKittrick 2006). However, we could also see that "black femininity and Black women's politics . . . are not necessarily marginal, but are *central* to how we know and understand space and place [and politics]: black women's [politics] are workable and lived subaltern [realities], which tell a different [political] story" (McKittrick 2006, 62) (emphasis in original).

Suggestions for Future Research

Future investigations could develop this line of inquiry on the state of research on Black political women in several ways. First, although I utilized the periods 1970–1985, 1986–2003, and 2004–2008, in order to better enable comparisons with previous research, recalibrating results for each discipline along decades may yield beneficial results. Second, a fuller examination could entail a review of journals focused on gender and/or race and ethnicity, such as *Politics & Gender* in political science, *Gender & Society* in sociology, and *Feminist Economics* in economics, to understand the ways in which these subfields within disciplines have opened up research opportunities and/or positively redirected and expanded research on race and gender in mainstream journals, as well. Third, we can further examine the impact of and necessity for post-positivist methodologies in examining Black political women.

Of course, the recent increased attention to intersectionality in political science, as evidenced, for instance, by special symposia in *Politics & Gender* in 2007 and 2012, as well as pre-conference workshops and panels on the subject, ostensibly promises to produce a greater volume of research about Black women as political actors and Black gender politics, but there is a reason to approach this expectation with some caution. As I argue elsewhere (Alexander-Floyd 2012), the interpretations of intersectionality now gaining currency are in fact a "post"-Black feminist formulation that displaces and/or deprioritizes research on Black women. Indeed, as previously indicated, research has already begun to expose the relative inattention to Black women in current intersectionality research in the discipline. I suggest further examination of the various fields in order to provide examples of the ways in which scholars, particularly in political science and sociology, have operationalized intersectionality in their research, including ways that at times hinder liberatory, Black feminist scholarship on Black women.

Ultimately, it is important to detail the extent and nature of the limitations on scholarship in various disciplines not only for issues of exposure, but also to provoke decisive action to substantively redirect the methodological and political priorities of the discipline. Undoubtedly, the current interpretation of intersectionality within the discipline, without a change of direction, will ironically further invisibilize Black women as political actors. A truly interdisciplinary approach to intersectionality in the discipline—not one that accommodates intersectionality to prevailing paradigms, but truly transforms what we think we can know and the means by which we can come to know it—will be a central means of enacting the type of Perestroika-like movement that is necessary to assert a Black feminist frame of reference for political science.

Notes

1. I use the term "Black political women" to denote women of African descent in terms of their political subjectivity and engagement in formal and informal politics. It is inspired by Jewel Prestage's (1991) seminal work, "In Quest of African American Political Woman."
2. For a discussion of Black feminist "home-making" and spatial politics, see Zenzele Isoke's, "The Politics of Homemaking: Black Feminist Transformations of a Cityscape," *Transforming Anthropology* 19 (2): 117–30.

References

Agnew, John. 2011. "Space and Place." In *The SAGE Handbook of Geographical Knowledge*, ed. John Agnew and David Livingstone, 316–43. Los Angeles, CA: SAGE.

Alexander-Floyd, Nikol. 2007. *Gender, Race, and Nationalism in Contemporary Black Politics*. New York: Palgrave Macmillan.

———. 2012. "Disappearing Acts: Reclaiming Intersectionality in the Social Sciences in a Post-Black Feminist Era." *Feminist Formations* 24, no. 1: 1–25.

Barriteau, Eudine. 2003. "Theorizing the Shift from 'Woman' to 'Gender' in Caribbean Feminist Discourse." In *Confronting Power, Theorizing Gender: Interdisciplinary Perspectives in the Caribbean*, ed. Eudine Barriteau, 27–45. Jamaica: University of the West Indies Press.

Bay, Mia. 2008. "Looking Backward in Order to Go Forward: Black Women Historians and Black Women's History." In *Telling Histories: Black Women Historians in the Ivory Tower*, ed. Deborah Gray White, 182–99. Chapel Hill, NC: The University of North Caroline Press.

Blatt, Jessica. 2012. "Race, Rights, and the Origins of American Political Science." Paper presented at the annual meeting of the Southern Political Science Association, New Orleans, LA, January.

Carroll, Susan J., and Linda M. G. Zerilli. 1993. "Feminist Challenges to Political Science." In *Political Science: The State of the Discipline*, ed. Ada Finifter, 55–76. Washington, DC: The American Political Science Association.

Dill, Bonnie Thornton, and Ruth Enid Zambrana, eds. 2009. *Emerging Intersections: Race, Class, and Gender in Theory, Policy, and Practice*. New Brunswick, NJ: Rutgers University.

Hancock, Ange-Marie. 2004. *The Politics of Disgust: The Public Identity of the Welfare Queen*. New York: New York University Press.

Hine, Darlene Clark. 2008. "Becoming a Black Woman's Historian." In *Telling Histories: Black Women Historians in the Ivory Tower*, ed. Deborah Gray White, 42–57. Chapel Hill, NC: The University of North Carolina Press.

Jacobs, Harriet. 2009. *Incidents in the Life of a Slave Girl*. Cambridge, MA: Belknap Press.

Jones, Mack H. 1972. "A Frame of Reference for Black Politics." In *Black Political Life in the United States: A Fist as the Pendulum*, ed. Lenneal Henderson Jr., 7–20. San Francisco, CA: Chandler.

———. 1977. "Responsibility of Black Political Scientists to the Black Community." In *Black Political Scientists and Black Survival*, ed. Shelby Lewis Smith, 9–17. Detroit, MI: Balamp Publishing.

Jordan-Zachery, Julia. 2007. "Am I a Black Woman or a Woman Who Is Black?: A Few Thoughts on the Meaning of Intersectionality." *Politics & Gender* 3, no. 2: 254–63.

Ladner, Joyce, ed. 1973. *The Death of White Sociology*. New York, NY: Random House.

McCormick, Joseph. 2009. "NCOBPS: The First of Our Forty Years." In *Racial Americana?: Continuities and Changes in Racial Politics (Annual Meeting Program)*, 27–43. Houston, TX: National Conference of Black Political Scientists.

McKittrick, Katherine. 2006. *Demonic Grounds: Black Women and the Cartographies of Struggle*. Minneapolis, MN: University of Minnesota Press.

Monroe, Kristen, ed. 2005. *Perestroika!: The Raucous Rebellion in Political Science*. New Haven, CT: Yale University Press.

Possing, Dorthe. 2010. *A Politics of Place: How Young Muslims Frame Global and Local Events in Online Communication*. Global Migration and Transnational Politics, Working Paper, George Mason University, 11 April.

Prestage, Jewell. 1991. "In Quest of the African American Political Woman." *The Annals of the American Academy of Political and Social Science* 515: 88–103.

Walcott, Rinaldo. 2001. "Caribbean Pop Culture in Canada: Or, the Impossibility of Belonging to the Nation." *Small Axe* 5, no. 1: 123–39.

Walters, Ronald. 2003. *White Nationalism, Black Interests: Conservative Public Policy and the Black Community*. Detroit, MI: Wayne State.

White, Deborah. 1985. *Ar'n't I a Woman: Female Slaves in the Plantation South*. New York: W. W. Norton and Company, Inc.

———. 2008. "My History in History." In *Telling Histories: Black Women Historians in the Ivory Tower*, ed. Deborah Gray White, 85–100. New York, NY: W. W. Norton and Company.

Wilson, Ernest J. 1985. "Why Political Scientists Don't Study Black Politics, But Historians and Sociologists Do." *PS: Political Science & Politics* 18, no. 3: 600–7.

Wilson, Ernest J., and Lorrie A. Frasure. 2007. "Still at the Margins: The Persistence of Neglect of African American Issues in Political Science, 1986–2003." In *African American Perspectives on Political Science*, ed. Wilbur C. Rich, 8–23. Philadelphia, PA: Temple University Press.

"I Ain't Your Darn Help": Black Women as the Help in Intersectionality Research in Political Science

Julia S. Jordan-Zachery
Providence College

At a social function for my daughter's fifth-grade class, I had a rather interesting interaction with another mother. Before I can get to the details of the interaction, I need to explain the context. I was engaged in a conversation with one mother; we share an interest in reading and were discussing our recent selections. As we were conversing, another mother joined us and began to speak about her "absolute love" of Stockett's (2009) novel, *The Help*. My response to her adulation was, "I find the book very problematic and simplistic. I should say that this is probably because I do research on such issues."

The mother replied, "Who gives a f**k what you think! The book is brilliant." Her response left me stunned for a number of reasons, beyond the fact that it seemed inappropriate. For one, we were the only women of color among the approximate fifteen families in attendance. I was the only Black mother present—the other two were moms of Latino descent. Second, the outburst came from a woman who lived in New York City. One could suppose that this exposed her to the use of immigrant women as nannies, which could discourage disrespectful behavior toward Black women. Third, this is a woman who tells her story of poverty and homelessness, and a desire that we all treat each other with respect and dignity.

Ironically, while attending a professional conference, I had a somewhat similar discussion, which diminished Black women's identities and contributions. At an American Political Science Association (APSA) conference, a White female colleague told me that I should feel proud that Black women had made such a contribution—intersectionality—to the discipline. This was in response to my questioning of the ever-expanding use of intersectionality, and more importantly, the omission of Black women in such studies. At a prior APSA meeting, I was told that should Black women attempt to exclusively hold onto the concept of intersectionality, it will go the way of the term "Holocaust," which in her imagination limited the resonance and impact of the term outside of the Jewish community. Consequently, if Black academicians resisted the traveling and reimagining of intersectionality, based on the logic of her argument, then there would be less support for the specific injustices suffered by Black women.

How and why are these conversations relevant to this special edition on Black women and politics? My conversations, separated by time and space, speak to the politics

19

of identity. While these are individual encounters, they capture what I believe is part of a larger trend on the treatment of and response to Black women. The conversations, intentionally or not, reify and maintain discursive systems that create truth regimes, which serve as forms of regulation (Foucault 1978). The mother of my daughter's classmate and my colleagues attempted to regulate, and to some extent, mute my voice. They engaged in a project of omission. This omission project is experienced in the sociocultural, political, and academic realms. According to Sesko and Biernat (2010), Black women are being rendered invisible in a sociocultural way. In comparison to other gendered and/or raced groups, Black women tend to go both unnoticed and unheard. Black women are also "disappearing" as research subjects within our "leading" journals (see Alexander-Floyd 2012 and her essay in this volume) and within intersectionality research.

This research note investigates how the politics of research results in the further marginalization of Black women. Generally, politics is thought to involve the relationship between social actors and the state. Ignored in such conceptualizations are other interactions and the exercise of power and use of force. Therefore, the conversations I recounted above and the ever-evolving use of intersectionality in political science research might not be thought of as politics. However, these phenomena speak to practices, systems of knowledge, and cultural norms that serve to uphold racialized-gendered hierarchies. As such, they are a form of politics.

The question guiding this analysis is how can the politics of knowledge production influence the material reality of doubly marginalized groups in general, and Black women more specifically. Others, such as Cohen (1999), Hancock (2004), and Ernst (2010), address the lack of Black women's voices in policy formation and show how such omission perpetuates harm to Black women. These and other researchers critically analyze the relationship between identity and policy responses and they make substantive contributions to our understanding of intersectionality; however, there remains a gap in our research efforts. Unlike these influential works, I focus on meta-questions and analyses of political science intersectionality research. As I argue below, there is an omission project occurring in published political science research generally and within intersectionality research specifically. Black women as research subjects are being omitted. This is the gap that remains in our research—it has not focused on how and why Black women are being omitted in social science research and specifically within intersectionality research. Alexander-Floyd (2012) offers one of the few research-length articles on this issue of the disappearance of Black women in social science research in general. This project complements hers, as I focus primarily on the discipline of political science and intersectionality research specifically. Social science research in general, and in particular intersectionality research do not exist in a vacuum; instead, they embody power hierarchies evident in the wider society. I posit that Black women, vis-à-vis the use of intersectionality as a theory and approach, are being muted. Consequently, their movement for social justice is stymied. As a result, the purpose of intersectionality, as envisioned by Black feminists, becomes subverted and a victim of race/ethnicity, class, gender, and sexuality hierarchies.

In recent years, intersectionality as a theoretical concept has permeated various fields of study within political science. In discussing the impact of intersectionality on feminist work, Risman (2004, 442) says "there is now considerable consensus growing that one must always take into consideration multiple axes of oppression; to do otherwise presumes the whiteness of women, the maleness of people of color, and the heterosexuality of everyone." Often pitched as a theory that allows us to speak for and understand the experiences of marginalized groups, intersectionality tends to be celebrated as an all-encompassing theory. In exploring the ever expanding popularity of intersectionality, Nath (2009) suggests that intersectionality has become popular because,

> (1) The analytic insights offered by theories of intersectionality are so profound and perhaps so intuitive that their widespread incorporation into feminist scholarship is, to use a colloquial phrase, a "no brainer." (2) . . . [T]he analytic insights of intersectionality theorizing have been so theoretically rich and complex, that their decentering of the essential female subject has been, again, a "no brainer." (3) . . . The profundity of this type of theorization means that those affiliated with it automatically gain theoretical legitimacy.

The increasing use of intersectionality as a research tool, theoretical concept, and so forth, has not been without debate (see Kwan 1997 for a discussion on some perceived limitations of intersectionality). Indeed, this discussion on the merits and challenges of intersectionality theory is fascinating and thought provoking. However, there is something missing from this discourse. What is missing is an understanding of how such research embodies politics and power dynamics that render some groups invisible and results in the muting of some voices. Research is a political act. The theories employed and the manners in which they are deployed and the method and methodological approaches, like a picture, tell a story. These texts "as elements of social events have causal effects, *i.e.*, they bring about changes . . . in our knowledge . . . our beliefs and our attitudes, values and so forth" (Fairclough 2003, 8).

To explore the politics of intersectionality research and what I call an omission project, I start by examining the relationship between the novel, *The Help*, and intersectionality research. This allows us to contextualize what is occurring in political science. It shows how these cultural and academic phenomena at times mirror each other and also reinforce and normalize the treatment of Black women. I follow this section with the theoretical orientation of the article—grounded in Black feminism and group muted theory. Next, I present the data on how Black women are treated in intersectionality research and conclude with a discussion of the findings. In my discussion, I do not seek to offer a specific theory or some comprehensive approach to addressing the omission of Black women. Instead, my goal is to explore the ways in which Black women are treated in intersectionality research with the hope of stimulating a discussion on how our politics of research might be more inclusive. At first glance, my approach may not appear to follow the typical academic mode of production: how we generate knowledge and make knowledge claims. That is because I have used this approach as a means of disrupting knowledge claims and approaches often assumed to be best suited for knowledge production. As Collins (2000, 252) asserts, "like other subordinate groups, African-American women have not only developed a distinctive Black women's standpoint, but have done so by using alternative ways of producing and validating knowledge." My approach, in conjunction with my use of first-person stories and encounters, fits with Black feminist conceptualizations of epistemology.

Black Women as Bridges: *The Help* and Intersectionality

What are the similarities between the conversations I had at the social meeting and the one I had at the political science meeting? The parallels between the novel and my APSA conversations are not obvious until we start to look at the increasing popularity of intersectionality among scholars in political science and unpack how Black women were used in the novel. There is a parallel between Black women's role in *The Help* and Black women's role in political science. In each instance, both sets of Black women are used to advance others' dreams and desires, even if simply to provide (cultural/theoretical) legitimacy, while often remaining in the shadows. Intersectionality research, similarly to *The Help*, appears to give a nod to the voices of Black women; however, upon closer inspection, Black women's voices are not necessarily heard.

The Help deploys historical narratives of the contented, silent, and "dignified" Black woman. This fictional portrayal tapped into a cultural and political moment of nostalgia—a desire for the "beauty" and "simplicity" of the past. This yearning for nostalgia requires Black women to play the role of Mammy—the docile enslaved woman who cared for and protected White interests. We cannot avoid the politics of this particular understanding of Black womanhood because "fictionalized creations of black women are not innocent; they do not lack the effect of ideological force in the lives of those represented in that black women are rendered as objects and useful commodities in a very serious power struggle" (Bobo 1995, 36).

The popularity of the novel eventually led to its adoption for the big screen. In 2011, the much anticipated movie was released. This occurred in conjunction with an intense marketing campaign designed to encourage women to not only dress like the characters, but to also eat like them. For example, the Home Shopping Network (HSN) launched a site (which coincided with the release of the movie) featuring products inspired by the movie and novel. Such products included kitchenware and clothing items designed around "Southern Belle" styles. One could aspire to dress in the fashion (out of uniform) of the maids or the more "high"-end floral ensembles of the more economically well-off women. To some extent, the lives of Black women are available for consumption with little thought of the daily, lived realities of these women.

Often touted as a story of interracial, intra-class friendship, *The Help*, both film and novel versions, is really a story of White women's voice—particularly the main character's search for an alternative experience. Similarly, intersectionality, as currently deployed, also represents this type of search for something other—it is, in part, a desire to move beyond traditional understandings of identity politics. Thus, intersectionality and the voices of Black women become an avenue for others to seek freedom from the "norm." Black women serve as a bridge between both worlds. What is often neglected in this quest to seek alternatives is what happens to Black women who serve as the "help." Particularly, what is missing is how Black women's bodies, psyches, and intellects serve not for their advancement, but the advancement of others—whether in terms of tenure and promotion, other forms of job security, or simply just as a means to a more "comfortable" life.

Skeeter, the main character of the novel, was able to find her alternative—she got the job in New York that allowed her to escape the confines of White womanhood as dictated by the Southern culture—by co-opting the voices of Black women. Meanwhile, Aibileen

Clark, the Black maid, who served as a bridge between Skeeter and the other maids, was dismissed from her job and left to live in the South. Furthermore, although Aibileen was officially "recognized" as the author of the self-help column published in the local newspaper, she was required to write under a pen name, Miss Myrna. Thus the readers remained unaware of the author's true identity. Aibileen assumed "formal" authorship of this column after Skeeter left town (Stockett 2009).

Interestingly, while Skeeter was the author of this column, Aibileen's wisdom was used to respond to the readers' letters. Skeeter benefited, in multiple forms, from Aibileen's knowledge. Aibileen legitimized Skeeter a writer. Skeeter claimed the notoriety and benefits, while Aibileen went unacknowledged. The voice of this woman remained hidden behind the image of a White woman/persona. This fictitious Black woman, like her real-life counterparts, was forced to exist in the place where she was simultaneously seen while remaining invisible. Although living in the midst of the Civil Rights Movement, where Black women were tormented on a daily basis, Aibileen displayed no anger toward the theft of her intellect or her freedom. Maybe this is a result of no one "giving a f**k" what she thinks (in the words of the mother I spoke to at the social), or it is a result of those in power choosing not to allow her to speak, or when she spoke, choosing to ignore what she said, thereby discrediting any critique she might have offered. This is the omission project; Black women are there while not being there. It is this nebulous state that makes a critique of this project such a challenge.

Skeeter, by appropriating Aibileen's knowledge, was able to escape to the North. Aibileen was left in the South without a job, living in poverty, and having to confront sexism and racism. Although Aibileen served as the bridge that allowed Skeeter to escape the South (read: identity politics) to the North, her labor, physical and intellectual, could not be used for her own advancement, neither could it be used for the advancement of the larger Black community (read: intersectionality as part of a freedom project). However, at the end of the novel, Stockett tells us that Aibileen's spirit was not broken. Stockett invoked the notion of the strong and often "content" Black woman—in the sense that she did not challenge multiple oppressive structures, but simply focused on getting by in the current context. This is the message I often receive from some colleagues when I question how intersectionality is used in political science research. I am told to be content and not question the politics of research.

This issue of "North"/"South" is really a question of representation and identity. It involves the politics of a "ranking" of oppression as opposed to a quest for freedom for all. When others challenge my questioning of the use of intersectionality and "The Help" by suggesting that I am incessantly angry (the trope of the angry Black woman) and by suggesting that I want to claim intersectionality as the domain of only Black women, they are missing the larger issue of the politics of research and the politics of cultural representation. For me, the questioning of the use of intersectionality is not to claim it as the primary domain of Black women. Instead, it asks, where are Black women in the excitement about intersectionality? When intersectionality loses its attractiveness, who will study Black women and how will we study Black women? Will Black women as research subjects be left in the "South" as researchers continue their journey to the "North" as was the case with main character Eugenia "Skeeter" Phelan and Abilene Clark, her help? Will Black women be constructed simply as having a strong sprit? Will this construction, one of strength, be used as a marker of their great contribution to political science? Like *The Help*, the increasing popularity of intersectionality can be the result of a number of forces. However, if there is no questioning of power relations and how identities are constructed so that benefits are not equally distributed, then Black women and their lived experiences will be, like Aibileen Clark, left to live in the South with an unbroken sprit and a nod to their contributions.

Theoretical Foundation: Silences, Muting, and Omissions

The theoretical concept of intersectionality has as its foundation Black women's experiential knowledge—this is not to suggest that they are the only group that can claim the use of intersectionality. While some researchers take their meaning of intersectionality from Crenshaw's (1989, 1991) understanding of the concept, it is possible to trace a much longer history. Black women, although they might not have explicitly employed the term intersectionality, have historically expressed its core tenets. For example, Maria Stewart in 1832 spoke of the intersection of race and class in the lives of Black women (see Logan 1995). In the more recent iterations of the concept, such a history has been erased as a result of omission. Current research, beyond ignoring the early writings of Black women, while citing the work of more contemporary scholars does not necessarily, systematically, and critically engage the scholarship. In her critique of this movement Alexander-Floyd (2012, 2) says, "barely a decade into the new millennium, a new wave of raced-gendered occultic commodification is afoot, one focusing not on black female subjectivity per se, but on the concept of intersectionality."

Consequently, Black women who have theorized their experiences are treated like Aibileen of *The Help* in a substantial number of the research papers I analyze. The result is that they are simultaneously seen while remaining invisible in intersectionality research. This research invisibility is multipronged. Invisibility, in the words of Alexander and Mohanty (1997, xii), occurs as a result of "token inclusion of our text." Such "inclusion" tends to be non-transformative in nature and is often done with little critical engagement. Another form of invisibility occurs as a result of who serves as research subjects. As I discuss elsewhere (Jordan-Zachery 2012), there is "a failure among researchers to recognize intra-group differences among marginalized groups." I assert,

> We tend to ignore how intersectionality is experienced and lived among different members of the same group. Furthermore we tend to concentrate our research efforts among a select group of Black women; thereby, leaving untouched the lived realities of the majority of Black women—every-day, non-elected Black women. (407)

Such invisibility results because "while the social location of racially marked otherness creates conditions of possibility for epistemic privilege in terms of intersectional theorizing, this does not necessarily foreclose the achievement of an antiracist feminist standpoint to white women and others" (Clark Mane 2012, 76). Clark Mane and others expose how Black women, while appearing to speak, are actually silenced and muted. There is an intimate relationship between silence and forgetting. As intersectionality travels, the silencing and muting of Black women in research can create a situation for forgetting why Black women centered intersectionality as a tool for analyzing and responding to the material realties they confront on a daily basis.

Group muting theory offers a lens to understand and analyze the treatment of Black women in intersectionality research. This theory seeks to represent marginalized groups whose voices and experiences often are silenced. Being muted should not be conflated with silence. Instead, muting should be seen as the hindrance of the communicative outlets and abilities of a marginalized group at the hands of those in power. The process of muting suggests that some groups are denied representation, as they are limited in their ability to speak and in their ability to choose how they want to speak. Furthermore, some groups are denied representation based on how others choose to see them or not see them. As argued by Orbe (2005, 65–66), the muted group theory is a foundational starting place for "theorizing from the margins."

The muted group theory, similar to intersectionality, suggests that marginalized groups' perceptions and interpretations of reality are influenced by the dominant groups' constructions. This works, as argued by Kramarae (1981), because each society constructs "template structures," which are a series of beliefs, values, and opinions that collectively work to define a particular worldview. These "template structures" provide society with the "language" images, symbols, and so forth that are then used to construct and understand reality (see Ardener 1975). Template structures are relied upon, explicitly and implicitly, to determine who should serve as research subjects and also the producers of knowledge. Such structures can be deployed in the process of silencing some members of the community/group. They play a role in the omission project.

According to Sheriff (2000),

> Unlike the activity of speech, which does not require more than a single actor, silence demands collaboration and the tacit communal understandings that such collaboration presupposes. Although it is contractual in nature, a critical feature of this type of silence is that it is both a consequence and an index of an unequal distribution of power, if not of actual knowledge. Through it, various forms of power may be partly, although often incompletely, concealed, denied, or naturalized. Although the type of silence I refer to may be a more or less stable and widely shared cultural convention, it is constituted through, and circumscribed by, the political interests of dominant groups. (114)

There are two forms of silences that result from the muting process taking place in intersectionality research. One can be overt; this is the complete absence of Black women as research subjects and/or the recognition of their contributions. Another type of silence tends to be more covert in nature. Covert silence, and the resulting omissions, allows for a form of memorializing the contributions of Black women. It is the type of silence that is part of speech, thereby making it hard to identify and critique. An example of covert omission involves the citation of some works without any critical engagement of the scholarship. Regardless of the form of silence, both types ignore the narratives of Black women. Our scholarship—cultural and academic—excludes these narratives. Below, I explore how Black women are treated in intersectionality research.

Finding Black Women: Article Selection Criteria

For the period 1996–2010, I analyze four journals to determine how Black women are treated as research subjects. I focus on journal-length articles because it allows me to identify trends and because "publications in leading journals are an important marker of professional status and a key conduit for the diffusion of ideas" (Munck and Snyder 2007, 339). The number of journal articles is considered as an indicator of the extent to which the scholarly community accepts Black women, as research subjects. Beyond this, I also consider how Black women are treated within these scholarly journals as another indicator of their acceptance. Combined, the count of articles and the nature of the research show the trends and statues of research on Black womanhood.

Articles were selected from four journals, two of which, according to Garand and Giles (2003) are among the top-ranking journals. These journals are: *The American Political Science Review* (APSR) and the *Journal of Politics* (JOP). The other two journals focus on women and/or gender. *The Journal of Women, Politics & Policy* (formerly *Women & Politics*) and *Politics & Gender* complete the journals used in this analysis.

Using a series of keywords, each journal was searched and the resulting articles recorded. The key words included: Black women, African American women, and intersectionality. To determine whether articles on intersectionality were relevant to the study, I employed a US based understanding of intersectionality as developed by Black women. Intersectionality, one manifestation of Black feminism in the United States, is rooted in the simultaneity and multiplicity of oppressions (race, class, gender, and sexuality among others) and relationality (emphasis is placed on the relation between the everyday lives of Black women and sociopolitical and historical structures and processes). Given this understanding of intersectionality, I excluded articles that looked at women outside of the United States. Furthermore, I excluded book reviews, and articles in the Critical Perspective section of *Women, Politics & Policy*. This was done to ensure that the data would be comparable across the journals.

After the list of data was complied, the articles were read to determine whether indeed they centered on Black women and/or intersectionality. The articles were categorized using the following typology: Intersectionality (these are articles that focus primarily on the concept of intersectionality with no reference to Black women); Intersectionality and Black womanhood (these articles not only employ intersectionality, but also discuss Black women); Black women as a means (such articles are not about Black women, but employ Black women to tell a larger story); Black women (Black women are the singular focus of these articles); and Comparative (in these articles, Black women serve as a comparative group to discuss race, gender, and politics/policy).

Trends in Scholarship

Among the fifty-nine articles analyzed, the number of articles centered on Black women and/or intersectionality as the subject of the research was rather scarce. There were five articles utilizing the concept of intersectionality (see Table 1). Of these articles, three focused on Latinas, one employed intersectionality to discuss the policy-making process and one was a comparative analysis. Further analysis reveals that four of these five articles were published in *Women, Politics & Policy* and one was published in *Politics & Gender*. In terms of research on intersectionality and Black womanhood as a singular research topic, there were two such articles and both were published in *Politics & Gender*. Articles categorized as "using Black women as a means" accounted for nine publications. In these articles, there was a mention of Black women, not as part of an attempt to understand their political/policy lived experiences, but to use them to tell a larger story that often had nothing to do, directly, with Black women.

Table 1.
Black Women as Research Subjects in Political Science, 1996–2010

Black women as a singular research subject, with no explicit use of intersectionality, accounted for fifteen articles in total. Twelve of these articles were published in *Women, Politics & Policy*. *Politics & Gender* and *JOP* published two and one, respectively. The nature of these articles varied and included analyses of Black feminist thought, and the impact of policies—such as the war on drugs. The major subject areas centered women either as voters, candidates, and/or representatives.

Black women, in the majority of articles (twenty-eight), were treated in a comparative manner. Again, a disproportionate number were published in *Women Politics & Policy* (twenty articles). The other eight articles were published in *Politics & Gender* (5), *JOP* (2), and *APSR* (1). It is worth noting that not all comparative articles treated Black women in the same manner. Additionally, among this body of research only one article focused on girls as a subject. The others centered around Black feminist/standpoint theory, political behavior, and/or institutions. Comparative studies can be informative; however, they can also be limiting (see hooks 1991). Such studies can reinscribe differences and encourage further marginalization of Black women as they can result in "a God trick . . . that mode of seeing that pretends to offer a vision that is from everywhere and nowhere equally and fully" (Haraway 1988, 584). Although Black women are used in some of these studies, they are employed to call attention to other concerns other than the concern of the "structural sources of inequality" (Guidroz and Berger 2009, 70). Such studies can mask differentials in power relations between and within groups. This is not to suggest that all dimensions of comparative studies are inherently problematic for Black women.

Further examination of the trends shows that the *APSR* is apt not to publish research on Black women as singular research subjects and neither is it likely to publish work on intersectionality. The *JOP*, similarly to the *APSR*, tended not to include articles within which Black women are treated as singular research subjects. If, indeed, *APSR* and *JOP* are recognized as two of the top ranking journals in political science, and if such rankings are key in tenure decisions, the omission of Black women among published articles sends the message that such research is not valued and, as such, should not be pursued. The other trend suggests that Black women are valuable research subjects provided they are part of a comparative study. Again, the message is that research that privileges Black women, as a singular research topic is not valued, in terms of published research.

Beyond the fact that Black women as singular research subjects receive minimum attention in the published articles, how they are studied can also be limiting in our understanding of their lived reality. Among the publications studied, there was minimum attention paid to Black female centered organizations. Neither was attention paid to Black women's experiences with various public policies. During the time period analyzed, there was one article that centered Black lesbians (Fogg-Davis 2006). Finally, there were no publications that focused on Black women's public opinions. These trends suggest a rather narrow understanding of Black women's politics.

Discussion

Spelman (1997) discusses White women's deployment of rather vivid images of slavery to describe their own suffering. She argues that while the language of the enslaved was being appropriated, the suffering of actual slaves receded from their view and ultimately their consciousness. According to Spelman (1997, 113–17), suffragists who appropriated the language of enslaved individuals denied differences, by claiming commonality of experience, between themselves and the enslaved. While recognizing the utility of intersectionality, researchers seem to be engaging, consciously or unconsciously, in a similar manner to those described by Spelman. They are engaging in the same tactic used by the fictitious character, Skeeter, discussed above. *The Help*, in an analogous way to what is occurring within intersectionality research in political science with the study of Black women, if not challenged, is apt to treat Black women in a manner parallel to the White women suffragists described by Spelman. As a result, the experiences of Black women will remain lost, while their voices become appropriated in the construction of an identity of sameness and commonality. Consequently, essentialist presumptions can become implicit in our discussions of intersectionality.

The template structures used to engage in group muting specify viable research and research subjects. Consequently, some researches who might want to engage in certain types of research projects are discouraged and ultimately silenced. Or these researchers might be muted in the sense that they are forced, by the "rules of the game," to limit the nature of their research. Such silencing can result from covert or overt actions. I have experienced both types of silencing in my career. As a young professor, I was told by a colleague not to focus my research on Black women. According to him, I would be "pigeon holed" and my career would be stunted. Several years later, I face the challenge of finding spaces that are receptive to publishing my research and institutions that will view such work as valuable. As the data suggest, the top journals are less than likely to publish works on Black women and on intersectionality. Some institutions, implicitly or explicitly, value journal rankings and will give more "points" when hiring and during promotion and tenure decisions to research appearing in these high-ranking journals. This politics of research results in the marginalization of Black women and others who might desire to study intersectionality and Black womanhood.

This silence does not only affect what happens in academia, it also has implications for how we understand politics and Black women's reality. The muting process results in some research questions going unexplored. Questions such as: how are Black women who are not elected to office engaging and grappling with issues of intersectionality? How are they defining and responding to a multitude of issues that influence their daily lives? How they are defining themselves tends to be ignored. Including Black women in our studies of politics, by centering on their social, political, and cultural understandings, can broaden and (re)shape notions of how we study and ultimately understand politics. Such a framing has practical ramifications, as it allows us to further explore policies that target, directly and indirectly, Black women and their communities.

In my attempts to raise these issues, I have been dismissed. Some have dismissed my concerns about the treatment of Black women in cultural, social, and political realms by suggesting that I am not being realistic and at times appear incessantly and inappropriately angry. Such dismissals result in the failure to grasp a few critical aspects of intersectionality. One is accountability. Intersectionality requires us to be accountable in terms of how we treat the process of knowledge production and the producers of that knowledge. Beyond this, intersectionality also requires us to be accountable in terms of how knowledge is used to challenge power relations, which involves not minimizing differences and silencing the voices of those who have been "Othered." Second, to assume that Black women are to be satisfied with simply making a contribution to the larger field of political science is to lose sight of why Black women speak to the realities of living at the margins of many axes of oppression. This has long been a concern of Black women, both inside and outside of the academy. Black women have long been concerned about their representation and have fought valiantly to have their voices heard.

Black women want to be more than the "help" of political science and the subfield of women and politics. While I cannot speak for all Black women given that I do not have the requisite scientific data for support, I still make the claim that simply being satisfied with making a contribution to political science is not and has never been the goal of critical Black feminists. Faced with the possibility of the loss of voice and ultimately representation, I will not, like Aibileen, remain content dwelling in the South (read lack of progression and equality). Instead, I will remain passionate by questioning the distribution of power and holding myself and other researchers accountable for public treatments of Black women.

At the end of *The Help*, the main character goes on to realize her dreams. She escapes. However, the Black women who helped her, while risking their lives and livelihood were left to live with sexism, classism, and racism. The question that we have to confront as intersectionality traverses different spaces, is, will Black feminist theorists and, by default, Black women face a similar fate? Will they be forgotten and left to live within the same age-old axes of oppression, as intersectionality becomes *the help* of mainstream political science?

References

Alexander, M. Jacqui, and Chandra T. Mohanty. 1997. "Introduction: Genealogies, Legacies, Movements." In *Feminist Genealogies, Colonial Legacies, Democratic Futures*, ed. M. J. Alexander and C. T. Mohanty, xiii–xlii. New York: Routledge.

Alexander-Floyd, Nikol. 2012. "Disappearing Acts: Reclaiming Intersectionality in the Social Sciences in a Post-Black Feminist Era." *Feminist Formations* 24, no. 1: 1–25.

Ardener, Edwin. 1975. "Belief and the Problem of Women." In *Perceiving Women*, ed. S. Ardener, 1–17. London: Malaby Press.

Bobo, Jacqueline. 1995. *Black Women as Cultural Readers.* New York: Columbia University Press.

Clark Mane, Rebecca L. 2012. "Transmuting Grammars of Whiteness in Third-Wave Feminism: Interrogating Postrace Histories, Postmodern Abstraction, and the Proliferation of Difference in Third-Wave Texts." *Signs* 38, no. 1: 71–98.

Cohen, Cathy. 1999. *The Boundaries of Blackness: AIDS and the Breakdown of Black Politics.* Chicago: University of Chicago Press.

Collins, Patricia Hill. 2000. "Black Feminist Epistemology." In *Black Feminist Thought: Knowledge, Consciousness, and the Politics of Empowerment*, 251–72. New York: Routledge.

Crenshaw, Kimberlé. 1989. "Demarginalizing the Intersection of Race and Sex: A Black Feminist Critique of Antidiscrimination Doctrine, Feminist Theory and Antiracist Politics." *University of Chicago Legal Forum*: 139–67.

———. 1991. "Mapping the Margins: Intersectionality, Identity Politics, and Violence against Women of Color." *Stanford Law Review* 43, no. 6: 1241–99.

Ernst, Emily Rose. 2010. *The Price of Progressive Politics: The Welfare Rights Movement in the Era of Colorblind Racism.* New York & London: New York University Press.

Fairclough, Norman. 2003. *Analysing Discourse: Textual Analysis for Social Research.* London: Routledge.

Fogg-Davis, Hawley G. 2006. "Theorizing Black Lesbians within Black Feminism: A Critique of Same-Race Street Harrassment." *Politics & Gender* 2: 57–76.

Foucault, Michel. 1978. *The History of Sexuality: An Introduction.* Vol. 1. New York: Pantheon Books.

Garand, James C., and Micheal W. Giles. 2003. "Journals in the Discipline: A Report on a New Survey of American Political Scientists." *PS: Political Science and Politics* 36, no. 2: 293–308.

Guidroz, Kathleen, and Michele Berger. 2009. "A Conversation with Founding Scholars of Intersectionality Kimberlé Crenshaw, Nira Yuval-Davis, and Michelle Fine." In *The Intersectional Appraoch: Transforming the Academy through Race, Class & Gender*, ed. M. T. Berger and K.Guidroz, 61–78. Chapel Hill, NC: University of North Carolina Press.

Hancock, Ange-Marie. 2004. *The Politics of Disgust: The Public Identity of the Welfare Queen.* New York: New York University Press.

Haraway, Donna. 1988. "Situated Knowledges: The Science Question in Feminism and the Privilege of Partial Perspective." *Feminist Studies* 14, no. 3: 575–97.

hooks, bell. 1991. "Narratives of Struggle." In *Critical Fictions: The Politics of Imaginative Writing*, ed. P. Mariani, 53–61. Seattle, WA: Bay Press.

Jordan-Zachery, Julia S. 2012. "Blogging at the Intersections: Black Women, Identity, Lesbianism." *Politics & Gender* 8, no. 3: 405–14.

Kramarae, Cheris. 1981. *Women and Men Speaking: Frameworks for Analysis.* Rowley, MA: Newbury House Publishers, Inc.

Kwan, Peter. 1997. "Intersections of Race, Ethnicity, Class, Gender & Sexual Orientation: Jeffrey Dahmer and the Cosynthesis of Categories." *Hastings Law Journal* 48: 1257–92.

Logan, Shirley W. 1995. *With Pen and Voice: A Critical Anthology of Nineteenth-Century African American Women.* Carbondale, IL: Southern Illinois University.

Munck, Gerardo, and Richard Snyder. 2007. "Who Publishes in Comparative Politics? Studying the World from the United States." *PS: Political Science and Politics* 40, no. 2: 339–46.

Nath, Nisha. 2009. "Rediscovering the Potential of Feminist Theories of Intersectionality." Paper presented at the Candian Political Science Association Conference, Ottawa, ON.

Orbe, Mark. 2005. "Continuing the Legacy of Theorizing from the Margins: Conceptualizations of Co-Cultural Theory." *Women & Language* 28, no. 2: 65–66.

Risman, Barbara J. 2004. "Gender as a Social Structure: Theory Wrestling with Activism." *Gender & Society* 18, no. 4: 429–50.

Sesko, Amanda K., and Monica Biernat. 2010. " Prototypes of Race and Gender: The Invisibility of Black Women." *Journal of Experimental Social Psychology* 46: 356–60.

Sheriff, Robin E. 2000. "Exposing Silence as Cultural Censorship: A Brazilian Case." *American Anthropologist, New Series* 102, no. 1: 114–32.

Spelman, Elizabeth. 1997. *Fruits of Sorrow.* Boston, MA: Beacon Press.

Stockett, Kathryn. 2009. *The Help: A Novel.* New York: Penguin Group.

(Black) Papa Knows Best: Marion Barry and the Appeal to Black Authoritarian Discourse

Rosemary Ndubuizu
Rutgers University

In the early fall of 2007, Marion Barry, councilmember of Washington, DC, Ward 8, and former (four-time) mayor of Washington, DC, sauntered into a community meeting. He was there to meet with Barry Farm public housing residents and discuss the city's plan to transform their distressed and historically under-resourced 432-unit public housing community into a 1,500-unit mixed-income development.[1] After Barry had transformed the community meeting into a quasi-public rally supportive of his leadership, he insisted that their public housing community needed to be physically demolished and culturally transformed; no longer, he claimed, will the Barry Farm community be a symbol of cultural depravity, violence, and crime.

Eventually, one Barry Farm resident, who was a participant in Organizing Neighborhood Equity (ONE DC), a DC-based housing and jobs organizing group, quietly stood up and questioned the details of the plan.[2] She queried, "How are we sure that we will get one-to-one replacement? What is the legal enforcement of our right to return?" Barry snapped, "Of course, you will get to come back!" and immediately interrogated her involvement with ONE DC. He castigated her for aligning herself with an "anti-community" political organization, and condemned ONE DC as an outside group that was purportedly meddling in neighborhood affairs. Unlike these "outside" interest groups, Barry reassured the residents that he had their "true" interests in mind. Barry's caustic inquisition eventually made her cry. She quickly withdrew from political organizing work, later admitting to ONE DC staff that she was terrified of Barry's possible retribution and feared public censure for failing to support Barry's political agenda.

This story is one of many examples, but I ultimately share this story to highlight how Barry paternalistically interacts with dissenting Black women, while simultaneously muting intraracial and democratic debate.[3] His public performance of punitive paternalism is also evident within his public policy platform. I submit that three of Marion Barry's recent and widely publicized policy initiatives promoted between 2007 and 2011 reveal his troubling conservative gender politics. Furthermore, Barry leverages his conservative gender politics as a discursive tool to attain mainstream attention. His paternalistic politics also grants him support from unlikely political bedfellows, chiefly the conservative right.

To answer the question of how and why Marion Barry wields conservative gender politics to enhance his creditability and visibility requires a discussion about how race-first public officials pursue prominence in a post-civil rights era. Recent scholarship on Black officials analyzes how younger Black politicians like Barack Obama and Corey Booker promote racially transcendent politics in order to secure broad electoral and crossover support (Gillespie 2010). Conversely, Barry represents the older cohort of Black officials who rose to prominence during the Civil Rights Movement. These older leaders often utilize race-first politics and lack crossover support because they typically support controversial issues like affirmative action and mandatory set-asides for minority contractors. Gillespie (2010) contends these older leaders are declining in number and popularity. Gillespie is right. The number of civil rights politicians is decreasing; yet, Black male politicians like Marion Barry remain active in local politics. Therefore, the research question becomes: how do race-first politicians like Barry remain relevant in the post-civil rights era?

In this post-civil rights era, race-first politicians can attain a form of political attention typically reserved for racially transcendent politicians, while still employing explicit racial rhetoric, so long as they adopt certain popular racialized and gendered figures and/or narratives—such as the welfare queen trope or the Black Cultural Pathology Paradigm (Alexander-Floyd 2007; Jordan-Zachery 2009). Marion Barry's recent promotion of welfare reform, demolition of public housing developments, and a proposed moratorium on rental housing demonstrate his sensitivity to this discursive power. These policies clearly illustrate his paternalism, gender-bias, and desire for political and media attention. His policies also reveal his ideological investments in what I call Black authoritarian discourse. Although this concept is expounded upon later in this text, I define Black authoritarian discourse as ideological speech that intertwines scripts of conservative Black paternalism and culturally based assumptions of Black deviance that discipline poor Black women for not adhering to conservative, class-based models of femininity, motherhood, and upward mobility. Barry's use of Black authoritarian discourse evinces his (often futile and short-lived) attempts to seek mainstream attention within a post-civil rights era. This ideological narrative also reveals a gender imperative inherent in masculinist Black politics that Black feminists have historically critiqued (Beal 1970; Wallace 1978; Alexander-Floyd 2007; Jordan-Zachery 2009). My project builds on this Black feminist legacy by exposing the problematic and harmful effects of Barry's traditionalist and masculinist Black politics. Indeed, I argue Barry leverages Black authoritarian discourse to act as a self-appointed Black patriarch who seeks mainstream attention by promoting policies that discursively punish and reprimand poor Black women.

In what follows, I outline the recent scholarship on Black (male) officials' leadership styles. Then, I review recent Black feminist literature on how gender and racial tropes inform Black politics and public policy debates. Next, I use critical discourse analysis to scrutinize how Marion Barry uses Black authoritarian discourse to increase his political visibility through his endorsement of welfare reform and public/rental housing reform. I conclude my analysis with a discussion about how Barry strategically employs Black masculinist tropes of redemption, victimization, and reputation to legitimize his conservative gender policies within his majority-Black electoral ward.

Black Leadership Styles and the Need for a Black Feminist Analysis

Adolph Reed proffers a sharp critique of the Black political leadership structure that arose during the civil rights movement. In his classic work, *The Jesse Jackson Phenomenon*, Reed (1986) analyzes Jesse Jackson's 1984 presidential campaign to document the perils of this model of leadership. Reed claims protest leaders like Jesse Jackson lost their political efficacy once they transitioned into electoral politics, and condemns this strategy as ineffective because it relies on the problematic and liberal assumption that Black progress is primarily based on Black middle-class integration into positions of authority. Reed claims this capitalistic narrative also limits politicians' scope of change, thereby inhibiting their ability to advance structural reforms. Reed also censures the race-first Black officials' assumption that the Black community is an undifferentiated group that privileges race above all other categories of difference. Reed submits that this race-first posturing elides critical discussions about how these officials often promote their middle-class and business interests. This class bias becomes most evident in these politicians' ardent fight to protect affirmative action provisions, high-status appointments, and set-asides for minority contractors (65).

Reed claims this style of race-first leadership arose in the 1890s (read: Booker T. Washington) when White elites transferred resources through self-appointed Black spokesmen. He asserts that this practice facilitated the growth of "group-primalist" or "organic" leaders who base their leadership on claims of racial authenticity. This form of leadership also requires the affective performance of charisma. Reed submits that these charismatic Black protest politicians often advance symbolic rather than programmatic reforms. He also maintains that the mainstream media promote the fallacy that Black people prefer symbolic politics and racial spokespersons. Reed comments that ". . . the orthodox media tacitly colluded with his [Jesse Jackson's] exaggerated contention that he was running to be recognized as paramount national Black spokesman, an office for which no election ever has been held" (110).

Similar to Reed, Johnson (2007) reviews and critiques key civil rights activists' strategic transitions from protest to electoral politics as a leading medium for social change in his monograph, *Revolutionaries to Race Leaders: Black Power and The Making of African American Politics*. He contends texts like Cruse's *The Crisis of the Negro Intellectual* (1967) popularized race-first political rhetoric and vanguard politics. Johnson insists that this political approach ultimately failed because "such assertions of Black vanguardism shared a tendency to downplay the ideological and political diversity among 'the wretched of the earth' and overinvest in the revolutionary potential of subaltern minorities and colonized peoples at the expense of other social forces" (18). As such, Johnson argues that a race-first and vanguard strategy forces African American politicians and activists to "close ranks" and minimize intragroup differences (88).

Reed and Johnson's review of these protest leaders is astute, and they convincingly critique this model of leadership. Despite their insightful critique, there are limitations. Even though all of the leaders they apprise are men, they do not explicitly address how gendered tropes inform Black leadership. For instance, if charisma and racial authenticity are embodied characteristics of Black (male) leaders, then how do gender norms inform their political positions?

Gillespie also builds upon this literature about Black leadership. She avers that there is another "wave" of Black politicians who emerged after the protest elite cohort.[4] In *Whose Black Politics? Cases in Post-Racial Black Leadership*, Gillespie (2010) offers an alternative model to analyze this new cohort of Black leadership. She insists that these new leaders fundamentally differ from previous ones because of their ability to advance racially transcendent campaigns. She claims younger politicians like Newark Mayor Cory Booker and President Barack Obama appropriate this strategy by avoiding race-specific issues and emphasizing politics that appeal to the broader (non-Black) electorate. She characterizes these new officials as "ambitious politicians with more moderate politics" (13). Their moderate and racially transcendent politics often boost their crossover appeal. Crossover appeal, for Gillespie, means that these younger politicians "build political alliances that circumvent the traditional Black establishment, and deliberately work to establish more diverse appeal, outreach, and power centers among the electorate" (Gillespie 2012). Critics Dixon (2012) and Reed (2008) decry these younger politicians' enhancement of their crossover appeal when they espouse neoliberalist positions like the privatization of public services. These critics argue that ideological discourse plays a critical role in crossover appeal. Put differently, they contend that these younger politicians appropriate neoconservative discourse in order to gain political legitimacy and widespread support. They also lament that these younger politicians tend to avoid race-explicit political conversations about Black mass incarceration, Black unemployment, and foreclosures. Sinclair-Chapman and Price (2008) wonder if these younger leaders actually *transcend* race and suggest these leaders simply *manipulate* existing gender and racial tropes differently than their race-first predecessors. In brief, these scholars recognize that ideological discourse informs crossover appeal and Black leadership generally. Because ideological discourse characterizes Black leadership, it is important to review how older politicians like Marion Barry manipulate ideological discourses in order to gain political prominence.

In order to explore how gendered and racialized narratives inscribe political debates, I turn to Black feminist scholarship. Nikol Alexander-Floyd's (2007) book, *Gender, Race and Nationalism in Contemporary Black Politics*, documents how Black Nationalism and masculinity scripts instruct Black politics. Alexander-Floyd insists that certain narratives like the Black Cultural Pathology Paradigm (BCPP) shape Black politics. She describes BCPP as a "popular set of assumptions of Black family breakdown and cultural deviance" (3). She argues that Black officials leverage BCPP discourses to transform race-first politics into the politics of Black male loyalty.

Other Black feminists document how stereotypes about poor Black women sway public policy. For example, Roberts (1998) documents how politicians used negative stereotypes (e.g., Black crack cocaine users) to police Black women's bodies and curtail their reproductive choices. Jordan-Zachery (2009) examines how politicians manipulate and deploy images and symbols like the Mammy, the urban teen mother, and welfare queen to advance punitive welfare, crime, and family reforms. In short, Black feminist scholars' work provides the intellectual groundwork to analyze how gendered and racialized messages affect Black politicians' agendas.

In order to examine how gendered and ideological discourse shapes Black leadership, I examine Marion Barry's recent campaign to become the national advocate for welfare reform, his publicized support for public housing demolition, and his legislative attempts to ban rental housing.[5] As previously noted, some political scientists may question my selection of Barry as a representative case study for paternal Black leadership because of his age or controversial political and personal history, but I suspect Barry's cultural paternalism is often shared with younger politicians (Reed 2008). As media-appointed racial spokespersons, Black male politicians are typically compelled to explain the (cultural and rarely structural) underpinnings of Black poverty to mainstream and non-Black audiences. Consequently, Black officials may strategically use policy as a class-based and morality-enforcing device, sanctioning citizens who do not adhere to cultural codes like social and economic mobility, two-parent households, and so forth (Alexander-Floyd 2007, 2012; Jordan-Zachery 2009).

Following Julia Jordan-Zachery's application of Critical Discourse Analysis (CDA) in her monograph in *Black Women, Cultural Images and Social Policy* (2009), I use a similar methodological approach to study Barry's discursive exploitation of Black pathology scripts. As previously stated, Jordan-Zachery uses CDA to identify how public officials use gendered images and class-based and Black deviance tropes to justify punitive family welfare reforms. Discourse scholar, van Dijk (1993), describes CDA as tool to examine how dominance and social inequality are (re)produced in discourse. He explains, "Power and dominance are usually organized and *institutionalized*. The social dominance of groups is thus not merely enacted, individually, by its group members [. . .] It may also be supported or condoned by other group members, sanctioned by the courts, legitimated by laws, enforced by the police and ideologically sustained and reproduced by the media or textbooks" (emphasis in the original, 255). In short, van Djik avers that CDA analytically exposes "the intricate relationship between text, talk, social cognition, power, society and culture" (253). Similar to Jordan-Zachery, I argue that policy reform relies on imagery and symbols, but my project focuses on how politicians create images of themselves. I examine how Barry attempts to (re)create a particular image of his leadership through his public advocacy for welfare and rental housing reforms. Because CDA assumes that a person's discourse is never arbitrary, I unpack the ideological assumptions, limitations, and contradictions inherent in Barry's policies and speech (Jordan-Zachery 2009). Further, I analyze how Barry legitimates his policies by appealing to conservatives, media, and academic discourse (van Dijk 1993).

I use CDA to reveal how Barry's policies rely on Black authoritarian discourse. I define this discourse as speech or text that relies on assumptions of Black cultural deficiency, Black paternalism, and class-based performances of parenting and upward mobility. Discourse scholar, Goldschläger (1982), argues that speakers of authoritarian discourse generally seek to conserve power, demand complete obedience, and monitor the thoughts and wills of others. He qualifies authoritarian discourse as "statements whose goal is to direct the life and social behavior of the receiver, placing him under the guidance and authority of the emitter" (11). Briefly put, speakers of Black authoritarian discourse exploit prevailing assumptions of Black authenticity and heteronormative respectability, enforce hierarchical and patriarchal relations with Black constituents, silence intraracial differences, and appropriate mainstream scripts about Black deviance—particularly gendered, racialized, and maligning narratives about low-income urban Blacks. To be sure, Black authoritarian discourse is a contemporary redeployment of historical narratives about Black idleness and racial uplift (Hartman 1997). More specifically, Black politicians who deploy this discourse typically agree with many Americans who claim poor people have easier lives because of their access to demonized entitlements like welfare, public housing, and food stamps (Pew Research Center 1998, 2012). Accordingly, Black authoritarian discourse assumes Black officials can demand behavior modification in exchange for government resources. I argue this discourse affords Barry visibility and continued political popularity because it resonates with widespread assumptions about the disciplinarian role that the government should play in curbing poor people's supposed exploitation of the "benevolent" state. My interpretative methodology attends to how Barry leverages this Black authoritarian discourse to enhance his own image as a reputable political actor.

Marion Barry: The Political Engine That Will Not Quit

At age seventy-six, Marion Barry remains in Washington, DC politics. His political career has spanned more than forty years. In 1965, Barry moved to Washington, DC, to continue his organizing duties with the Student Nonviolent Coordinating Committee (SNCC). He entered politics in 1971 after winning a seat on DC's school board. In 1975, he became DC's at-large city councilmember. Then, he served three consecutive terms as Mayor and delivered the 1984 presidential nomination speech for Jesse Jackson, Sr. This ascending list of political accomplishments was interrupted by Barry's famous drug arrest in 1990. Pundits assumed Barry's electoral career was finished, but Barry had different plans (Alexander-Floyd 2007). After serving a six-month prison sentence, Barry ran for the city council seat in DC's majority-Black Ward 8 in 1992 and won. He led a redemption-themed campaign with the popular slogan, "He May Not Be Perfect, But He is Perfect for D.C.!" Two years later, Barry advanced his redemption-themed campaign once again when he announced his candidacy for the mayoral seat (Agronsky 1991; Plotz 1993; Barras 1998). Barry's reformed image supposedly endeared him to many African Americans, and he won the mayoral seat for a fourth time in 1994 with 50 percent of the vote (Plotz 1993; Jet Magazine 1994). During Barry's fourth mayoral term, DC was placed in federal receivership and his mayoral powers were severely abridged. After leaving public office in 1999, Barry stated that he would retire from politics. Yet, less than ten years later, he returned and ran for the city council of Ward 8, winning 70 percent of the vote. In 2012, with 87.98 percent of the total vote, he won his third consecutive term as city councilmember for Ward 8.

Barry's forty years in public office may be notable to some scholars due to his uncanny ability to win reelection campaigns despite his controversial political history. But, what is particularly noteworthy is his frequent return to Ward 8. As previously mentioned, Barry first ran for the Ward 8 councilmember seat in 1992. Since then, Barry has been elected as a councilmember of Ward 8 three more times. The demographics of Ward 8 may explain Marion Barry's enduring electoral connection. The residents of Ward 8 are overwhelmingly Black. In 2010, 94 percent of all residents were Black and close to 40 percent of the residents earned income at or below the poverty line (Neighborhood Info DC 2012). This ward also has one of the highest levels of joblessness in the United States—25.2 percent of all residents are unemployed (Homan 2011). Metaphorically, Barry's frequent return to Ward 8 signals his ideological investment in Black Nationalism and race-first leadership.[6] During his 2007–2011 tenure as the Ward 8 councilmember, Barry has touted specific legislative priorities, including employment opportunities for returning citizens, affordable homeownership, and redevelopment of existing subsidized communities (e.g., HOPE VI developments). In pro-Barry rallies, Marion Barry has claimed that his policy agenda reflects his desire to materially "uplift" Ward 8 residents (Mummolo 2010).

Cut-Off Dependency: Barry's Campaign to Terminate Welfare Benefits

In November 2010, Barry made national news. In his interviews with Bill O'Reilly, Fox Business News, and local DC news outlets, Barry publicized his recent campaign: to terminate Temporary Assistance to Needy Families (TANF) assistance after five years. His bill also called for the elimination of childcare subsides. In his Washington Post Opinion editorial, Barry bemoaned that DC's TANF has "failed our residents for years"; he lamented that the policy's "result has been to enslave residents in joblessness and dependency on the government rather than lifting them up and giving them an opportunity to achieve self-sufficiency through job training and employment" (Barry 2010).

Barry led the media and political campaign to terminate welfare benefits after five years, instead of the bill's cosponsor, Yvette Alexander (an African American woman). Barry's sole advocacy for welfare reform exposes his leadership style and desire for media and political attention. In his effort to rally broad support for this bill, Barry uses Black authoritarian discourse. More specifically, he links race-first rhetoric and culture of poverty logic with class-based scripts of heteronormative respectability and Black paternalism. True to his race-first rhetoric, Barry uses provocative race-explicit commentary in his op-ed to incite anger and galvanize broad support. Moreover, Barry insinuates that he is a modern-day Moses, rescuing welfare receipts from the hellish fate of "welfare dependency." Since he also claims the side of racial justice and sound rationality, Barry summarily dismisses his political opposition as incompetent do-gooders who keep TANF recipients "enslaved, without jobs and without hope" (Barry 2010; Suderman 2012a).

Although Barry never directly names these welfare recipients as mainly Black women or mothers in his op-ed, he identifies these long-term TANF recipients as society's "most vulnerable" members and encourages others, notably Mayor-elect Vincent Gray, to help him transform these "vulnerable" TANF recipients into paid workers. Discursively ignoring the empirical point that Black *mothers* comprise well over 90 percent of DC's TANF caseload, Barry tacitly emphasizes his symbolic role as a benevolent, rational, and Black patriarch who innocuously seeks to curb Black women's unruly dependency on the state (Acs and Loprest 2003). With this figurative subject position, Barry can gently but sternly break these Black women's welfare dependency and compel them to become better versions of themselves—namely heteronormative, wage-earning, and, thus, respectable mothers.

Barry's Black authoritarian discourse certainly relies on the controversial assumption that wage work instills a politics of propriety, which is presumptively absent in poor (Black) mothers (Joyner 2006). Barry shares conservative political scientist Lawrence Mead's sentiments about welfare (Mead 1993). Like Mead, Barry argues that citizenship requires employment, and his publicity campaign for welfare reform translated into a bid to recruit more service jobs for DC's poor. Barry petitioned Wal-Mart and similar retail service corporations to come to Ward 8 and "improve" the moral stock of poor Black women through employment. Justifying African Americans' employment in the service sector, Barry nostalgically notes, "There was a time in the African American community, even during segregation, when 90 percent of the waiters were Black. This is an excellent opportunity for residents to learn menus, to *learn courtesy* and make up to $200 to $300 a day" (DePuyt 2010; italics mine). Similar to conservatives, Barry's rhetoric romanticizes history to compel putatively lazy Black welfare recipients to submit to any wage work. He implies welfare recipients today lack the morality and dignity their ancestors earned through their paid work. Never mind that racism and segregation remain institutionalized and continue to restrict living-wage job opportunities and equitable pay (Conrad 2008).

Since Barry assumes that Black women are supposed to be the cultural bearers of morality, he uses welfare reform as an opportunity to teach these mothers how to embody the appropriate morals and lifestyle practices. Put differently, he uses his political position to discursively enforce a respectability standard for these Black women by assuming that their incorporation into the formal economy would teach them the values that they lack, namely civility and hospitality.[7] The irony begs commentary. Marion Barry's morally questionable lifestyle choices, including decades-long substance dependency and extramarital affairs, are ignored when he condemns Black mothers for not learning "normal" lifestyle practices.[8] As a Black male politician, he assumes his metaphorical and literal exploitation of women is not subject to the same moralistic critique he directs at poor Black women. Consequently, Barry uses policy to create a fictive, hierarchal, and symbiotic union with poor Black women. As their self-appointed Black patriarch, he could also castigate them and dole out sympathy and protection only to the most deserving Black women (Alexander-Floyd 2012).[9]

Barry's neoconservative rhetoric is striking, but his inability to recognize his theoretical limitations is significant. First, he assumes that poor (Black) mothers' care work is not "real" work, unless they earn an income outside the home.[10] As such, their care work is rendered invisible and inconsequential. Since poor single mothers lack the resources to hire care workers, they must invariably consider their care work secondary to their wage work (Mink 1998). Second, Barry ideologically assumes western normative ideals of self-sufficiency and autonomy. Feminist philosopher Young (2002) contends that self-sufficiency is a utopian desire, rarely replicable in society. Young insists that humans are connected through a web of interdependent relationships. Feminist scholar Fineman (2002) argues that self-sufficiency and autonomy hide a heteronormative imperative. She claims, "As an ideological construct, the private [heterosexual and middle-class] family masks the universal and inevitable nature of dependency and allows the public and government officials to frame rhetoric in terms of idealizing capitalistic individualism, independence, self-sufficiency and autonomy" (224). Furthermore, they suggest that the welfare reform rhetoric, like Barry's, appropriates the sinister ideological belief that poor and single Black women's noncompliance with the state's expectations to work outside the home and create nuclear families is metaphorically tantamount to treason.

Barry's legislative campaign to reform welfare eventually failed. Barry's colleagues refused to consider the bill because it had far-reaching consequences: close to forty percent of DC's approximately 17,000 welfare recipients would be denied services.[11] Nevertheless, Barry's bill did allow him to become a media darling for a short time (DePuyt 2010; Sherman 2010). Several conservative pundits wrote op-eds supporting Barry's recent crusade to end Black women's supposed dependency on the state. In "On Welfare, an

Unlikely Voice of Reason," Michael Tanner, a Senior Fellow at the Cato Institute, cites the demographics of Ward 8 as an indisputable signifier of Barry's expertise about welfare and Black communities. Tanner (2010) then recommends that other Democrats listen to Barry's putative race knowledge. Tanner admits that he has found an unlikely ally in the fight to abolish welfare, and he is not alone. In an anonymous Washington Post editorial, the conservative pundit applauds Barry's welfare reform advocacy and underscores his policy reversal on welfare—but Barry's adoption of neoconservative beliefs should not be interpreted as happenstance; he strategically deploys this policy to advance his credibility as a relevant politician ("Questions about Welfare in the District" 2010). Claiming to be an aspiring "national welfare reform advocate," Barry utilizes his victimized and redemptive narrative to legitimize his Black authoritarianism, which ultimately garners him political and media attention.

Undoubtedly, Barry discursively pimps poor Black women to improve his image because he recognizes that the negative images of poor Black women metaphorically make them the perfect political scapegoat. Unlike Black males who have a redemptive masculinity trope, these poor Black women are treated as politically expendable and non-redeemable. Barry's advocacy of welfare reform also suggests that there are no nuanced ways of understanding Black women's poverty in political discourse—perhaps the only way poor Black women can demonstrate their "redemption" is through their explicit submission to the state and Black paternal authority.

Tear Down the "Dysfunction": Barry's Campaign to Reform Poor Black Women's Homes

Barry's Black authoritarian discourse also emerges in his support of HOPE VI/New Communities and suggested ban on future rental housing development. In 2006, the DC city council passed a resolution approving the future demolition and redevelopment of Barry Farm into a mixed-income housing development (New Communities 2012).[12] Barry lauded the passage of the bill, suggesting it would herald a different and "better" future for DC's poor. Some DC officials colloquially refer to New Communities as a more "humane" version of the bipartisan-supported Housing Opportunities for People Everywhere (HOPE VI), the Housing and Urban Development's program.[13]

One of the communities, Barry Farm public housing, is located in Ward 8. Over the last several decades, Barry Farm has gained notoriety as a "troubled" neighborhood bedeviled with crime and poverty. Justifying his support for Barry Farm redevelopment, Marion Barry carps that the "national government's policy of building housing for poor people stacked all together, sociologically and culturally" has failed DC residents (Muller 2011). His comment reveals his ideology: he appropriates the bipartisan political rhetoric that public and subsidized housing enables "concentrated poverty" and encourages "underclass" behavior, specifically single mothers, "absent" fathers, illegal substance use, teen pregnancy, and violence. His remark also suggests that he appreciates new urbanism scholarship, which undergirds this political ideology.

New Communities and HOPE VI share an ideological commitment to New Urbanism. This architectural philosophy advocates for "streetscapes, aesthetically continuous with surrounding areas that would inspire pride and community in their residents" (Duryea 2006, 567–68). In the 1980s, urban planner Fainstein (2010) argues academic and political conversations about the "underclass" infiltrated urban planning discourse; therefore, New Urbanist-inspired mixed-income housing became a positive alternative to public housing.

A luminary figure in underclass scholarship, sociologist Wilson argues that the spatial concentration of poor Black people results in the development of "group-specific cultural traits (orientations, habits and worldviews as well as styles of behavior and particular skills) that emerged from patterns of racial exclusion and that may not be conducive to factors that facilitate social mobility" (Wilson 2009, 2). Wilson offers a provocative argument about the cultural traits learned in these environments, but he ultimately ignores the political ideology at play in his rhetoric. Black underclass scholarship often assumes that poor people are personally responsible for their impoverishment (Reed 1992; Gordon 1997; Crooms 2001).[14,15] Steinberg (2010) critiques the concentrated poverty theory underlying HOPE VI and similar redevelopment projects. Here Steinberg problematizes the concentrated poverty theory's epistemological logic:

> [Housing policy advocates] make the fatal mistake of treating concentrated poverty as a factor sui generis [. . .] With a sleight of hand, all these powerful structural forces that involve major political and economic institutions are conflated into a single factor—concentrated poverty, which is now identified as *the* central problem in terms of analysis and social policy. (219, emphasis in original)

Furthermore, Steinberg submits that these housing policies fail to address the structural reasons for poverty and, in fact, reinforce the racist assumption that urban Black people are responsible for intergenerational poverty. He cites the fact that the state's lack of intervention in rural communities, which confront similar challenges, as evidence of the state's racially biased assumptions of Black cultural dysfunction.[16,17]

A few critics of HOPE VI/New Communities highlight how the housing policy exploits the myth that these homes deserve to be demolished because these primarily Black female-headed households do not adhere to the traditional and class-based two-parent household model (Duryea 2006; Fritz 2009). Indeed, DC's Office of Planning and Economic Development's webpage identifies concentrated poverty and the high number of Black female-headed households as two justificatory examples for New Communities. Thus, the Moynihan assumption that Black female-headed households enable dysfunction informs HOPE VI/New Communities policy. In "Rethinking Gender in U.S. Housing Policy," Fritz (2009) adds, "U.S. housing policy in the twentieth century is inextricably linked to perceptions of gender and the single family home, and the traditional nuclear family has been rendered a hegemonic entity" (62).

The federal endorsement of New Urbanism probably informed Barry's choice to support the demolition and redevelopment of the Barry Farm community. His initial mayoral campaign in 1974 touted the need to re-invest in public housing and encouraged residency in vacant public housing (Barras 1998). But by the early 2000s, Barry changed his tune, lamenting that public housing became a hotbed of cultural dysfunction (Muller 2011). Barry's political support of New Urbanism and New Communities also reveals his investment in Black authoritarian discourse. As a patriarchal "race leader," he can tell public housing residents how they should structure their homes. Ergo, Barry advocates for state intervention in the restructuring of Black women's homes and behavior modification partially due to the Moniyhan/Malthusian contention that poor and single Black women are unable to raise culturally adjusted children. And now armed with underclass scholarship and new urbanism, Barry can advance his policies as legitimate, empirically based and, therefore, sound, conveniently eschewing a democratic and public debate about how his housing policies harbor a problematic and ideological bias.

This gendered understanding of housing policy also explains Marion Barry's recent push to ban future development of rental housing in Ward 8 (DePillis 2011). In defense of his bill, he argued, "The American dream is to own a home. And Black people have not gotten the American dream as much as they need to. Somebody can rent for 20 years, and has no equity in their unit at all" (DePillis 2011). Undeniably, renters usually lack ownership equity. But *organized* renters can exercise influence over the direction of their rental community through tenant associations and advocate for shared owner-ship partnerships. Organizing groups like ONE DC help DC residents understand their tenants' rights, strengthen community ties and, if desired, can assist residents with the purchase and conversion of their buildings into limited equity cooperatives, which help ensure long-term affordability (Gordon Nembhard 2009). Barry's failure to mention these alternative ways for renters to increase their ownership equity signals his troubling conceptions of homeownership and citizenship. In this media interview, Barry suggests that rental communities like Barry Farm enable crime because these residents, unlike homeowners, have no stake in their neighborhoods. He states, "Renters will allow drug dealers in the neighborhood. It's a fact. It's a doggone fact" (Barry, quoted in DePillis 2011).[18] Perhaps anticipating questions about whether his age and long-term drug use have impaired his mental faculties, Barry responds: "I've thought about this; it's not a kneejerk reaction" (DePillis 2011).

Again, Barry's Black authoritarian discourse is evident. Complaining that 75 percent of Ward 8 residents are renters, Barry insinuates institutional and racial injustice when he suggests that African Americans have been imprisoned within and handicapped by the rental market (DeBonis 2012). To be sure, residential segregation and economic marginal-ization exacerbate Black poverty, but Barry's housing policies clearly ignore the multiple forms of ownership that residents can use to build (community) wealth. Instead, Barry uses housing policy to demand single-family homeownership, a particular embodiment of capitalistic and liberal success. As such, he manipulates narratives about residential and economic oppression to justify his patriarchal, liberal, and capitalistic project. Similar to his welfare reform crusade, he fails to explicitly announce the renters' race, class, and gender background, albeit he speaks of renters as a culturally troubled group. But since he frequently touts renter statistics of Ward 8 in his media correspondence, he must know that unmarried Black women head three out of four households in Ward 8 (Craig 2010). As the Black paternal leader of Ward 8, Barry assumes that he can tell Black women that they need to reconfigure their lives and finances so they can attain the "American dream" of single-family homeownership.[19]

Barry's legislative bid to prohibit rental housing development failed. This time, Barry did not garner as much public attention and support as he did with his welfare reform bill (DePillis 2011). Nevertheless, his bill and subsequent media interviews provided Barry the opportunity to exercise his Black authoritarian discourse, while also implying poor Black women, as leaseholders, are crime enablers. Ideologically similar to Patrick Moyni-han's 1965 controversial report on Black poverty, Barry suggests that the persistence of Black poverty is primarily a cultural and personal problem rather than a structural one.

In short, Barry uses housing and welfare policy to tout his simplistic and symbolic vision of Black liberalism: he presumes if poor Black women simply marry, renounce welfare, work at Wal-Mart or other service-oriented jobs, and buy a house, then his selective understanding of the civil rights movement's goal—poor Black people's integration into the middle class—would be realized.[20]

Why Do Black People Still "Love" Barry?

A Washington Post poll of 1,002 DC residents in 2012 cited Marion Barry as the highest-rated official in the nation's capital ("Washington Post Poll" 2012). The poll notes 81 percent of Black residents in DC positively view Barry's leadership, while only seven percent of White residents agree with this perspective. Understanding the source of Barry's persistent popularity among Black people is a complicated question, but the answer lies in part within Barry's sophisticated utilization of Black masculinity tropes.

In "Cultural Politics of Black Masculinity," Gordon (1997) cites two tropes of masculinity that Black men employ in order to secure acceptance and recognition within Black communities: reputation and respectability. Black males demonstrate "respectability" through their "hard work, economic frugality and independence, community activism, mutual help and uplift, personal responsibility, religious faith, and conservative styles of self-presentation" (41). These men can earn a positive "reputation" through "acts of sexual prowess, rejection of (especially White) authority, gratuitous violence, virtuosity in expressive culture, extraordinary command of language, and living by wits and guile" (43). In politics, Barry gains reputation and credibility when he invokes his numerous and widely publicized heterosexual relationships, victim narrative of drug abuse, and imprisonment (Carbado 1997; Gordon 1997). He also gains respectability because he links narratives of racial victimization with stories of civil rights activism and decades-long public service. But Barry also uses an injury-based narrative to advance a biblically inspired redemption narrative. As the heroic prodigal son of Washington, DC, he can personify features of Black deviance, fallibility, and redemption while retaining the prerogative of paternalism, because his embodiment and narrative approximates Black people's (narrow and gender-biased) racial story (Alexander-Floyd 2012, 140–41). Indeed, Barry frequently enlists Black churches and mosques to perform his rituals of redemption (Barras 1998; Mummolo 2010). Posturing as a redeemed and reputable heterosexual subject, Barry uses legislation to treat Ward 8 as his personal fiefdom, unilaterally imposing his traditionalist standard of middle-class respectability on all Ward 8 residents. Ironically, his performance endears him to some of his constituents because his behavior is registered as an authentic form of "wounded Black masculinity," a subjecthood worthy of the Black community's (particularly Black women's) protection and support (Carbado 1997; Alexander-Floyd 2007). Ultimately, his performance of Black wounded masculinity minimizes or silences Black women's agency and subject complexity. His race-based narratives of injury and authenticity continue to garner favor among Ward 8 residents, particularly (elderly) Black women (Craig 2012; Suderman 2012ab). Barry's campaign manager, a sixty-eight-year-old Ward 8 African American woman, Sandy Allen, explains Barry's sustained fame, "Marion is one of the greatest politicians that I have ever known. [African Americans] feel that he is one of them. He has not gotten so far above them that he does not understand their plight" (Nuckols 2012).[21] A Ward 8 grandmother concurs, "We love Mr. Barry because he's the only person we can talk to. He's been through the same things we've been through. He's a good man" (Plotz 1993). Clearly, these Black women embrace Barry because they consider him heroic and an authentic representation of Blackness. Perhaps, these women willingly accept Barry's masculinist and socially conservative ideologies because they read Barry as a steadfast yet fallible leader who remains committed to helping Ward 8 residents actualize their (sub)conscious desire for recognition as legitimate and *normative* subject-citizens. For them, Barry's political style signals his commitment to making sure that poor Black individuals reform their lives so they can effectively mimic middle-class and heteronormative subjects, implicitly hoping that they will approximate White conceptions of liberal citizenship—a performance-based discourse that relies on historical binaries, like White morality/Black immorality and Black idleness/White industry (Hartman 1997). Because the proper embodiment of liberalism has always been tied to whiteness, Barry eagerly steps in as a Black interlocutor of liberalism, reminding Black people, particularly Black women, that they can *possibly* gain respect and inclusion within the American body politic if they freely submit to the state's microregulation of their lives and homes. To be sure, some women worry that Barry exploits their support. Ward 8 Democrats' President, Reverend R. Joyce Scott, recently ended her long-term support of Barry.[22] But a few months before Rev. Scott publicly opposed Barry's 2012 reelection bid, she tempered her criticism with words of affection: "We feel [Barry] has taken our support for granted. *We love you* [*Barry*], but we're concerned about the way you've handled the community the last four years, or the lack thereof" (Suderman 2012b; italics mine). But even with the rising number of disgruntled Barry critics, many African American Ward 8 residents insist that Barry is the only man with the experience and the trust of the Ward 8 community.[23]

Rethinking the Role of Gender in Black Leadership Styles

In order to remain politically relevant, Barry appropriates Black authoritarian discourse, which naturalizes the demonization of poor Black women. There is, therefore, a conceptual link between discourse, political visibility, and gendered performances. Future research is needed to explore how gender, discourse, crossover appeal, and/or political visibility intersect. In other words, how do Black officials use gender tropes and discourse in order to increase their visibility as a "racially transcendent" or a race-first leader? Are there certain political discourses that Black men can use but women cannot? These questions can broaden the scope of the analysis, as they relate to Black leadership models.

Younger politicians like Barack Obama and Cory Booker may perpetuate similar discourses in their attempt to become and remain crossover leaders who retain strong Black support. Political viability may demand that Black male politicians utilize heteronormative and Black deviance tropes. Obama's Black fatherhood speech in June 2008 clearly suggests that his political viability increased because of his use of paternalistic and Black pathology narratives (Reed 2008). Perhaps, research in this area will inspire scholars, activists, and organizing groups like ONE DC to offer and popularize organizing strategies that discredit Black politicians' undemocratic authoritarianism and reject the political, hegemonic condemnation of Black communities, specifically (poor) Black women.

Notes

1. The public housing name Barry Farm has no relation to Marion Barry.
2. ONE DC is a nonprofit, which organizes long-time and low-income residents of color in support of living wage jobs and affordable housing. I currently volunteer with ONE DC. From 2007 to 2010, I was a paid community organizer with ONE DC. This story was recounted to me by a colleague and resource organizer, Dominic Moulden. More information about ONE DC can be found on its website: www.onedconline.org.
3. Contrary to Barry's defamatory characterization of ONE DC, ONE DC boasts a primarily Black and citywide membership. Indeed, ONE DC's historical organizing campaigns began in Shaw, a Northwest DC neighborhood, but gradually expanded its work into other sections of Washington, DC. Clearly, Barry sought to demonize ONE DC to galvanize community support for his political position.
4. Gillespie uses a "wave" analogy to document the differences between Black leaders. However, many feminists have long critiqued this practice as deceptive because the wave analogy often mutes variation and interconnection (Laughlin et al. 2010). In Gillespie's article, the wave analogy suggests that there is a dominant form of elected official, but elides discussion about why there are older politicians who still remain in public office. There is little discussion about the interaction and connection between older and younger politicians.
5. I understand that Barry's attempt to attain public attention may not be limited to these policies alone.
6. Read E. Frances White (1990) and Alexander-Floyd's (2007) work on the problematic gender politics of Black Nationalisms.
7. Barry's comment that Black women need to learn manners is similar to Newt Gingrich's comment that young poor (Black) children need to learn the "dignity" of hard work. Gingrich contends that poor neighborhoods (read: Black/Brown mothers) simply breed criminals: "Really poor children, in really poor neighborhoods have no habits of working and have nobody around them who works so they have no habit of showing up on Monday. They have no habit of staying all day, they have no habit of I do this and you give me cash unless it is illegal" (Huisenga 2011).
8. I do not seek to condemn or evaluate the morality of Barry's or anyone else's sexual choices. I just seek to explore the contradiction and hypocrisy of his personal practices in contrast to his political claims about poor Black women's lifestyle choices.
9. In his op-ed, Barry stipulates that only Black women who suffer the most severe barriers to employment should be granted leniency under his revised welfare reform bill. (Barry 2010).
10. During the recent national debate about whether 2012 Republican Presidential candidate Mitt Romney's wife earned wages—if her care work was a "real" work—Obama and other Democrats rallied to her defense. It is notable that these same people enforce a double standard with single poor mothers. Their work is not care work because they do not fit the normative, nuclear family model. In response to this national debate, Maureen Dowd queries in her editorial, "So the dignity of work only applies to poor moms?" (Dowd 2012).
11. But shortly thereafter in December 2010, DC city council approved budget cuts to TANF, specifically agreeing to gradually cease providing assistance for unemployed parents who received TANF assistance for more than five years by 2014 (Shapira 2012). It is not clear whether Barry's welfare reform campaign motivated this particular TANF reform. The bill's passage does suggest that punitive and antisocial welfare politics continue to be a politically popular approach for liberals and conservatives alike.
12. Four public housing communities were selected to be a part of DC's massive redevelopment effort to attack "high rates of poverty and unemployment" and remove the "blight and deterioration of the housing stock" (New Communities 2012).
13. DC's Office of Planning and Economic Development's webpage lists its guiding principles for the redevelopment of these communities: one-for-one replacement; the opportunity to return/stay; mixed-income housing; and build first (New Communities 2012).
14. Even Wilson chides politicians' narrow interpretation of his scholarship: he condemns them for eschewing complex structural reasons for poverty and problematically assuming the spatial proximity of nonpoor people near poor people will effectively reduce poverty (Wilson 2009).
15. One curious omission in this "underclass" scholarship is why the scholarly gaze and onus of social change are placed on poor bodies in the first place. This scholarship (Wilson 1987; Denton and Massey 1993) often assumes that poor Black bodies "own" social dysfunction. How social dysfunction is defined is political and ideological too—certain moral acts like out-of-wedlock childbirth or imprisonment are highlighted, but not others. For instance, does adultery, gambling, or divorce count? Do these acts inhibit the development or sustainment of nuclear and upwardly mobile families (assuming this is the signifier for morality, normalcy, and progress)? Are poor Blacks always socially inclined to commit

all types of social dysfunction? This omission suggests that there is a Malthusian and racialized logic at play. Much of this scholarship problematically reinforces the government and societal gaze on poor (Black) bodies, because they are marked as indelibly different and deficient.

16. The replacement units are often used as an alternative affordable housing definition, which often makes the "affordable" units less affordable for the original residents. Organizing Neighborhood Equity (ONE DC) advocates for housing that is affordable for residents who earn less than $50,000 a year. This organization focuses on this level of affordability, because in rapidly changing cities like Washington DC, the definition of affordability given by the Department of Housing and Urban Development (HUD) encompasses the metropolitan area. Therefore, DC holds one of the highest area median incomes (FY 2012—$106K for household of four) in the nation. Developments use this calculation to determine the level of affordability, and many new affordable units target households with fifty to sixty percent Area Median Income (AMI), effectively diminishing the possibility for extremely low-income families from moving into these new developments. Without vouchers or deep subsidies, affordable housing essentially becomes a code word for middle-class housing.

17. Also, this logic of cross-class interaction belies the evidence about HOPE VI developments. Admittedly, HUD and public housing administrators often poorly track the number of residents who originally lived in public housing after it was demolished (Popkin et al. 2004). Nevertheless, there are some general observations that can be made from the data that do exist. Nationally, less than a third of residents return to HOPE VI redevelopments (Duryea 2006). In one of the few comprehensive tracking studies for eight of the early HOPE VI sites, researchers found that public housing residents and nonpoor residents rarely interact (Popkin et al. 2004). Additionally, another study confirms that demolition of public housing does not necessarily deconcentrate poverty: less than a third of the original residents moved into HOPE VI housing, half lived in public housing elsewhere, and another third lived in subsidized housing with vouchers (Kingsley, Johnson, and Pettit 2003). The culture of poverty logic is also evident in HOPE VI/ New Communities' re-entry criteria. Akin to welfare reform, HOPE VI often requires that poor residents demonstrate their "cultural readiness" to live near nonpoor people. They can return if they adhere to re-entry criteria (i.e., employment, drug testing, criminal background). Residents who do not comply are often denied the opportunity to return to the new development.

18. Barry's ideological commitment to positivism is striking. For decades, feminists and other philosophers have challenged the positivist assumption that facts are objective, value-free, and indisputable (Hawkesworth 2012).

19. Barry makes no mention about how the predominately minimum wage Wal-Mart jobs he advocates for could actually decrease a parent's ability to save and buy a home, especially when one considers DC's high cost of living and Wal-Mart's non-unionized and minimum wage jobs.

20. This is similar to Murray's (2008) three-step anti-poverty program, which Rick Santorum advocated on his 2012 bid for the Republican presidential nomination. The three steps are graduating from high school, delaying pregnancy until marriage, and working.

21. In 2004, Marion Barry ousted Sandy Allen in his Ward 8 election campaign. But by 2012, Sandy Allen became Marion Barry's campaign manager.

22. Even though Barry did not technically win Ward 8 Democrats' endorsement in 2012, he garnered 40 percent of the electoral vote, more than other Ward 8 candidates (Suderman 2012a).

23. A DC resident framed his support for Barry in terms of race (i.e., Barry) loyalty: "When Mr. Barry was mayor, everyone over the age of fourteen had a job. He looks out for people and the least we can do is look out for him" (Muller 2012).

References

Acs, Gregory, and Pamela Loprest. 2003. *A Study of District of Columbia's TANF Caseload.* Washington, DC: Urban Institute.

Agronsky, Jonathan. 1991. *Marion Barry: The Politics of Race.* New York: British American Publishing.

Alexander-Floyd, Nikol. 2007. *Gender, Race and Nationalism in Contemporary Black Politics.* New York: Palgrave Macmillan.

———. 2012. "'But, I Voted for Obama': Melodrama and Post-Civil Rights, Postfeminist Ideology in Grey's Anatomy, Crash, and the 2008 Barack Obama Presidential Campaign." *National Political Science Review* 13: 23–39.

Barras, Jonetta Rose. 1998. *The Last of the Black Emperors: The Hallow Comeback of Marion Barry.* Baltimore, MD: Bancroft Press.

Barry, Marion. 2010. "A Needed Conversation on Welfare in D.C." *Washington Post*, November 20, Section Opinion.

Beal, Frances M. 1970. "Double Jeopardy: To Be Black and Female." In *The Black Woman: The Anthology*, ed. Toni M. Bambara, 109–22. New York: Washington Square Press.

Carbado, Devon W. 1997. "The Construction of OJ Simpson as a Racial Victim." *Harvard Civil Rights-Civil Liberties Law Review* 32: 49–565.

Conrad, Celicia. 2008. "Black Women: The Unfinished Agenda." *The American Prospect*, September 20. http://prospect.org/article/black-women-unfinished-agenda (accessed April 4, 2012).

Craig, Tim. 2012 "Another Battle for Marion Barry." Washington Post, March 22.

_____ 2010. "Bill Would Place 5-Year Limit on Welfare in D.C." *Washington Post*, November 15.

Crooms, Lisa. 2001. "The Mythical, Magical 'Underclass': Constructing Poverty in Race and Gender, Making the Public Private and Private Public". *Journal of Gender, Race & Justice* 5, no. 1: 87–129.

Cruse, Harold. 1967. *The Crisis of the Negro Intellectual: A Historical Analysis of the Failure of Black Leadership*. New York: Morrow.

DeBonis, Mike. 2012. "Marion Barry's Crusade against Rental Housing Moves to St. Elizabeth's." *Washington Post*, November 29, Section Local.

Denton, Nancy, and Douglas S. Massey. 1993. *American Apartheid: Segregation and the Making of the Underclass*. Cambridge, MA: Harvard University Press.

DePillis, Lydia. 2011. "Barry: No More Renters in Ward 8!" *Housing Complex Blog*. Washington, DC: Washington City Paper, July 11.

DePuyt, Bruce. 2010. "Marion Barry Discusses Welfare Reform, Wal-Mart's Plan to Expand Here." *NewsTalk with Bruce DePuyt Blog*, November 19. http://www.tbd.com/blogs/news-talk/2010/11/marion-barry-discusses-welfare-reform-wal-mart-s-plan-to-expand-here-4890.html.

Dixon, Bruce A. 2012. "Cory Booker and the Hard Right's Colonization of Black American Politics." *Black Agenda Report*, May 23.

Dowd, Maureen. 2012. "Phony Mommy Wars." *New York Times*, April 17, Section Opinion. http://www.nytimes.com/2012/04/18/opinion/dowd-phony-mommy-wars.html?_r=0 (accessed April 18, 2012).

Duryea, Danielle Pelfrey. 2006. "Gendering the Gentrification of Public Housing: HOPE VI's Disparate Impact on Lowest-Income African American Women." *Georgetown Journal on Poverty Law & Policy* 12, no. 3: 567–93.

Fainstein, Susan S. 2010. *The Just City*. Ithaca, NY: Cornell University.

Fineman, Martha L. A. 2002. "Masking Dependency." In *The Subject of Care: Feminist Perspectives on Dependency*, ed. Ellen K. Feder and Eva Feder Kittay, 215–44. Lanham, MD: Rowan and Littlefield Publishers, Inc.

Fritz, Marie J. 2009. "Rethinking Gender in U.S. Housing Policy." *The Good Society* 18, no. 2: 62–68.

Gillespie, Andra. 2010. "Meet the New Class: Theorizing Young Black Leadership in a 'Postracial' Era." In *Whose Black Politics? Cases in Post-Racial Black Leadership*, ed. Andra Gillespie, 9–42. New York: Routledge.

———. 2012. *The New Black Politician: Cory Booker, Newark, and Post-Racial America*. New York: New York University Press.

Goldschläger, Alain. 1982. "Towards a Semiotics of Authoritarian Discourse." *Poetics Today* 3, no. 1: 11–20.

Gordon, Edmund T. 1997. "Cultural Politics of Black Masculinity." *Transforming Anthropology* 6, nos. 1–2: 36–53.

Gordon Nembhard, Jessica. 2009. *When Traditional Asset Building Is Not Enough: A Comment on 'Enabling Families to Weather Emergencies and Develop.'* Washington, DC: Urban Institute.

Hartman, Saidiya. 1997. *Scenes of Subjection: Terror, Slavery, and Self-Making in Nineteenth-Century America*. New York: Oxford University Press.

Hawkesworth, Mary. 2012. "Truth and Truths in Feminist Knowledge Production." In *The Handbook of Feminist Research: Theory and Practice*, ed. Sharlen Nagy Hesse-Biber, 92–118. Los Angeles, CA: Sage.

Homan, Timothy. 2011. "Unemployment Rate in Washington's Ward 8 is Highest in US." *Bloomberg*, March 3.

Huisenga, Sarah. 2011. "Newt Gingrich: Poor Kids Don't Work 'Unless It's Illegal.'" *CBS News*.

Jet Magazine. 1994. "Marion Barry Makes a Mayoral Comeback, Wins Democratic Mayoral Primary." *Jet Magazine*, October 3.

Johnson, Cedric. 2007. *Revolutionaries to Race Leaders: Black Power and the Making of African American Politics*. Minneapolis, MN: University of Minnesota Press.

Jordan-Zachery, Julia S. 2009. *Black Women, Cultural Images, and Social Policy*. New York: Routledge.

Joyner, James. 2006. "Marion Barry Tested Positive for Cocaine Use." *Outside the Beltway Blog*, January 11. http://www.outsidethebeltway.com/barry_tested_positive_for_cocaine_use_in_the_fall/

Kingsley, G. Thomas, Jennifer Johnson, and Kathryn L. S. Pettit. 2003. "Patterns of Section 8 Relocation in the HOPE VI program." *Journal of Urban Affairs* 25, no. 4: 427–47.

Laughlin, Kathleen A., Julie Gallagher, Dorothy Sue Cobble, and Eileen Boris. 2010. "Is It Time to Jump Ship? Historians Rethink the Waves Metaphor." *Feminist Formations* 22, no. 1: 76–135.

Mead, Lawrence. 1993. *The New Politics of Poverty: The Nonworking Poor in America*. New York: Basic Books.

Mink, Gwendolyn. 1998. *Welfare's End*. Revised ed. Ithaca, NY: Cornell University.

Muller, John. 2011. "Is Barry Farm Going Dutch?" *Greater, Greater Washington Blog*, November 18. http://greatergreaterwashington.org/post/12777/is-barry-farm-going-dutch/

———. 2012. "Crowded Field Seeks to Unseat Barry". *East of the River Magazine*, March. http://www.capitalcommunitynews.com/PDF/20-23_EOR_0312.pdf (accessed April 5, 2012).

Mummolo, Jonathan. 2010. "Marion Barry to Supporters: I'm Not Going Anywhere." *Washington Post*, March 3, Section D.C. Wire.

Murray, Charles. 2008. "Guaranteed Income as a Replacement for the Welfare State." *Basic Income Studies* 3, no. 2: 1–12.

Neighborhood Info DC. 2012. "DC Ward (8) – Population." http://www.neighborhoodinfodc.org/wards/nbr_prof_wrd8.html (accessed April 4, 2012).

"New Communities." 2012. Office of Planning and Economic Development. http://dmped.dc.gov/DC/DMPED/Programs+and+Initiatives/New+Communities (accessed April 4, 2012).

Nuckols, Ben. 2012. "Marion Barry Gears Up for Another Campaign: 'They Can't Touch Me Politically.'" *Huffington Post*, January 5. http://www.huffingtonpost.com/2012/01/05/marion-barry-election-dc-council_n_1185648.html (accessed April 5, 2012).

Pew Research Center. 1998. *Conservative Opinions Not Underestimated, But Racial Hostility Missed*. Washington, DC: Pew Research Center.

———. 2012. *Partisan Participation Surges in Bush and Obama Years: Trends in American Values: 1987–2012*. Washington, DC: Pew Research Center.

Plotz, David. 1993. "The Resurrection of Marion Barry." *Washington City Paper*, September 10. http://www.washingtoncitypaper.com/articles/8453/the-resurrection-of-marion-barry (accessed April 3, 2012).

Popkin, Susan, Bruce Katz, Mary Cunningham, Karen D. Brown, Jeremy Gustafson, and Margery Austin Turner. 2004. *A Decade of HOPE VI: Research Findings and Policy Challenges*. Washington, DC: Urban Institute.

"Questions about Welfare in the District." 2010. *Washington Post*, November 17, 2010, Section Opinion.

Reed, Adolph. 1986. *The Jesse Jackson Phenomenon: The Crisis of Purpose in Afro-American Politics*. New Haven, CT: Yale University Press.

———. 1992. "The 'Underclass' as Myth and Symbol: The Poverty of Discourse about Poverty." In *Stirrings in the Jug: Black Politics in Post-Segregation Era*, 179–98. Minneapolis, MN: University of Minnesota Press.

———. 2008. "Obama No." *The Progressive*, May. http://www.progressive.org/mag_reed0508 (accessed April 5, 2012).

Roberts, Dorothy. 1998. *Killing the Black Body: Race, Reproduction and the Meaning of Liberty*. New York: Vintage.

Shapira, Ian. 2012. "Longtime D.C. Welfare Residents Prepare for a Life Off the Rolls." *Washington Post*, December 20, Section The District. http://www.washingtonpost.com/wp-dyn/content/article/2010/12/20/AR2010122005385.html (accessed November 26, 2013).

Sherman, Shantella. 2010. "Residents React to Barry's Proposal to Cap Welfare Benefits." *The Washington Informer*, November 24. http://washingtoninformer.com/news/2010/nov/22/residents-react-to-barrys-proposal-to-cap-welfare/ (accessed April 2, 2010).

Sinclair-Chapman, Valeria, and Melanye Price. 2008. "Black Politics, the 2008 Election, and the (Im) possibility of Race Transcendence." *PS: Political Science and Politics* 41, no. 4: 739–45.

Steinberg, Stephen. 2010. "The Myth of Concentrated Poverty." In *The Integration Debate: Competing Futures for American Cities*, ed. Chester Hartman and Gregory Squires, 213–28. New York: Routledge.

Suderman, Alan. 2012a. "The Barry in Winter: Barry Is Running for Re-Election. Is Anyone Paying Attention?" *Washington City Paper*, March 23. http://www.washingtoncitypaper.com/articles/42392/the-barry-in-winter-marion-barry-is-running-for-re/full/ (accessed November 26, 2013).

———. 2012b. "Correction: Ward 8 Dem Boss Will Take Barry to Back Room for Tail Kicking." *Washington City Paper*, February 21. http://www.washingtoncitypaper.com/blogs/looselips/2012/02/21/clarification-ward-8-dem-boss-will-take-barry-to-back-room-for-tail-kicking/ (accessed April 2, 2012).

Tanner, Michael. 2010. "On Welfare, an Unlikely Voice of Reason." *National Review Online Blog*, November 24. http://www.nationalreview.com/articles/253857/welfare-unlikely-voice-reason-michael-tanner (accessed March 30, 2012).

Van Dijk, Teun A. 1993. "Principles of Critical Discourse Analysis." *Discourse & Society* 4, no. 2: 249–83.

Wallace, Michelle. 1978. *Black Macho and the Myth of the Superwoman*. New York: Verso.

"Washington Post Poll." 2012. *Washington Post*, December 28. Washington, DC. http://www.washingtonpost.com/wp-srv/politics/polls/postpoll_20120717.html (accessed 26, 2013).

White, E. Frances. 1990. "Africa On My Mind: Gender, Counter Discourses and African American Nationalism." *Journal of Women's History* 2, no. 1: 73–97

Wilson, William Julius. 1987. *The Truly Disadvantaged: The Inner City, the Underclass, and Public Policy*. Chicago: University of Chicago Press.

———. 2009. "More Than Just Race: Being Black and Poor in the Inner City." *Poverty and Race Research* 18, no. 3: 1–9.

Young, Iris Marion. 2002. "Autonomy, Welfare Reform, and Meaningful Work." In *The Subject of Care: Feminist Perspectives on Dependency*, ed. Ellen K. Feder and Eva Feder Kittay, 40–60. Lanham, MD: Rowan and Littlefield Publishers, Inc.

"Talking" about Gender While Ignoring Race and Class: A Discourse Analysis of Pay Equity Debates

Julia S. Jordan-Zachery
Providence College
Salida Wilson
Independent Scholar

Introduction

On January 29, 2009, President Barrack Obama signed into law the Lilly Ledbetter Fair Pay Act. As argued by President Obama, this bill was in honor of a diverse group of women, including his grandmother "who worked in a bank all her life, and even after she hit that glass ceiling, kept getting up again," and his young daughters "because I want them to grow up in a nation that values their contributions, where there are no limits to their dreams" (quoted in Stolberg 2009). President Obama's framing—one of inclusiveness and homogeneity—is particularly relevant as it captures how US elected officials tend to see and talk about gender workforce based discrimination. In speaking of the benefits of this Act, President Obama seemingly privileged universal claims about women and, as such, normalized specific experiences with workplace discrimination of which pay inequity is one manifestation. He invokes rhetorical devices of sameness among and between women. These are commonly used rhetorical devices in the discourses of pay equity—that women share a common social position, regardless of race and class, which informs their experiences with pay inequity.

Obama, like other elected officials, sees this Act in a race-neutral and essentialist manner. He assumes that his (White) grandmother like his (Black) daughters would receive equal benefit and protection under this Act. Such notions of race and gender neutrality permeate much of society's understanding of democratic processes. However, this notion of neutrality sometimes does not manifest itself in the policymaking process. Policy makers, when politically expedient, can use differences (real or perceived) in the policymaking process. Consequently, some groups of women, depending on the issue, can be rendered invisible and hypervisible in such processes. One example of such an occurrence is reflected in our conversations on HIV/AIDS. Black women were rendered invisible in the original framing of HIV/AIDS, although they were affected and infected rather early in the history of the disease (Hammonds 1992; Cohen 1999). Often, Black women, via their hypervisibility, are used to tell the story of crack-abusing pregnant/

parenting women. These women generally receive harsher penalties in comparison to White substance-abusing pregnant/parenting women (Roberts 1997).

Through an analysis of fair pay and pay equity discourses, we explore how diverse policy makers, in terms of gender, race, and political ideology, address differences, between and within groups of women. As argued, recognizing variations between and within groups of women in the policymaking process can enhance the effectiveness of policies targeting women. The purpose of this research is not to analyze or explain under what conditions are marginalized women rendered invisible or hypervisible in the policy process. Neither are we necessarily interested in the epistemology intentionality, nor rationalization of policy makers' decision to employ particular frames in their discourse on fair pay and pay equity. Instead, we concentrate on the frames themselves and how power dynamics and hierarchies are employed. According to Entman (1993, 52) "[to] frame is to select some aspects of a perceived reality and make them more salient in a communicating text, in such a way as to promote a particular problem definition, causal interpretation, moral evaluation, and/or treatment recommendation." Our focus is on describing how diversity, via the use of rhetorical devices, is recognized in the policy process, via the framing of fair pay and pay equity, and how the effectiveness of the policy is enhanced or lessened by ignoring differences between and within groups of women. This analysis contributes to our larger discussions on critical policy analysis.

Fair pay and pay equity serve as relevant categories for analyzing how rhetorical devices of heterogeneity between and within groups of women are addressed in the policymaking process. Our analysis of fair pay and pay equity discourses, however, not only informs our understanding of the policymaking process, but also has the potential to substantially impact the lives of women targeted by the policy. While having been constructed as a means of ensuring that women are treated equally and fairly in the work force, it also has implications for poverty. Pay equity can serve as an anti-poverty strategy. Our analysis centers the fair pay/pay equity discourses of the 110th Congress and is bounded by the period 2007–2008. Before analyzing the fair pay and pay equity discourses, we present a brief review of the impact of pay inequity across various groups of women. This is followed by a presentation of Black feminist philosophy and epistemology that serve as means of understanding gender and for critiquing policy. Black feminist thought is useful because it focuses on the intersectionality of various social locations and the impact of such intersectionalities on the lived realties of women. Next, we offer the approach to the study, which employs a critical discourse analysis of congressional floor debates on the general subjects of fair pay and pay equity. Through the lens of Black feminism, we explore the rhetorical devices of essentialism, White solipsism, and identity construction, which are heavily influenced by the experiences of White women, that run throughout the fair pay and pay equity discourses. White solipsism, as defined by Rich (1979, 299), refers to "the predisposition to think, imagine, and speak as if whiteness was the only way to describe the world." Finally, we discuss the value of employing an intersectional approach, grounded in Black feminist thought, to the framing of policy issues.

Work-Based Discrimination Is Not the Same for All: Gender, Race, and Disparity

In the policymaking process, the lived experiences of marginalized and minoritized women (Black, Latina, Asian American, and First American) can be ignored by classifying women as a homogeneous group, thereby operating from a position of gender equality and neutrality. As in the case of pay equity, there seems to be a tendency to construct Black women[1] as comparable, and indeed the same as their White counterparts. Meanwhile, ignored and often masked are the disproportionate inequalities experienced by Black women. This inattention to the variance of experiences, resulting from the intersection of gender, race, and class, can potentially compromise the effectiveness of public polices targeting women, directly or indirectly.

Despite substantial gains made by Black women, they still face wide economic disparities in comparison to White women. Historically, "African American women are worse off than white women. This holds true when comparing the median earnings of white and African American full-time, full-year workers at every education level, and when comparing poverty rates and unemployment rates" (Institute for Women's Policy Research [IWPR] 2005, 29). Additionally, IWPR (2005, 29) reported, "African American women working full-time, full-year earned $26,992 in median annual earnings, compared with $32,036 earned by comparable white women workers." Furthermore, this report suggest that even when Black women earned more than White women in the same professions it was because they worked more hours (IWPR 2005, 29). Men in full-time management, professional, and related occupations had weekly earnings of $1,268 (in 2010). Women in comparable positions earned $915 a week, approximately 75 percent of men's earnings (US Bureau of Labor Statistics 2010). During the first quarter of 2010, it was reported that men employed in full-time sales and related occupations earned $832. Women in the same occupational fields earned $508, about 62 percent of men's earnings (U.S. Bureau of Labor Statistics 2010).

The US Bureau of Labor Statistics (2012) informs us, "Earnings growth has been sharpest for White women, outpacing that of their Black and Hispanic counterparts." Within groups of women, we continue to see a downward trend in their economic position. Black women's greater work efforts have not been enough to lessen the disproportionately high poverty rates experienced by these women.

> Poverty rates were particularly high, at more than one in four, among black (25.6 percent), Hispanic (25.0 percent), and Native American (26.4 percent) women. Rates for white, non-Hispanic women (10.4 percent) and Asian women (12.2 percent) were also considerably higher than the rate for white, non-Hispanic men (8.1 percent). (National Women's Law Center 2011)

Women headed families have also experienced increased poverty. Sullivan (2008) asserts, "The data [2003 U.S. Census Bureau Report on Poverty] indicate women's poverty rate—especially single mothers—increasing for a third straight year. The numbers show a jump in child poverty that was the largest in a decade." The 2010 Census poverty data show a continuation of this trend (National Women's Law Center 2011). Among the nation's poor, African Americans and Latinos are disproportionately represented. Within the groups, African American and Latino women, relative to men, are more likely to be poor. These data make evident the persistent racial inequality trends and significant variations among Black and White women. More importantly, the data demonstrate the imperative need for policy makers to explore patterns and differences in the socioeconomic status of all groups and classes of women when framing and formulating polices.

Seeking Equity and Justice for Women

The Equal Pay Act of 1963, in tandem with the Civil Rights Act of 1964 and affirmative action policies, seeks to address labor market discrimination. At the core of the Equal Pay Act is gender discrimination. Accordingly, the Equal Pay Act mandates "equal pay for equal work," by requiring that individuals who are performing essentially the same jobs (with allowance for differentials based on piecework, seniority, and other factors) receive comparable wages. Through the years, as a result of legislative changes and amendments and court decisions, the scope of the Equal Pay Act of 1963 has broadened (see Acker 1989; Young 2005). Equal pay is often thought of as a tool for not only addressing labor force gender discrimination, but also for addressing poverty among women. It has been argued that pay equity, when fully recognizing and accounting for the fact that not all women experience discrimination in the same manner, can effectively lessen the incidence of poverty among a substantial number of women (Hoynes, Page, and Stevens 2006; Stone and Kuperberg 2006).

In this long fight for equal pay, the Lilly Ledbetter Fair Pay Act was introduced in the 110th Congress. This act successfully made it through the House, but not the Senate. The Lilly Ledbetter Fair Pay Act was in response to the Supreme Court decision (5–4) that ruled against Lilly Ledbetter. A similar bill was subsequently introduced and successfully enacted. The enacted Act expands worker's rights to sue, in cases of pay discrimination, and it "relaxes" the statute of limitations for such suits by restarting the six-month clock each time the worker receives a paycheck. The passage of this Act was in response to the Supreme Court's decision, which stated that a plaintiff could only bring an Equal Pay claim 180 days after the initial discriminatory decision to pay a female worker differently than her male counterpart. Many herald this Act as a key step in addressing gender pay equity and its resulting impact on women's economic stability. While the benefits of the Act are indeed still unfolding, we argue that the framing of the Act is limiting, and as such, its impact might be stymied.

Theorizing about and Categorizing Women: A Black Feminist Perspective

This study examines the floor speeches and extended remarks (later referred to as text) of various Congress members through a Black feminist critical perspective. Intersectionality, as theorized by Black feminists, is employed to deconstruct categories of gender that are used to frame the fair pay/pay equity debate. Black feminist thought offers a different understanding of how power, via discourse, is organized, maintained, and perpetuated (see Crenshaw 1994). Black feminist scholars, among others, have long challenged the generalization around identity markers, such as gender, and the implicit notion of a "linked fate" (Dawson 1995). Heyes (2002, 4–5) says that there is an "illegitimate generalization about identity," which puts a distinct identity characteristic as the main focal point on this single axis, as if being African American, for example, is "entirely separate from being [a] woman." Scholars such as Spelman (1988) argue that single axis construction of identity forces its subjects to select a distinct characteristic, such as women or African American, as their defining feature. Consequently, some individuals, and we argue that policy makers fail to recognize that women may identify as "heterogeneous selves with multiple identities" (Heyes 2002, 5).

Black feminists support the view that differences do exist among distinct races and classes of women. Higginbotham's work, for instance, reveals how Black women, regardless of socioeconomic status, were excluded from the dominant society's definition of "lady," and how the "gender identity of black women were inextricably linked to and determined by racial identity" (1992, 254). Likewise, the critical race theorist Crenshaw (1989) coined the term intersectionality to explain and describe the lived experiences of African American women, specifically in terms of legal prescriptions that only focus on either race or gender. Over time, intersectionality theory has been expanded to show how certain differences that result from race, class, and gender, among other oppressive structures, cannot be separated into single entities. In other words, the different experiences of women should be specific to their racial, class, and gender status and not generalized and grouped into one uniform category. Black feminists, among others, emphasize that these differences among women cannot be segregated because diverse groups of women experience divergent degrees of oppression, which ultimately changes the experiences of living as a woman in society (Collins 1990). These cultural patterns of oppression are not only interrelated, but are bound together and influenced by oppressive structures of society (Collins 2000). More importantly, these oppressive and interlocking structures of society combine to keep Black women and other disadvantaged groups from performing at their highest capacities. Consequently, Black women and other marginalized individuals are kept in subordinate positions that reinforce negative stereotypes and their inequitable social position.

Historically, one of the first instances where this configuration of gender difference was witnessed was during slavery when courts ruled slave women "outside the statutory rubric 'women'" (Higginbotham 1992, 257). Since Black women were not considered "true women" in the eyes of the courts, laws that protected White women did not shield Black women. Instead, such laws often resulted in the exploitation of Black women's bodies; primarily through physical labor and sexual advances (see Roberts 1997; Solinger 2000). In her discussion of *State of Missouri vs. Celia*, Higginbotham (1992, 257–58) shows the vulnerability of slave women's bodies to White men's sexual advances. In *State of Missouri vs. Celia*, Celia was sentenced to death after killing her master, who routinely raped her. The same statutes that protected White women from attempts of rape or defilement did not include Celia, since she failed to embody the ideals of true womanhood. Therefore, the laws, both written and unwritten, about the roles of Black and White women were as follows: Black women were expected to be workers and breeders, while White women were put on a "pedestal" and protected.

One continues to see the disparate treatment, via this race-gender identity construction, of women of different racial groups even in the labor force. The notion of work ethic is sometimes used to differentiate Black and White working-class women (see Hagler 1980). Focusing on the notion of work ethic, and who has it and who does not, allows for a distinction to be made between these groups of women. Thus, White working class women are elevated above Black working class women. Although this standard of the "good" woman was not similarly experienced along class lines, Palmer (1983) asserts that White women in general benefited from such distinctions between women. As posited by Palmer Euro-American women benefited either materially or symbolically as the distinction between good women and bad women was racialized. In her analysis of Black and White female mill workers of similar socioeconomic backgrounds, Byerly (1986) argues that the women had drastically different experiences. The different experiences, according to her, resulted from racial hierarchies. As part of a hegemonic ideology these distinctions work to blur class lines, even if symbolically (see Mullings 1994).

Byerly (1986), Collins (1990, 2000), Higginbotham (1992), and others reveal how the differently interpreted gender meanings for both groups of women shaped and continue to shape their economic, political, and social conditions. These scholars challenge the notion of the homogeneity of womanhood and instead contend that Black women were never equal to their White female counterparts. Although historical and literary evidence suggests that women are heterogeneous, policy makers continue to treat women, in certain contexts, as a homogeneous population. This focus on women as a homogenous group is often problematic because it addresses the interests of only one group of women, White and middle class (Spelman 1988).

Such an approach, we argue, fails to recognize intragroup differences among and between categories of women. In essence, by not recognizing intragroup differences policy makers are failing to acknowledge, "That the social construction of target populations has a powerful influence on public officials and shapes both the policy agenda and the actual design of policy" (Schneider and Ingram 1993, 334). Consequently, in promoting gender neutrality, for example, there is a failure to recognize how race and class influence women's experience in the paid labor force. For purposes of this research, intersectionality theory is used to contrast the more simplified conceptualizations of single systems of identity construction, which tends to use as its springboard the notion of womanhood based on the experiences of White middle-class women. Utilizing intersectionality in this manner allows us to contribute to the discussion on critical gender policy analysis.

Approach to the Study

We analyze the discourse of US Senate and House members as they debated fair pay and pay equity. Data were gathered via the online Thomas search engine from the Congressional Record. This analysis involved identifying and extracting complete transcripts relating to pay equity or fair pay. The temporal search parameters were limited to the 110th Congress—2007–2008. Our search yielded 173 "articles" that included the phrases in exact order (the search returned text containing all the search words near each other in any order; such results were excluded from the study). The data are comprised of actual remarks given on the floor of the House and Senate and Extensions of Remarks (not spoken on the floor) that were entered into the Congressional Record. Articles related to congressional procedures and those honoring individuals were eliminated from the analysis. We also ensured that there was no duplication among articles. As a result, we use sixty "articles" in our analysis.

We utilize an Interpretative Phenomenological Approach (IPA) to unpack the rhetorical devices that are employed by policy makers to provide legitimacy for their claims. These rhetorical devices include essentialism, White solipsism, and identity construction. In addition, we examine how their frames bolster a broader economic agenda designed to lift women out of poverty. Central to IPA is the belief that individuals seek to make sense of their experiences. Consequently, an analysis of responses can shed light, even if partially, on how they made sense of the experience. Beyond this, IPA recognizes that there is an interaction between the participants' accounts of their experiences and the researcher's interpretive framework(s); hence, the analysis is both phenomenological and interpretive (Smith, Flowers, and Larkin 2009).

According to Smith, Flowers, and Larkin (2009, 3), "IPA studies usually have a small number of participants and the aim is to reveal something of the experience of each of those individuals." Following this, we provide an in-depth analysis of sixty texts. In determining the adequacy of the sample size, we employed theoretical sampling, which focuses on the saturation of information—there is a redundancy of information and no new themes emerge—to determine if there was a need to increase the sample size (Morse 1994). Narrative thematic analysis was used to explicate the various themes running throughout the texts. This approach used an emergent protocol to develop codes. This protocol involved interactive readings of the texts. Taylor and Bogdan (1984, 131) suggest that themes are defined as units derived from patterns such as "conversation topics, vocabulary, recurring activities, meanings, feelings, or folk sayings and proverbs."

Our analysis of the texts involved the use of a critical discourse analysis (CDA). The discourse analysis examined the relationship and contexts of how the term "woman" was constructed in the policy frames. As part of the process of conducting the CDA, we closely looked at "all of the thinking about the issue, the language used to discuss the issue, and the values and beliefs relevant to the issue" (Ahern, Conway, and Steuernagel 2004, 9). In other words, the analysis focused on the patterned way of representing the phenomena of women in the policymaking world.

CDA, as opposed to a content analysis, was chosen because it allows for a "deeper" analysis of the impact of gender and racial hierarchies in the policy-making process (see Fischer 2003). We opted for CDA as opposed to a more positivist approach because such approaches often fail to capture the "inculcation of values and the validation of status" as these variables "cannot be measured according to rational techniques, especially since the latter require that everything be made explicit and unambiguous" (Yanow 1996, 6). As defined by van Dijk (2001), CDA is

> A type of discourse analytical research that primarily studies the way social power abuse, dominance, and inequality are enacted, reproduced, and resisted by text and talk in the social and political context. With such dissident research, critical discourse analysis takes explicit position and thus wants to understand, expose and ultimately resist social inequality. (352)

Van Dijk captures what separates CDA from other forms of discursive analyses. This method facilitates the analysis of opaque and transparent structural relationships of power and control manifested in language (Weiss and Wodak 2003). Discourse analysis, in general, has been criticized as being too interpretive and subjective (Widdowson 1995), and therefore, the generalizability of the findings is viewed as suspect. The reader should note that we analyze the fair pay and pay equity discourses within a specific time frame and draw conclusions on the basis of this singular analysis alone. Of equal or greater importance to what we uncover in our analysis is the incorporation of Black feminist theory in our understandings of policy analysis. By offering a critical Black feminist approach to policy analysis, we engage in and further a discussion of how we understand intersectionality in policymaking.

We noticed that the frames of the policy-targeted populations—these are the "people whose behavior is linked to the achievement of desired ends" (Schneider and Ingram 1993, 335)—are consistent over time. The central focus was not necessarily on the construction of the issue—pay equity/fair pay. Instead, we focused on how the policy-targeted groups were constructed. Thus, our analysis of the frames was guided by the following: how do Congress members recognize differences between groups of women in their discourse on pay equity? Our analysis is based on the three most dominantly used frames: Universal Woman; Coloring Inequity; and Families Matter.

Congress Members' Talk about Women and Fairness

In framing social issues, policy makers often rely on existing race, gender, and class hierarchies to suggest that their particular definition of an issue is accurate. They can select, consciously or not, particular categories of interest to highlight in the framing of an issue. Therein lies the relationship between language and power (see Fairclough 2000). Words are combined to form a text in order to reflect a particular view and or belief. Words do not simply assume their meaning in an independent manner; instead, words, singularly and together, assume meaning through social interaction within a system of hierarchical relations. Fairclough (2000) asserts that discourse is shaped and constrained by (a) social structures—class, status, gender, and so forth, and by (b) culture and (c) discourse—the words we use—which helps to shape and constrain our identities, relationships, and systems of knowledge and beliefs. To determine how differences between women are addressed in the policymaking process, we consider the various frames used to discuss the issue of pay equity and fair pay. Black feminist thought allows us to unpack hierarchical relations embedded in the discourses of elected officials. It is by the exploration of the langue used that we can begin to understand how essentialism, White solipsism, and identity construction are integrated into the framing of pay equity and fair pay. Below, we explain how these rhetorical devices, as reflected in the general themes of Universal Woman, Coloring Inequity, and Families Matter, work to reinforce race and gender divisions.

Universal Woman

As expected, Congress members relied on the discourse of gender equity by highlighting the differences in earnings between men and women (representative frames are presented in Table 1).[2] While gender equity is accentuated as an objective in this frame, it fails to recognize gendered realities that are raced and classed. In attempting to show disparity, Congress members cited statistics that grouped all women, regardless of race, class, and/or nature of employment together. Embedded in this frame is essentialism as its point of departure is the experiences of a specific group of women and men—Euro-Americans. There is expediency in relying on statistics, as used by Representative Moore, for example (see Table 1). However, this linear approach, albeit efficient, fails to recognize the lived experiences of various women.

The frame of homogeneous womanhood does not disaggregate experiences. For example, in the article "Why is her pay check smaller?" Fairfield and Roberts (2010) show that pay inequity varies by occupation. Among food preparation workers, women

Table 1.
Universal Woman

"... in 2008, when women make on average only 77 cents for every dollar made by their male counterpart, the importance of the Paycheck Fairness Act is clear" (Shea-Porter (D-NH) 2008, 1731; see also National Committee on Pay Equity a,b).

"... according to the National Committee on Pay Equity, working women stand to lose $250,000 over the course of their careers because of unequal pay practices. While women's wages and educational achievements have been rising, there's still a sizeable gender wage gap. This is a national disgrace" (Hare [D-IL] 2007, H6014; see also National Committee on Pay Equity a,b).

"The House has passed legislation to right this wrong, and the other body will follow this week. While a weakening economy weighs heavily on women and families across America, and when women are still only earning 77 percent of what men earn, this is not the time to curtail women's access to fair pay. That is why this Congress must pass into law the Paycheck Fairness Act. With the support of more than 227 cosponsors, my bill would help women confront discrimination in the workplace, give teeth to the Equal Pay Act by prohibiting employers from retaliating against employees who share salary information with their coworkers, allow women to sue for punitive damages and the recovery of back pay and create a new grant program to help strength the negotiation skills of girls and women" (DeLauro [D-CT] 2008, H2558; see also National Committee on Pay Equity a,b).

"in 2006, women earned 77 cents for every dollar earned by men" (Moore [D-WI] 2008, 675)

make 8 percent less than men. However, among pharmacists, women make 15 percent less than men (Fairfield and Roberts 2010). The use of percentages aggregates women's experiences regardless of class and educational background. So, there is no distinction made between lower-income, middle-income, and upper-income earners both between and within groups of women. Can we safely assume that all these women experience labor force discrimination in the same manner and that the impact is the same regardless of social location? The failure to recognize intragroup differences can also result in a "blanket" type of approach to addressing inequality not only between men and women but also between women of different groups. This tendency to suggest that there is a unitary experience in gender-based employment discrimination gives way to White solipsism and the practices and manifestations of essentialism.

Coloring Inequity

Congress members recognized, at a basic level, that not all women are the same. Indeed, the multiple floor debates reflect how some elected officials took the time to highlight these differences. This was done primarily by distinguishing between women, thought of as White women, and women of color (see Table 2).

In the attempts to color the discourse, similar to the frame that resulted in universalizing women's experiences with pay inequity, there was little attempt to differentiate among women of color. The discourse analysis shows that, although they were named, minoritized women were often treated as either one or two groups. If there were distinctions made, then women of color were constructed, primarily, as being either African American or Latina (see Table 3). One can argue that Congress members attempt to efficiently frame the discourse on pay equity by focusing on the numerically larger minority groups.

Table 2.
Coloring Inequity

"While the Equal Pay Act was intended to prevent pay discrimination in the workplace, 45 years after it was signed by President Kennedy, women, and especially women of color, continue to take home significantly less pay than men for the same work" (Hirono [D-HI] 2008, H7690).

"Women earn about 77 cents for each dollar earned by men, and the gap is even greater for women of color. In 2004, African-American women earned only 67 percent of the earnings of White men, and Hispanic women earned only 56 percent" (Kennedy [D-MA] 2007, S2700; see also National Committee on Pay Equity a,b).

"The wage gap is most severe for women of color. It is absolutely inexcusable that women, and especially minority women, earn a fraction of what men earn from the same job. African American women earn just 63 cents on the dollar, and Latinos earn far worse at 57 cents. In my own State of California, black women working full time year-round earn only 61 percent and Latinos 42 percent of the wages of white men" (Lee [D-CA] 2008, H7685).

Table 3.
Families Matter

"Mary Norton understood that the wage gap is not just a women's issue it is a family issue. When women earn less for equal work, families are forced to do more with less. Affording all of life's expenses is challenging enough-it shouldn't be made harder as a result of women being shortchanged on payday" (Holt [D-NJ] 2008, H1695).

"To all cynics who dismiss equal pay as just another women's issue, I want to point out that the wage gap not only hurts women, it hurts families. It hurts children being raised by single moms who have to work two jobs to make ends meet when one might suffice were she to be paid equally with her male coworkers. . . . Currently, single women who are heads of households are twice as likely to be in poverty as single fathers. Again, currently single women who are heads of households are twice as likely to be in poverty as single mothers. This is a fact that we must face here and remedy. And we know that pay equity for women is closely linked to eradicating poverty" (Slaughter [D-MN] 2008, 7637; see also National Committee on Pay Equity a,b).

"Madam Speaker, today, as we observe Equal Pay Day, I rise with my colleagues and professional women everywhere to say: Women are the face of pay equity . . . . Equal pay is not solely a women's issue, it's a family issue; when women aren't paid equally, their families pay the price. There are long-term consequences too: lower pay means less Social Security and less saved for retirement" (Speier [D-CA] 2008, E687).

"When women earn less, their entire family suffers. When we allow women to be paid unequal wages for equal work, we as a society are tolerating discrimination. That is why we must take action to close the wage gap, and treat all workers equally" (Capps [D-CA], 2008, E669).

However, we have to ask how might the inclusion of the experiences of Asian descended women change how we discuss pay equity? According to the National Committee on Pay Equity (n.d.)

> In 2010, the earnings of African American women were $32,290, 67.7 percent of all men's earnings (from 67.5 percent in 2009), and Latinas' earnings were $27,992, 58.7 percent of all men's earnings (up from 57.7 percent in 2009). Asian American women's earnings at $41,309 dropped from 90 percent of all men's earnings in 2009 to 86.6 percent in 2010.

Showing the divergent experiences of women of color with pay equity raises a number of questions (several of which are beyond the scope of this analysis). However, consider the following: How do we explain the disparity between Latinas' experiences relative to Asian Americans? Can it be explained via education and or immigration status? Why is it that Asian American women's earnings are falling relative to men? While we do not pretend to have the answers to these questions, we would argue that a Black feminist approach, one that allows us to look critically at the intersectionality of multiple identities and experiences, would help us to begin to craft a response.

Additionally, it is worth noting that there exists minimum comparison of these women to the men in their respective racial and/or ethnic groups. White men and or White women served as the comparison group by which the experiences of women of color were framed. This particular use of identity is but another example of solipsism that in turn gives way to essentialism. Simply relying on a large "N" to tell the story does not mean that the stories and experiences of other women of color such as First Americans and Asian Americans are not important. Including Asian American women, for example, in the framing of pay equity allows us to expand our understandings on the functioning of race, class, and gender and labor force discrimination.

Patriarchy was used in another attempt to color the discourse of pay equity and experiences of women of color (particularly African American women) with pay discrimination. While we are not making the claim that this patriarchal frame was relied on extensively by Congress members, we do believe that it is important to explore such framing. It speaks to an understanding of identity, particularly racial identity, and some of the larger discussion on how to address poverty among Black women. Take for example the frame used by Delegate Norton (African American, Democrat) who said,

> Recently, I thought we were seeing progress when the census reported last year that Black, college educated women actually earned more than white, college-educated women, although the overall wage gap for Black women, at 65 percent, remains considerably larger than the gap for white women. No explanation was offered for the progress for Black women, but other data and information suggest that even when women seem to catch up it may not be what we had in mind. I suspect that African American women are represented disproportionately among the 50 percent of all multiple jobholders who are women. (2007, E854)

In attempting to contextualize the work habits of Black women, Representative Norton also claimed,

> I am certain that this progress for African American women also tells a tragic story. The decline in marriageable Black men, eaten alive by ghetto life, also means that many college educated Black women are likely to be single with no need for even the short time out for children that many white women often take that may affect their wages as compared with Black women. (2007, E854)

In explaining the experiences of Black women, Delegate Norton suggested that the problems faced by Black women in the labor force are related to the shortage of "marriageable Black men." In essence, Delegate Norton, as do other Congress members of color, relies on what Alexander-Floyd (2007) refers to as the narrative of the "endangered black man." Alexander-Floyd's discussion of masculinity scripts and Black nationalism within Black politics helps to understand how Congress members, while speaking of gender inequality, can indeed support a rather masculinist approach to policy. As she argues, the narrative of the Black Cultural Pathology Paradigm (BCPP), in part, shapes Black politics. Accordingly, BCPP "centers on ideological assumptions of wounded Black masculinity (alternatively described as the plight of Black male/endangered Black male or the Black male crisis) and the breakdown of the Black family" (3). BCPP privileges maleness in the understandings of the ills that plague the Black community. Policy then suggests that the key to solving issues confronted by Black women involves first fixing the Black man by allowing him to assert his maleness—that is practice patriarchal norms—thereby increasing his marriageability quotient. The result of using this frame is that, similar to the families matter frame (discussed below), the needs of Black women are considered important only because of their connections to others, particularly Black men, in society. Even those who consider themselves as representatives of Black women or other minoritized women and speak on their behalf, in general, can employ the ideology of BCPP.

Families Matter

In addition to the above referenced frames, Congress members also relied on the frame of Families Matter, which couches women's pay inequity in terms of their roles as caregiver and provider. Families Matter suggests that fair pay/pay equity is essential because women's incomes are necessary, not only for their survival, but for the survival of the entire family—often an extended family including elderly parents (see Table 3 for representative examples of this frame). As such, women were characterized not just in the role of emotional and moral guardian of the family, but also as a key economic contributor. If we unpack this frame, we uncover how it too essentializes the notion of "family" and women's worth/value to society.

As used, this frame does not allow for distinctions to be made between African American, Latina, Asian American, and White solo parents (a distinction that is often made in other policy areas, at times implicit, such as welfare). When a distinction was made, it was made along the line of the married versus unmarried working-woman caregiver. Sometimes, solo-parenting women were singled out and used to frame the wider impact of the wage gap, as was done by Representative Slaughter (see Table 3).

The Families Matter frame serves the role of rehabilitating the women, as it is designed to cast women and the issue of pay equity as worthwhile—something that others should be concerned about. However, this frame is limiting in its construction of womanhood. Women are reduced to their "biological" and implicit "natural" role. By linking women to motherhood (i.e., their perceived value to society), policy makers appear to be engaging a rehabilitation project for these women. The framing of the issue in this manner suggests that if we are not concerned about pay equity solely out of concern for women, then we need to think of the families for which these women are responsible. This approach is used to expand the scope of conflict and draw individuals into the issue (see Schattschneider 1960; Haider-Markel and Meier 1996). However, this attempt to expand the scope of conflict marginalizes groups of women. For example, excluded are those women who, for various reasons, do not choose this role. We are left wondering: are they not important? Additionally, this frame ignores the hierarchy of mothers—based on racial categorizations that are used to differentiate mothers and the impact of such differentiation on their access to resources (see Roberts 1997; Solinger 2000). For example, Black women, as a result of the intersection of race, class, and gender, are often not provided with the protections to be "good" mothers and women although they are judged by the standards of the hegemonic image of the "good" woman.

Another rehabilitative aspect of this Families Matters frame centers on the use of the solo-mother image and consequently the woman as provider. The use of this frame raises a number of questions including: which group of solo mothers are they talking about? Are these women simply rehabilitated because of their connection to the workforce? Similar to the Universal Woman frame discussed above, this frame fails to include the lived experiences of various solo mothers. For example, in the recent economic turmoil, solo-parenting women have had different experiences with maintaining employment. Sherman, Fremstad, and Parrott (2004) state, "the steepest employment losses from 2000 to 2003 were for black mothers." According to Insight: Center for Community Economic Development,

> . . . women who maintain families—the vast majority of whom are single mothers—have the highest unemployment rate of all women. Fifteen percent of black single mothers were unemployed in 2009, as were 11.6 percent of Hispanic single mothers, compared with 6.6 percent of black and 9.7 percent of Hispanic married women, the ethnic group with the highest unemployment rate for married women. This high unemployment rate for married Hispanic married women results in a smaller gap between the unemployment rates of Hispanic married and unmarried women than for blacks and whites. (2010)

Additionally, not all solo mothers are constructed as worthy of assistance. Take for example the Black solo mother (often constructed as the matriarch). Black female solo parents, particularly those who were dependent on government assistance, were constructed as negative and in need of fixing because "the image of the Black matriarch serves as powerful symbol to both Black and White women of what can go wrong if White patriarchal power is challenged. Aggressive, assertive women are penalized—they are abandoned by their men, end up impoverished, and are stigmatized as being unfeminine" (Collins 1990, 77).

In the discourse on pay equity, this historical understanding of the Black solo parent is ignored. This category of women, solo parents, is not racialized in the Families Matter frame. However, in the past, solo mothers, particularly the poor and welfare dependent, have been racialized (see Neubeck and Cazenave 2001). In this current discourse, it is suggested that this group of women suffer, more so than other women because they are caregivers without partners—they are sole providers. So, in essence, there is a connection between poverty and marital status. However, what is missing is the often-negative construction of these women (see Hancock 2004; Jordan-Zachery 2009). It appears that this image of solo-parenting women, because it is deracialized, is now rehabilitated in the "post-welfare" era. By deracalizing solo mothering, these women are now constructed as playing by the rules because they are working and are considered worthwhile policy targets (see Schneider and Ingram 1993). One has to wonder how such rehabilitation relate to and fit in with the simultaneously occurring discourse on family and family formation. Reminiscent of the Moynihan (1965) thesis of the 1960s, solo parents, especially poor women of color, are often viewed as the source of all that is wrong with their communities. Maybe this is why there was little effort made to differentiate among solo-parenting women in terms of race, because doing so would result in the centering of a group of "tainted" women. However, by deploying an essentialist frame, there is a failure to recognize that all solo-parenting women do not share the same experience. Black solo mothers tend to be poorer relative to white solo mothers.

Why We Need an Intersectionality Approach to Pay Equity

As a tool of social control, women have been encouraged to recognize only one area of human difference as legitimate, those differences which exist between women and men . . . we have recognized and negotiated those differences . . . But our future survival is predicated upon our ability to relate within equality . . . Now, we must recognize differences among women who are our equals, neither inferior or superior, and devise ways to use each other to enrich our visions and our joint struggles. (Lorde 1984, 122)

Audre Lorde, in her call to recognize differences, is asking us to resist essentialism. Furthermore, she argues that recognition of differences within the category of woman is an act of liberation. A Black feminist approach to policy analysis allows us to see how discourse, designed to liberate, can actually result in oppression.

In this current discussion on pay equity, previous existing hierarchies among and within groups of women are rendered invisible, even as officials putatively work to dismantle wage discrimination. Failing to recognize the more complex levels of class, race, and gender hierarchies makes for simplified policy deliberation, but does not, of course, render them any less potent in the lives of women. Indeed, while all women, in theory and in practice, are affected by the wage gap, it does not affect all women equally. Differences, resulting from factors such as race, ethnicity, class, and age among others, influence a woman's experiences with labor force discrimination. The cost of such discrimination is high. The result is that these women's financial security, relative to men, is often lessened. Many women who are living in poverty or who are on the cusp of poverty are severely impacted by this so-called wage gap (Hoynes, Page, and Stevens 2006). However, in the framing of this issue, there seems to be an (often) unstated assumption that women, regardless of their racial and/or class location, share a common experience with economic strain and poverty that results from gender-based pay inequality. We contend that this is an erroneous assumption.

This notion of homogeneous womanhood masks a plethora of historical, socioeconomic, and ideological differences among different groups of women. This characterization obscures, rather than mirrors, the reality of women's heterogeneity. Employing an essentialist understanding to pay equity "will prove insufficient if and when applied to policy development" (Clarke 2004, 1). It is for this reason that we propose an intersectional approach. An intersectional approach would center the lived experiences of women, regardless of social location and account for and recognize differences between and among groups of women. We are not necessarily proposing that policy target particular groups (although we recognize the utility of doing such). Instead, an intersectional approach to policymaking (taking policy making as a process with multiple stages) suggests that the policy logic (often thought of as the problem definition stage) be intersectional in nature. We focus primarily on this stage of the policymaking because discursive structures and rhetorical devices are an integral part of the process of crafting an intersectional policy approach. It is in this stage where issues are framed and the consequent actions justified.

A focus on the policy logic process requires us to ask which pressure groups have worked to call attention to the particular social issue and how have they used their position to shape the discourse in a manner that reflects their interests. Rummens (2003) asserts,

Identification of different socially-situated perspectives will not only provide more precise information but also yield greater insights into systems of marginalization and oppression. This will assist policy makers and service providers alike to deliver more effective and efficient programs and services to better meet the needs of those individuals and groups most disadvantaged by social inequities. (25)

This might prove difficult in a political system that suggests that it has moved beyond group-based and race-based politics. Additionally, given that simple stories (see Stone 1989) are the norm in discussing complex issues, it might also prove difficult to tell the stories of multiple women. However, if we are to challenge, in a substantive way, inequality, we cannot let existing structures and norms prevent the integration of "new" ways of understanding reality.

Policy grounded in intersectional strategies would begin to offer a more comprehensive approach to addressing labor force discrimination. Such a policy/policies would recognize the racial and class composition of jobs and not simply focus on gender neutrality in terms of equal pay for equal work. Additionally, an intersectional approach can result in policy pluralism that addresses many of the challenges faced by various women. A pluralistic policy approach could include, but is not limited to, affordable childcare, access to quality education starting at the kindergarten level, rebuilding urban, and other economically depressed communities, affordable and safe housing, and an approach that facilitates occupational integration. An intersectional approach would begin to challenge the reproduction of inequality.

Notes

1. Our focus is on Black women, as we employ an understanding of intersectionality that grew from their lived experiences.
2. While we treat the frames in a singular manner, this is not to suggest that at any point, a Congress member could not deploy the frames simultaneously. We use a singular approach only to make the presentation of the data more readable.

References

Acker, Joan. 1989. *Doing Comparable Worth: Gender, Class, and Pay Equity.* Philadelphia, PA: Temple University Press.

Ahern, David W., Mary M. Conway, and Gertrude A. Steuernagel. 2004. *Women and Public Policy: A Revolution in Progress.* 3rd ed. Washington, DC: CQ Press.

Alexander-Floyd, Nikol G. 2007. *Gender, Race, and Nationalism in Contemporary Black Politics. New York:* Palgrave Macmillan.

Byerly, Victoria. 1986. *Hard Times Cotton Mill Girls: Personal Histories of Womanhood and Poverty in the South.* Ithaca, NY: Cornell University Press.

Capps, Lois. 2008. "Equal Pay Day." *Congressional Record* 154: 64, E669. Available from LexisNexis® Congressional (accessed January 12, 2012).

Clarke, A. Y. 2004. "Intersectionality and the Reproduction of Race and Class Hierarchies." Unpublished Doctoral Dissertation, Yale University, Connecticut. http://www.yale.edu/ccr/clarke.doc (accessed June 8, 2007).

Cohen, Cathy. 1999. *The Boundaries of Blackness: AIDS and the Breakdown of Black Politics.* Chicago: University of Chicago Press.

Collins, Patricia Hill. 1990. *Black Feminist Thought: Knowledge, Consciousness, and the Politics of Empowerment.* Boston, MA: Allen & Unwin Hyman, 221–38. http://www.hartford-hwp.com/archives/45a/252.html (accessed June 2, 2007).

———. 2000. *Black Feminist Thought: Knowledge, Consciousness, and the Politics of Empowerment.* 2nd ed. New York: Routledge.

Crenshaw, K. 1989. "Demarginalizing the Intersection of Race and Sex: A Black Feminist Critique of Antidiscrimination Doctrine, Feminist Theory and Antiracist Politics." *University of Chicago Legal Forum:* 139–67.

———. 1994. "Mapping the Margins: Intersectionality, Identity Politics, and Violence against Women of Color." In *The Public Nature of Private Violence: The Discovery of Domestic Abuse*, ed. Martha A. Fineman and Roxanne Mikitiuk, 93–118. New York: Routledge.

Dawson, Michael. 1995. *Behind the Mule: Race and Class in African American Politics*. Princeton, NJ: Princeton University Press.

DeLauro, Rosa. 2008. "Paycheck Fairness Act." *Congressional Record* 154: 65, H2558. Available from LexisNexis® Congressional (accessed January 12, 2011).

Entman, Robert. 1993. "Framing: Toward Clarification of a Fractured Paradigm." *Journal of Communication* 43, no. 4: 51–58.

Fairclough, Norman. 2000. *Language and Power.* 2nd ed. New York: Longman.

Fairfield, Hannah, and Graham Roberts. 2010. *Why Is Her Paycheck Smaller?* New York Times: http://www.nytimes.com/interactive/2009/03/01/business/20090301_WageGap.html (accessed December 21, 2011).

Fischer, Frank. 2003. *Reframing Public Policy: Discursive Politics and Deliberative Practices*. New York: Oxford University Press.

Hagler, D. Harland. 1980. "The Ideal Woman in the Antebellum South: Lady or Farmwife?" *Journal of Southern History* 46: 405–18.

Haider-Markel, Donald, and Kenneth Meier. 1996. "The Politics of Gay and Lesbian Rights: Expanding the Scope of Conflict." *The Journal of Politics* 58, no. 2: 332–49.

Hammonds, Evelynn. 1992. "Missing Persons: African American Women, AIDS and the History of Disease." *Radical America* 24, no. 2: 7–23.

Hancock, Ange-Marie. 2004. *The Politics of Disgust: The Public Identity of the Welfare Queen*. New York: New York University Press.

Hare, Phil. 2007. "Paycheck Fairness Act." *Congressional Record* 153: 91, 6014. Available from LexisNexis® Congressional (accessed January 15, 2011).

Heyes, Cressida. 2002. "Identity Politics." In *The Stanford Encyclopedia of Philosophy*, ed. E. N. Zalta. http://plato.stanford.edu/archives/fall2002/entries/identity-politics (accessed June 3, 2007).

Higginbotham, Evelyn B. 1992. "African-American Women's History and the Metalanguage of Race." *Signs* 17, no. 2: 251–74.

Hirono, Mazie. 2008. "Paycheck Fairness Act." *Congressional Record* 154: 129, 7690. Available from LexisNexis® Congressional (accessed March 12, 2009).

Holt, Rush. 2008. "Paycheck Fairness Act." *Congressional Record* 154: 130, 1. Available from LexisNexis® Congressional (accessed March 12, 2009).

Hoynes, Hilary W., Marianne E. Page, and Ann H. Stevens. 2006. "Poverty in America: Trends and Explanations." *Journal of Economic Perspectives* 20, no. 1: 47–68.

Insight: Center for Community Economic Development. 2010. *Lifting as We Climb: Women of Color, Wealth, and America's Future.* http://www.insightcced.org/uploads/CRWG/LiftingAsWeClimb-WomenWealth-Report-InsightCenter-Spring2010.pdf (accessed January 12, 2012).

Institute for Women's Policy Research (IWPR). 2005. Women's Economic Status in the States: Wide Disparities by Race, Ethnicity, and Region. http://www.iwpr.org/pdf/R260.pdf (accessed May 18, 2007).

Jordan-Zachery, Julia. 2009. *Black Women, Cultural Images and Social Policy*. New York: Routledge.

Kennedy, Edward. 2007. "Statements on Introduced Bills and Joint Resolutions." *Congressional Record* 146: 38, S2700. Available from LexisNexis® Congressional (accessed January 12, 2011).

Lee, B. 2008. "Paycheck Fairness Act." *Congressional Record* 154: 129, 7685. Available from LexisNexis® Congressional (accessed March 12, 2009).

Lorde, Audre. 1984. *Sister Outsider: Essays and Speeches*. Freedom, CA: The Crossing Press.

Moore, Gwen. 2008. "In Support of Equal Pay for Equal Work." *Congressional Record* 154: 129, 7637. Available from LexisNexis® Congressional (accessed March 12, 2009).

Morse, Janice. 1994. "Designing Funded Qualitative Research." In *Handbook of Qualitative Research*, ed. Norman K. Denzin and Yvonna S. Lincoln, 220–35. Thousand Oaks, CA: Sage Publications.

Moynihan, Daniel P. 1965. *The Negro Family: The Case for National Action*. Washington, DC: United States Department of Labor, Office of Policy, Research, and Planning.

Mullings, Leith. 1994. "Images, Ideology, and Women of Color." In *Women of Color in U.S. Society*, ed. Maxine B. Zinn and Bonnie T. Dill, 265–90. Philadelphia, PA: Temple University Press.

National Committee on Pay Equity. n.d.[a] *Questions & Answers on Pay Equity.* http://www.pay-equity.org (accessed January 14, 2012).

———. n.d.[b] *Wage Gap Statistically Unchanged.* http://www.pay-equity.org (accessed January 14, 2012).

National Women's Law Center. 2011. *National Snapshot: Poverty among Women and Families, 2010.* http://www.nwlc.org (accessed December 20, 2011).

Neubeck, Kenneth, and Noel Cazenave. 2001. *Welfare Racism: Playing the Race Card against America's Poor*. New York: Routledge.

Norton, Eleanor. 2007. "The Introduction of the Fair Pay Act of 2007." *Congressional Record* 154: 129, 7637. Available from LexisNexis® Congressional (accessed March 12, 2009).

Palmer, Phyllis M. 1983. "White Women/Black Women: The Duality of Female Identity and Experience in the United States." *Feminist Studies* 9, no. 1: 151–70.

Rich, Adrienne. 1979. *On Lies, Secrets, and Silence.* New York: W. W. Norton.

Roberts, Dorothy. 1997. *Killing the Black Body: Race, Reproduction, and the Meaning of Liberty*. New York: Vintage Books.

Rummens, Joanna A. 2003. "Ethnic Ancestry, Culture, Identity, and Health: Using Ethnic Origin Data from the 2001 Canadian Census." *Canadian Ethnic Studies* 35, no. 1: 10–25.

Schattschneider, Elmer E. 1960. *The Semi-Sovereign People: A Realist's View of Democracy in America.* New York: Holt, Rinehart, and Winston.

Schneider, Anne, and Helen Ingram. 1993. "Social Construction of Target Populations: Implications for Politics and Policy." *The American Political Science Review* 87, no. 2: 334–47.

Shea-Porter, Carol. 2008. "Paycheck Fairness Act." *Congressional Record* 154: 129, 7637. Available from LexisNexis® Congressional (accessed March 12, 2009).

Sherman, Arloc, Shawn Fremstad, and Sharon Parrott. 2004. *Employment Rates for Single Mothers Fell Substantially during Recent Period of Labor Market Weakness*. Center on Budget and Policy Priorities. http://www.cbpp.org/cms/index.cfm?fa=view&id=1986 (accessed May 30, 2009).

Slaughter, L. 2008. "Providing for Consideration of H.R. 1338 Paycheck Fairness Act." *Congressional Record* 154: 142, E1731. Available from LexisNexis® Congressional (accessed March 12, 2009).

Smith, Jonathon, Paul Flowers, and Michael Larkin. 2009. *Interpretative, Phenomenological Analysis: Theory, Method and Research.* Thousand Oaks, CA: Sage Publications.

Solinger, Rickie. 2000. *Wake Up Little Susie: Single Pregnancy and Race before Roe V. Wade.* New York: Routledge.

Speier, Jackie. 2008. "Observance of Equal Pay Day." *Congressional Record* 154: 142, 687. Available from LexisNexis® Congressional (accessed January 12, 2011).

Spelman, Elizabeth V. 1988. *Inessential Woman: Problems of Exclusion in Feminist Thought*. Boston, MA: Beacon Press.

Stolberg, Sheryl G. 2009. "Obama Signs Equal-Pay Legislation." http://www.nytimes.com/2009/01/30/us/politics/30ledbetter-web.html

Stone, Deborah. 1989. "Causal Stories and the Formation of Policy Agendas." *Political Science Quarterly* 104, no. 2: 281–300.

Stone, Pamela, and Arielle Kuperberg. 2006. "Anti-Discrimination vs. Anti-Poverty? A Comparison of Pay Equity and Living Wage Reforms." *Journal of Women, Politics & Policy* 27, nos. 3 and 4: 23–39.

Sullivan, Marianne. 2008. *Women's Enews*. Women's Poverty Deepens Amid Slow 2003 Recovery. http://www.womensenews.org/article.cfm/dyn/aid/1968/context/archive (accessed January 12, 2008).

Taylor, Steven J., and Robert Bogdan. 1984. *Introduction to Qualitative Research Methods: The Search for Meanings.* New York: John Wiley and Sons.

US Bureau of Labor Statistics. 2010. U.S. Department of Labor. *The Editor's Desk*, Weekly Earnings in First Quarter 2010 by Demographics. http://www.bls.gov/opub/ted/2010/ted_20100420.htm (accessed April 17, 2012).

———. 2012. Highlights of Women's Earnings in 2011, Report 1038. http://www.bls.gov/cps/cpswom2011.pdf (accessed January 17, 2013).

Van Dijk, Teun A. 2001. "Critical Discourse Analysis." In *The Handbook of Discourse Analysis*, ed. Deborah Schiffren, Deborah Tannen, and Heidi Hamilton, 352–71. Malden, MA: Blackwell Publishers.

Weiss, Gilbert, and Ruth Wodak, eds. 2003. *Critical Discourse Analysis Theory and Interdisciplinary*. New York: Palgrave Macmillan.

Widdowson, Henry. 1995. "Discourse Analysis: A Critical View." *Language and Literature* 4, no. 3: 157–72.

Yanow, Dvora. 1996. *How Does a Policy Mean? Interpreting Policy and Organizatinal Actions.* Washington, DC: Georgetown University Press.

Young, Iris M. 2005. "Justice and the Politics of Difference." In *Gender and Planning: A Reader*, ed. Susan S. Fainstein, 86–103. Piscataway, NJ: Rutgers University Press.

Influencing the Political Agenda from the Outside: A Comparative Study of Hausa Women's NGOs and CBOs in Kano, Nigeria

Adryan Wallace
University of Hartford

Introduction

Black feminist scholars have argued that expanding the definition of politics beyond formal processes is essential to capturing the contributions of Black women as political actors (Prestage 1995, 169–84; Berger 2004). Two key theoretical contributions, discussed in greater detail below, were generated from works rooted in the political experiences of African American women living in the United States, namely intersectionality (see, e.g., Crenshaw 1989, 1991; Springer 2002; Jordan-Zachery 2007) and syncre-nationalism (Glass 2006). In an effort to contribute to this literature, my article explores the ways in which Muslim women in Nigeria construct and deploy an inclusive politics that can be best understood through combining the two analytical frames. The Hausa are the largest predominately Muslim ethno-linguistic group in West Africa (Furniss 1996). The women who participated in my study in Kano, Nigeria, a state under Sharia law, articulate conceptualizations of politics inextricably linked to their self-defined identities as Muslim women.

I am not suggesting that there is a class of homogenous Hausa Muslim women or that these women utilize a single approach to political engagement. Instead, I posit that Hausa women are employing a particular strategy, which incorporates the perspectives of women across different levels of privilege. Internal power hierarchies among women are mapped onto their individual memberships in nongovernmental organizations (NGOs) and community-based organizations (CBOs). CBOs comprise women involved primarily in small-scale trading or women who are traditional birth attendants, and these groups may not register with local government areas (LGAs) or Kano state officials.

In order to evaluate the political significance of Hausa women's strategies, it is essential to understand the ways in which women are defining politics in relationship to their sociocultural contexts (Prestage 1995, 169–84). It is also critical that we expand the definition of politics beyond formal processes and analyze the spaces in which the full range of political mobility occurs (Prestage 1995; Berger 2004). Given that women have minimal presence in legislative bodies in Kano, Nigeria, the majority of their political engagements occur through their NGOs and CBOs.

The practice of politics that Hausa women employ is rooted within their Islamic identities, social locations, connections to other Hausa women in Kano, and a broader imagined global Muslim community. Therefore, weaving intersectionality and syncre-nationalism into a single theoretical frame, I analyze the impact of Islam on Hausa women's political activities. There are two dimensions of Hausa women's inclusive politics that are the focus of this study: (1) decision making by consensus and (2) establishing institutional mechanisms for women across social locations to represent their own interests to political institutions.

The three principal contributions of this study are: (1) theorizing about intersectionality and syncre-nationalism in combination, whereas each is typically theorized in isolation; (2) these two theoretical frames, derived from the experiences of African American women, might be applied to African Muslim feminists' conceptualizations of identity, and in an African context, as a means to prevent essentialization of the perspectives of Muslim women; and (3) I mainstream intersectionality into discussions of religion and politics, thus enabling an analysis of the relationships between individual agency and collective experiences. I argue that exploring the political activities of African Muslim women within the context of Sharia law provides insights into the interaction of religion, identity, and political behavior. I develop my argument along three fronts. First, I provide a theoretical framework that captures the special expression of syncre-national intersectionality employed by these Black political women. Second, using feminist and interpretivist methods, I illustrate the multiple ways in which Hausa women define an inclusive politics. Next, I analyze two particular approaches to inclusion used by their organizations, consensus building, and self-representation. I conclude that syncre-national intersectionality is a theoretical framework with the capacity to understand the complex and dynamic interconnections between identity and political praxis. The contributions of African Muslim feminist scholars to this frame are underscored throughout this work.

Syncre-National Intersectionality

Women's interpretations of the political role Islam has ascribed to them are central overarching components that are integrated into other elements of their identity (Imam 1997). Muslim women in Africa are depicted as passive or reactionary. This is an essentialist view heavily critiqued by feminist scholars (Imam 1997; Adamu 1999; Mama 2001). Rather than being passive or reactionary, Hausa women are negotiating difference among themselves in an effort to establish collective political aims. By using Hausa women's experiences as the central point of theorizing, my study places intersectionality and syncre-nationalism (which are derived from works of feminists of color in the United States) in direct conversation with scholarship by African Muslim feminists. This continues a tradition of intellectual exchange between feminists of color in the United States and feminists outside of the West (Fernandes 2013). Furthermore, this work disrupts narratives of Islam, civil society, and the nation-state, as constructed in the United States, that often serve as normative frames in the study of political behavior (Fernandes 2013). Intersectionality provides a fluid model of conceptualizing identity; syncre-nationalism further evaluates the ways in which expressions of Muslim identities have political and material implications within the nation-state. Combining both concepts is essential to my work.

It is nevertheless important that I clearly identify which components of intersectionality and syncre-nationalism I use.

Intersectionality provides a lens for analyzing the simultaneity of oppression and privilege by centering the experiences of women in the intersections of race, sex, gender, ethnicity, class, nationality, and sexuality (Spillers 1987; King 1988; Collins 1989, 745–73; Crenshaw 1989, 314–43; 1991, 1241–99; Higginbotham 1992; Springer 2002). The different combinations of intersecting categories, in addition to how they are shaped, developed, and deployed within national contexts, must be given special consideration to avoid assuming that these processes are the same for all women in general and women of African descent in particular (Kalu 1996; Coogan-Gehr 2011, 83–107). While intersectionality provides a useful frame for this study, it is imperative that the experiences of Hausa women and their approaches to addressing gender issues remain central. Additionally, the concept of intersectionality should not eclipse scholarship by African Muslim feminists or treat Western constructs of gender as normative (Ogundipe-Leslie 1994; Kalu 1996; Ojewusi 1996; Oyewumi 1998, 1049; Adamu 1999, 56–61; Mama 2001, 67–73; Imam 2003, 280–303; Fernandes 2013).

I blend intersectionality and Hausa feminisms, which also outline the construction of multiple sites of identities, in order to capture and include a broader transnational Islamic identity in my analysis. African feminists make two key contributions to our understanding of identity by interrogating (1) the relationships between the individual and other communities (religious, national, etc.) in which they retain membership and (2) gender constructs within religious frameworks (Mama 2001). Given that identity can serve as a site of oppression and resistance, African Muslim women actively contest externally constructed definitions of Muslim women by both their male counterparts and Western feminists (Lemu 1980; Ogundipe-Leslie 1994; Oyewumi 1998; Adamu 1999, 56–61; Mama 2001; Alidou 2005; Jamal 2007, 209–15; Kabir 2010). These internally derived constructs of identity have direct implications for Hausa women's conceptualizations of politics. The constant tension that African Muslim women experience as they are exposed to more conservative forms of Islam, coupled with the hegemony of Western feminists, is captured by Adamu's (1999) concept of the double-edged sword, which argues that African Muslim women address gender inequality and interpret their roles as Muslim women on their own terms. The ways in which Hausa women resist these efforts by defining their own roles within religious contexts is the second way African feminists broaden our conceptualization of identity. Imam carefully traces these constant contestations and redrawing of boundaries within Islam and argues that they should be read as political agency (Imam 1997). Salime (2011) investigates a similar dynamic in Morocco; however, she argues that liberal feminist and Islamist women's movements are symbiotic rather than combative. Their constant interaction has caused liberal feminists in Morocco to increase their knowledge of the Quran and caused Islamist women to advocate for more space from their male counterparts. Hausa women in Kano, Nigeria, also use approaches that contravene an imagined artificial tension between being Muslim and addressing gender inequality. During my interviews, participants deliberately framed gender equality on their own terms—which included mainstreaming their roles as mothers with their commitment to developing their respective communities through NGOs and CBOs. Completion of the responsibilities associated with childcare and development, prior to addressing broader issues of gender inequality and community development, reveal the significance placed on establishing continuity between their private (domestic) and public roles.

There are additional categories including lineage, ethnicity, and geographically bounded nationalities, knowledge of the Quran, and linguistic cleavages that also mutually construct identities of African Muslim women. More specifically, for Hausa women, shared membership in the global Ummah (Muslim community) influences their conceptualization of politics. Furthermore, the position of the majority of African countries in the global economy impact the myriad ways in which African women assert autonomy from Western feminist approaches to addressing gender issues.

This symbolic connection between feminism, Islam, and other markers of identity is captured by Glass's (2006) concept of syncre-nationalism. Glass uses syncre-nationalism to analyze the ways in which African American women created their own political spaces beyond the purview and control of the state to mobilize constituencies. I argue that Hausa women also maintain memberships in Islamic communities that are not territorially bounded, which further intersect with other identity categories. Hausa women also call their own collectives into being via their organizations in order to attain their inclusive political aims. However, I posit further that Hausa women have an interest in maintaining and synthesizing their ideological and geographic political communities because Islam emphasizes continuity between the public and the private.

Therefore, Hausa women create specific gendered political collectives within Muslim communities in an effort to address change in both sectors. A central component of these collectives represents a concerted effort to value multiple voices in the decision-making process (Imam 1997; Mama 2001). Hausa women's political communities forged across social locations assume that women are constantly negotiating the terms of their membership in the ideological nation through their lived experiences and daily activities in geographically bounded political, economic, and social spaces. Furthermore, their decisions to structure ways for women with less privilege to directly articulate their own interests to the state illustrate how their commitment to other Muslim women provides continuity between ideological community and political practice. Hausa women's emphasis on their role in the family is similar to the ways African American women in the nineteenth century strategically engaged the frames of Republican motherhood toward their own ends (Glass 2006). Each organization's activity becomes a mechanism to increase the visibility of grassroots and elite women's issues, creating a mandate for the government to address them. While motherhood is an overarching theme, the ways in which women outline their requirements vary with their social locations. Consequently, Hausa women propose solutions to these challenges that are shaped by their interactions with state, as well as with social and religious structures, and that are consistent with their particular interpretations of Islam (Adamu 1999). The experiences of Hausa women reveal that being a mother is critical, but there are also distinctive aspects about their roles as Muslim women that push Glass's conceptualization further.

More specifically, Hausa women in Kano are maximizing their political efficacy by moving between formal and informal political institutions, instead of focusing solely on embedding themselves within the state. Rather than just acting as surrogates, elite women also create spaces and establish institutional mechanisms for grassroots women to take advantage of moving between the public and the private. Additionally, Hausa women use their multiple roles as Muslim women, mothers, etc. to execute development agendas that function as "non-electoral" political activities that directly impact their communities. During participant observation, it was evident that cultivating the political literacy and advocacy capacity of grassroots women in CBOs has political implications and Islamic origins. My language training in Hausa allowed me to observe interactions and programming in the local language (Fernandes 2013). Placing CBO women in a position to help shape legislation, and monitor and address access issues to healthcare centers, gives them autonomy and political significance in their communities, which lasts long after the conclusion of an NGO sponsored development program. Providing accountability mechanisms for state and LGA officials further illustrates that Hausa women not only move between formal and informal political institutions, but they also use their locations to interact with different levels of government, the local and the state. In the following three sections of my paper, I argue that embedding myself in Kano for five months allowed me to understand the ways in which Hausa women define politics and examine two key strategies of political inclusion. These are: (1) relying on decision making through consensus and (2) ensuring that a diverse range of women can represent their own interests to the state.

Methods

In order to uncover the ways identity influences Hausa women's ability to devise an inclusive politics, I utilized ethnography and semi-structured interviews. They were designed to ensure that Hausa women's perspectives are the central point of theorizing about political action. Two Hausa women's NGOs in Kano, Nigeria, were selected for this study. They were the Federation of Muslim Women in Nigeria (FOMWAN) and the Grassroots Health Organization of Nigeria (GHON). I selected these organizations because each has relationships with smaller CBOs. Also, it is important to understand the distinct methods Hausa women use to create collective political community and expediency.

The women who participated in this study were not financially dependent on income from their NGOs. Their economic status allowed them to be more selective about programming choices and they were able to set their own agendas, including mainstreaming the needs of women from different socioeconomic backgrounds. In organizations where women are economically dependent on their NGOs for financial stability, they are less able to maintain an inclusive politics. Economic independence allows women to follow their own priorities rather adjusting their agenda to accommodate the funding agenda of donors. The consistency between the programs implemented by FOMWAN and GHON and their articulation of gender issues is demonstrative of their autonomy.

By focusing on FOMWAN and GHON it is possible to see how Hausa women are utilizing syncre-nationalist strategies by expressing resistance through the work of their civil society organizations (CSOs) to forge political alliances with other women under the larger rubric of an Islamic community. In Kano, Hausa women's organizations have collaborated at times with international NGOs and secular domestic groups with more liberal feminist orientations. Nevertheless, they have maintained their identities as Muslim women, as evidenced through the observation of their programming. The agency Hausa women exhibit in defining politics and advancing women's concerns vis-à-vis Islamic development frames was illustrated during interviews and through participant observation (Prestage 1995, 169–84; Shebadduin 2008; Salime 2011).

I spent five months collecting ethnographic data and conducting thirty-five interviews in Kano, Nigeria. In line with feminist, Black feminist, and other critical scholars, my study utilizes Black feminist theorization and interpretivist ethnographic methods to create a textured picture of the conceptualization of politics and the role of civil society groups in representing the interests of diverse groups of women (Schildkrout 1982; Callaway 1987; Mama 1996; Mikell 1997, 405; Norton 2004; Jordan-Zachery 2007; Kleinman 2007; Nagar and Geiger 2007, 267–78; Jourde 2009, 201–16; Kubik 2009, 25–52; Schatz 2009). I observed GHON, FOMWAN, and CBO programming, which allowed me to analyze two strategies for cultivating an inclusive politics. Learning Hausa allowed me to evaluate programs conducted in Hausa and English, which centered their perspectives and decentered normative Western constructs of gender, Islam and politics (Fernandes 2013).

The programs I observed were limited to those focused on accessing health facilities, and included several office visits to assess CBO engagements outside of specific programming. FOMWAN is operating in thirty-four states in Nigeria and has over five hundred affiliated organizations. GHON programs have on average fifteen people serving as members of the community development group tasked with increasing community access to health facilities. Approximately one-third of the members of the development groups are women. The development groups in turn conduct actual trainings for over one hundred community members in each LGA. Interviews of Hausa women illustrated the varied perspectives of women in different social locations regarding their types of political activities. In this study, participants involved in NGOs had completed postsecondary training, and approximately 30 percent had graduate degrees. The majority of participants in CBOs had completed primary school, fewer than 10 percent had completed secondary school, and none had attained university degrees. In large part, the different approaches to inclusive politics adopted by these organizations are attributable to three factors: (1) organizational structure of the group; (2) programmatic goals; and (3) institutional relationships between NGOs and CBOs. These organizations make a concerted effort to remain neutral in party politics and do not emphasize party affiliation.

Islam, Identity, and Political Praxis

Uncovering the ways in which Hausa women define politics and inclusive political engagement is central to expanding our understanding of politics as a series of sustainable interactions that can establish accountability mechanisms for the state. As Berger (2004) relates, it is important to illustrate the interrelationship between identity and political behavior. Here, we find that being part of a larger community of Muslim women, specifically living under Sharia law, has influenced the types of political roles women should occupy and the time in their lives when they conduct activities (Berger 2004). Excerpts from the Democracy Training Manual developed by the Muslim Sisters Organization, a part of the executive committee of FOMWAN, explicitly define women and politics, stating:

Women are leaders in their homes and helpers of their husbands. Women's leadership is still looked upon with skepticism, not because Islam does not approve, but because women are, according to Sharia, mothers and housewives whose main duty is to safeguard the unity and happiness of the family, which in the end will benefit the entire society.[1]

Each participant in this study stated that one of the key roles women play within the family is being a mother. Choosing to engage in activities through CSO activities after childbearing responsibilities have been fulfilled allows women to be more selective about their programming endeavors, because these women are often retired, and NGO ventures are not a primary source of income. These articulations of women's political roles exemplify Adamu's (1999) contention that Hausa women have created a distinctive construct of the political.

FOMWAN's work on the Maternal Health Bill represents one dimension of inclusive legislative activity where their connection to CBOs allowed their framing of the bill that addresses maternal health issues that impact women across social locations. FOWMAN uses motherhood as a mechanism to challenge the state to provide resources to women. Motherhood, while appearing consistent with normative conceptions of women's roles, also becomes subversive, because these mothers are making political claims on the state (Glass 2006). Lastly, given the type of political communities Hausa women cultivate, they further complicate the overly simplistic construction of Hausa women by the state and instead articulate a range of perspectives, experiences, and priorities (Imam 1997; Mama 2001). More specifically, their process of establishing collective agendas, via consensus rather than majority rule, stems directly from Islam. I am not arguing that the completely equal representation of all members of FOMWAN is possible; nevertheless, their close proximity to women at the grassroots level coupled with their organizational structure significantly increases the likelihood that many grassroots interests are incorporated into their agendas.

Haj Hassan, the head of FOMWAN's Kano branch, also indicates that she feels confident in FOMWAN's ability to partner with the state or an international development organization if it is in their interests because FOMWAN maintains its own set of resources for programming. She refers to the ability of FOMWAN to engage with different actors, given the level of privilege that she and other members of the Kano branch retain, allowing them to move among sectors. She explains:

> Well we network with all the NGOs (my question was about WIN) any NGOs, we work with WIN, FIDA, um SWAN all the NGOS on the ground. Whenever they have something for us we go, we attend their meetings, we attend their activities, they attend our activities, so yeah. And so we have a good rapport with NGOs we have with government and local government so. Yeah but you know you have to be patient and you know we, FOMWAN, does [sic] not have a . . . we don't have much demands. We demand for what we require. And we tax ourselves more than going to ask to beg for, so we tax ourselves more. So if you are going . . . if we are going to government we come with a project and we say okay this is what we have on the ground, what are you going to do to us, what's going to be your contribution? We would not just come and say, look we are going to build a school what's going to be your . . . , no we will get a space maybe we will start to lay the foundation and then we say okay this is what we have on the ground, not what's going to happen? So I think that is how FOMWAN is trying. (Haj Hassan, personal communication)

FOMWAN and women in similar NGOs are in a position of equal negotiating power with both their male and Western counterparts because they secure the majority of project funds before approaching potential partners. The economic privilege of women engaged in NGOs allows them to choose to partner with government ministries and other international or domestic groups in ways that maintain their ability to mainstream a myriad number of women's interests.

Consensus Building and Political Maneuvering

Hausa women's politics successfully incorporates multiple voices across hierarchies of privilege as part of their role as political agents. The emphasis on building communities through inclusion is evident in the decision-making processes of these organizations. The importance of being nominated for leadership positions rather than acquiring office through self-appointment is enshrined in the ways in which women from different NGOs and CBOs interact within FOMWAN.[2] The rule by shurah, which is specifically outlined as a component of Islamic political practice in contrast to the Western democratic practice of elections by majority rule, is reflected in the division of labor between NGOs and CBOs where women representatives from each division are selected and form the executive board that often devises programming aims (Glass 2006). I argue that this allows women from different levels of privilege to be integrated into programming discussions that address differences. This is important because women in CBOs often focus on basic needs that need to be mainstreamed into the strategic agendas of NGOs. The meetings at FOMWAN are structured to ensure that women from each echelon of society have their own interests represented. Additionally, they utilize consensus rather than majority rule for decision making.

FOMWAN, an umbrella organization, was best positioned to focus on addressing gender inequality in the health sector via the introduction of the maternal health bill. The bill was well received, yet it is still in committee because the emphasis is on implementation, which requires addressing logistical challenges, including dividing local and state jurisdictional duties. These issues of application have been an ongoing challenge since the state offered maternal service to women. The bill cosponsored by FOMWAN addressed these obstacles.

Since 2001, the Kano state offered free maternal health services, but there was no existing policy plan or law to regulate the terms and delivery of services. Therefore, this legislation that FOMWAN drafted, in collaboration with other CBOs and groups, helped ensure that obstacles impeding all women's equal access to state maternal health services are remedied. FOMWAN's direct efforts to maintain connections to CBO groups helped integrate concerns from grassroots women that are often excluded. These efforts are reflected in the ways the organizations facilitate collective exchanges. Given the organizational structure of FOMWAN, members of NGOs and CBOs are selected to represent the interests of their respective groups and in turn work together in committee, based on consensus, to devise the organization's larger platform. Even when services may be available, it is imperative that there be guidelines to ensure equal access, and it is important that grassroots women are able to actively participate in this element of the political processes.

Mainstreaming the priorities and perspectives of women from CBOs into this framework is politically significant because it represents FOMWAN's commitment to the political community of Muslim Hausa women. The insertion of multiple women's perspectives also further expands the range of politics Muslim women choose to engage (Imam 1997; Mama 2001), as evidenced by the head of FOMWAN Kano, namely Haj Hassan's, account of her organizations' collective role in the maternal health bill. She remarks:

A lot on advocacies, sensitization, mobilization and the greatest of all [what] FOMWAN achieved and helped the state government [with] was in polio eradication in their health sector. And also I was part of those that moved the government to sponsor a bill for maternal health. So the bill now is in the assembly. COMPASS helped us as Nigerian partners. (Haj Hassan, personal communication)

Haj Hassan's statement illustrates the ways in which Hausa women's agency in these organizations is an interaction between their identity as Muslim women and their deliberate approach to politics, which works across class divisions. This is reflective of syncre-national intersectionality.

Inclusion through Self-Representation

FOMWAN, by proposing the maternal health bill, created a space for women in NGOs and CBOs to devise legislation that mainstreamed elite and grassroots women's priorities through consensus. GHON, unlike FOMWAN, used another approach. GHON is a development organization. It works to ensure that the health needs of grassroots women, defined by local CBOs, are addressed at the local level. Additionally, GHON has equipped women in CBOs with connections to the formal LGA political institutions capable of resolving the issues that they face related to accessing healthcare facilities. These local women's groups are now able to engage the relevant political institutions to address their concerns regarding the improvement of health factors and other areas, if they choose to do so.

In addition to areas such as health, GHON highlights the broader contributions that women can make to society in the areas of development. Under Sharia, in this particular Islamic context, delineating between the public and the private is not pronounced; therefore, changes in any one sector have direct implications on the other. Sadia, an employee of GHON, states that historically women were ". . . considered to be more at home or their work must be involved [in] home and the family. They are not recognized in the educational, health and everything to do outside. But as time goes on our people were able to identify that women [have] roles to play even in the outside society" (Haj Sadia, personal communication). Hausa women are successfully translating their needs associated with domestic activities into political claims particularly in the areas of health (Imam 1997).

In addition to influencing legislative agendas, Hausa women's organizations also have the potential to provide multilevel feedback to the government and to enhance the mobilization efficacy of women in CBOs. These feedback loops constitute political work that holds the state accountable and makes Hausa women more visible as political actors (Berger 2004; Glass 2006). Through participant observation, I was able to see the interactions among women of different social strata and the ways in which these institutional relationships can be beneficial. Changing grassroots women's positionality within the state further illustrates NGOs institutional commitment to a politics that integrates all women in sustainable and reflexive political processes (Glass 2006). Hausa women further use Islam as outlined in the Human Rights in Islam Tree designed by Muslim Sister's Organization (MSO), which lists a total of twenty-seven rights for women, to create their own narrative about their rights to education, health, a clean environment, and to political participation using the Quran and hadiths (Imam 1997).

Ensuring that women and communities have access to health facilities is critical because it is part of a practical need as outlined by CBOs in the rural areas. The government has made efforts to increase access to health facilities, especially for populations in more marginal locations. GHON compiled reports that outlined the obstacles and solutions to increase the amount of access communities have to health centers, based on assessments taken during focus groups and workshops. The women's membership in a broader Islamic community is further influencing their interest in utilizing inclusive political strategies and treating grassroots women as counterparts with priorities that are at times different, but no less significant than those of elite women (Glass 2006). Therefore, I am arguing that collectively, Islam, along with other elements, helps shape Hausa women's definition of collective politics via consensus and self-representation.

The reports drafted by GHON will be submitted to the Kano state ministry of health and LGAs. Additionally, there will also be follow-up with the government and CBOs for over six months after the completion of the health center training program. GHON conducted these programs in three LGAs. Each program was conducted for five days. In each LGA community area, Albasu, Kunchi, Taruani, and GHON officials worked with local leaders to ensure that at least one women's group participated in the program and that there were female members of the local development community. If there was no development community in existence, they encouraged women to create one. It is politically expedient to create informal institutional structures to help women advocate for their interests related to accessing healthcare (Prestage 1995, 169–84; Berger 2004). Furthermore, GHON provided smaller women's groups with mechanisms to hold local political and health officials responsible for removing barriers to exercising their legal rights to maternal healthcare (including pre-natal care, access to health facilities, etc.). The practice of creating inclusive politics is also mapped onto new organizations GHON encouraged women to form. Beyond this particular program for health centers, these groups are now positioned to address other issues with traditional and community leaders in addition to officials in contemporary government institutions. The intersecting nature of factors that impede healthcare access, including economic vulnerability, further allows some CBO groups to focus on other key areas of concern. Women from CBOs have used the techniques referred to above to make requests for small amounts of financial support from community leaders (i.e., small loans).

Participants in the program highlighted the ways in which attending the GHON training also serves to provide the women with authority in the community by being designated as key contact people or players in the formal political system (Berger 2004). Female members of CBOs, during later phases of the program, echoed this perspective. This also demonstrates how political linkages among women translate into consensus based political engagements. Furthermore, what is highlighted is a potentially key institutional relationship between NGOs with a focus on development issues, and government ministries. For example, Haladu, a program officer for the GHON, argues that part of the role of civil society is to partner with government and serve as a feedback mechanism regarding the ability of government to successfully deliver goods and services to its citizens. Their work on reproductive health provides opportunities for citizens to identify areas where their needs are unmet. It also provides an opportunity to highlight specific details about the occurrences of bottlenecks in addition to mapping areas where additional fiscal resources are required to address these conditions with the relevant government officials.

Haj Hadiza indicates that GHON allows the concerns of women in rural areas in Kano and other underserved segments of the city to reach the Ministry of Health and larger organizations, such as Pact Nigeria, which focuses on HIV prevention and improving the ability of citizens' to access health services (Haj Hadiza, personal communication). Additionally, the creation and empowerment of women's CBOs are important because they build skills to ensure that these groups can lobby LGA and traditional leaders around other issues impacting their quality of life. This is critically important to the sustainability of their programs. Second, GHON's work challenges the assumption that a relationship with the state, in terms of implementing programs, is synonymous with being co-opted by the state. I would argue further that their membership in an Islamic community serves as a buffer between the state and a space where political mobilization can occur beyond the purview of the state. GHON is able to provide feedback and address other factors that impact women's access to resources through blending formal and informal political processes as a means to interact with formal political institutions (Berger 2004). While it is possible that the organization can filter or alter the feedback of citizens, this was not obvious in direct observation of this particular organization.

There was a specific occasion when Haladu, a team member, during an advocacy visit with a traditional leader, insisted that women represent themselves rather than have one of the male elders represent them. This pivotal moment is a representative example of the ways in which NGO officials can alter the position of marginalized women, so that they are able to articulate their own interests rather than members of GHON serving as surrogates for grassroots women. Under these conditions, the position that GHON, the NGO, occupies, serves to benefit the local community-based women's group and its respective community writ large. For this reason, the women themselves become part of the committee that monitors the amount of access to health centers for all residents. Furthermore, each of the fifteen respondents from CBOs that I interviewed highlighted three key benefits of working with GHON: (1) feeling more empowered to advocate for their own interests; (2) having an affiliation with GHON made their communities take them more seriously when they were requesting support from local political authorities and community leaders; and (3) GHON facilitated relationships with officials who can assist them in accessing resources, for example, local hospital officials. GHON's work with the health facility clearly indicates the ways in which an inclusive politics can be sustainable.

Conclusion

Centering on the experiences of African Muslim women obviates tendencies to homogenize interpretations of women and politics in Islamic contexts, and instead illustrates the primary ways in which Hausa women address difference. By using syncre-national intersectionality as a single theoretical frame, I was able to analyze Hausa women's conceptualization of their political role and illustrate the impact of religion on identity and political behavior as evidenced in their specific form of inclusive politics. I expanded the conceptualization of identity by placing African feminist contributions, including the interrelationships between the individual and the community, and viewing interpretation as agency, into intersectional frameworks. Placing the work of African Muslim scholars in conversation with Black feminist scholarship culminated in syncre-national intersectionality, which is a theoretical frame capable of analyzing the political engagements of women of African descent within and outside of the United States. More specifically, I explored the ways in which Islam intersected with other women's identity categories and the impact on their political activities. There were two key elements of political praxis that this work revealed. First, Hausa women place emphasis on their roles as mothers, including development of the family and the community, and second women place importance on mainstreaming Hausa women's myriad of perspectives into political goals and activities. Decision making through consensus and the ability of NGOs to establish institutional relationships among women in grassroots organizations and the state are two key areas where inclusive politics are practiced by Hausa women. This case study in Kano provides a method to capture the agency of women as it relates to religious identity and politics and, furthermore, demonstrates that it is a dynamic, iterative, and continuous process. By practicing an inclusive politics, Hausa women are expanding the construct of Muslim women and their political activities, which directly challenges narrow external constructs often utilized by Western feminists.

FOMWAN and GHON cultivated institutional relationships with CBOs, allowing collective political agendas to be formed and implemented. FOMWAN focused on using consensus to craft legislation, while GHON connected women in CBOs with government structures capable of resolving issues in accessing goods and services provided by the state. Under this rubric, grassroots women are better able to represent their own interests rather than having women in NGOs function as surrogates. Moreover, this model creates an internal accountability mechanism among women because grassroots women have an independent information stream to government institutions that is not mediated by women in NGOs.

Finally, this study captured the ways in which Hausa women's individual identities as Muslim women shape their collective roles as political actors within their communities (Crenshaw 1991; Glass 2006; Jordan-Zachery 2007; Fernandes 2013). I argued that Hausa women's NGOs and CBOs frame and conduct an inclusive politics to address gender inequality in both domestic and public spheres because, in the Islamic context, the distinction between public and private spheres is less pronounced than that in the West. My data indicate that women with more privilege, access to fiscal resources, social capital, and formal and Quranic education engage in NGO work and women who are more economically vulnerable are members of CBOs.

Notes

1. MSO-Democracy and Governance Peer Educators Training Manual for Muslim Youths. The FOMWAN was founded by members of the MSO.
2. MSO-Democracy and Governance Peer Educators Training Manual for Muslim Youths.

References

Adamu, Fatima. 1999. "A Double-Edged Sword: Challenging Women's Oppression within Muslim Society in Northern Nigeria." *Gender and Development* 7, no. 1: 56–61.

Alidou, Ousennia. 2005. *Engaging Modernity: Muslim Women and the Politics of Agency in Postcolonial Niger*. Madison, WI: University of Wisconsin Press.

Berger, Michele. 2004. *Workable Sisterhood*. Princeton, NJ: Princeton University Press.

Callaway, Barbara. 1987. *Muslim Hausa Women in Nigeria: Tradition and Change*. Syracuse, NY: Syracuse University Press.

Collins, Patricia Hill. 1989. "The Social Construction of Black Feminist Thought." *Signs* 14, no. 4: 745–73.

Coogan-Gehr, Kelly. 2011. "The Politics of Race in U.S. Feminist Scholarship: An Archaeology." *Signs* 37, no. 1: 83–107.

Crenshaw, Kimberlé. 1989. "Demarginalizing the Intersection of Race and Sex: A Black Feminist Critique of Antidiscrimination Doctrine, Feminist Theory, and Antiracist Politics." In *Feminist Legal Theories*, ed. Karen Maschke, 23–52. New York: Taylor & Francis.

———. 1991. "Mapping the Margins: Intersectionality, Identity Politics, and Violence against Women of Color." *Stanford Law Review* 43, no. 6: 1241–99.

Fernandes, Leela. 2013. *Transnational Feminism in the United States: Knowledge, Ethics, and Power*. New York: New York University Press.

Furniss, Graham. 1996. *Poetry, Prose, and Popular Culture in Hausa*. Washington, DC: Smithsonian Institution Press.

Glass, Kathy. 2006. *Courting Communities: Black Female Nationalism and "Syncre-Nationalism" in the Nineteenth-Century*. New York: Routledge.

Higginbotham, Evelyn Brooks. 1992. "African-American Women's History and the Metalanguage of Race." *Signs* 17, no. 2: 251–74.

Imam, Ayesha. 1997. "The Dynamics of WINning." In *Feminist Genealogies, Colonial Legacies, Democratic Futures*, ed. M. Jacqui Alexander and Chandra Mohanty, 230–307. New York: Routledge.

———. 2003. *Women, Law and Islam in Nigeria*. Guelph: University of Guelph.

Jamal, Amina. 2007. "Islam: Islam and Modernities—Overview." In *Encyclopedia of Women & Islamic Cultures, Volume 5 Practices, Interpretations and Representations*, ed. Suad Joseph, 209–15. Boston, MA: Brill.

Jordan-Zachery, Julia S. 2007. "Commentary: The Practice and Functioning of Intersectionality and Politics." *Journal of Women, Politics & Policy* 28, nos. 3–4: 205–12.

Jourde, Cedric. 2009. "The Ethnographic Sensibility Overlooked Authoritarian Dynamic & Islamic Ambivalences in West Africa." In *Political Ethnography: What Immersion Contributes to the Study of Politics*, ed. Edward Schatz, 201–14. Chicago: University of Chicago Press.

Kabir, Hajara. 2010. *Northern Women Development: A Focus on Women in Northern Nigeria*. Vol. 1. Kano, Nigeria: Print Serve Limited.

Kalu, Anthonia C. 1996. "Women and the Social Construction of Gender in African Development." *Africa Today* 20: 269.

King, Deborah K. 1988. "Multiple Jeopardy, Multiple Consciousness: The Context of a Black Feminist Ideology." *Signs* 14, no. 1: 42–72.

Kleinman, Sherryl. 2007. *Feminist Fieldwork Analysis: Qualitative Research Methods*. London: Sage Publishers.

Kubik, Jan. 2009. "Ethnography of Politics: Foundations, Applications, Prospects." In *Political Ethnography: What Immersion Contributes to the Study of Politics*, ed. Edward Schatz, 25–52. Chicago: University of Chicago Press.

Lemu, Aisha. 1980. *A Degree above Them: Observations on the Condition of the Northern Nigerian Muslim Woman*. Karachi, Pakistan: Islamic Education Trust.

Mama, Amina. 1996. *Women's Studies and Studies of African Women during the 1990s*. Dakar, Senegal: CODESRIA.

———. 2001. "Challenging Subjects: Gender and Power in African Contexts." *African Sociological Review* 5, no. 2: 63–73. Plenary Address Nordic African Institute Conference: "Beyond Identity Rethinking Power in Africa," Upsala, October 4–7.

Mikell, Gwendolyn. 1997. *African Feminism: The Politics of Survival in Sub-Saharan Africa*. Philadelphia: University of Pennsylvania Press.

Nagar, Richa, and Susan Geiger. 2007. "Reflexivity and Positionality in Feminist Fieldwork Revisited." In *Politics and Practice in Economic Geography*, ed. Adam Tickell, Eric Sheppard, Jamie Peck, and Trevor Barnes, 267–78. London: Sage.

Norton, Anne. 2004. *95 Theses on Politics, Culture, and Method*. New Haven, CT: Yale University Press.

Ogundipe-Leslie, Molara. 1994. *Re-Creating Ourselves: African Women and Critical Transformations*. NJ: Africa World Press.

Ojewusi, Sola. 1996. *Speaking for Nigerian Women: A History of the National Council of Women's Societies, Nigeria*. Abuja: All State Publishing & Printing.

Oyewumi, Oeronke. 1998. "Deconfounding Gender: Feminist Theorizing and Western Culture, a Comment on Hawkesworth's 'Confounding Gender.'" *Signs* 23, no. 4: 1049–62.

Prestage, Jewel. 1995. "In Quest of an African American Political Woman." In *The Politics of Race: African Americans and the Political System*, ed. Theodore Rueter, 169–84. Armonk: ME Sharpe.

Salime, Zakia. 2011. *Between Feminism and Islam: New Political Transformations and Movements in Morocco*. East Lansing, MI: Michigan State University Press.

Schatz, Edward. 2009. *Political Ethnography: What Immersion Contributes to the Study of Politics*. Chicago: University of Chicago Press.

Schildkrout, Enid. 1982. "Dependence and Autonomy: The Economic Activities of Secluded Hausa Women in Kano, Nigeria." In *Women and Work in Africa*, ed. Edna Bay, 55–81. Boulder, CO: Westview Press.

Shebadduin, Elora. 2008. *Reshaping the Holy: Democracy, Development, and Muslim Women in Bangladesh*. New York: Columbia University Press.

Spillers, Hortense J. 1987. "Mama's Baby, Papa's Maybe: An American Grammar Book." *Diacritics* 17, no. 2: 65–81.

Springer, Kimberly. 2002. "Third Wave Black Feminism." *Signs* 27, no. 4: 1059–82.

Black Women's Pathways to the Statehouse:
The Impact of Race/Gender Identities

Nadia E. Brown
Purdue University

In 2013, out of 7,776 female state legislators serving nationwide, 364 are women of color; of these, 239 are African American women. Currently, women of color constitute only 4.9 percent of all state legislators (CAWP Fact Sheet 2013). In terms of Black female elected officials, although their numbers are disproportionate relative to the percentage of Black women in general, their presence in state legislatures is increasing. In fact, Bositis (2001) finds that the increase in the number of Black elected officials can be attributed to Black women. While overall women's election to state legislatures has begun to languish, African American women have steadily increased their numbers in state legislatures (Sanbonmatsu 2005; Scola 2006; Smooth 2006). Black women have achieved elected office more than Black men since 1990 (Orey et al. 2006).

However, while the United States has witnessed an increase in the number of Black women state legislators, little is known about the impact of their race/gender[1] identity on their campaigns and election, because much of the research on women's under-representation in elective office centers on White women's initial decisions to run for office (Lawless and Fox 2005, 2010).[2] The growing number of Black women elected officials speaks to the continued need to study this population. Thus, the focus of this study is African American female state legislators in Maryland. I rely on their narratives during a recent legislative session.[3] Maryland is an important site for study because, as of 2012, women accounted for 30.9 percent of the state legislature, and one of its two senators was a woman. The state ranks eighth in proportion of women serving in state legislatures nationwide, and during the 2009 and 2011 legislative sessions, it had twenty Black women state legislators. I focus here on how these women's race/gender identities influence their political campaigns for the Maryland state legislature.

Importantly, given the theoretical advance of Black women's studies and the ever increasing number of African American women state legislators, modern scholars point to the necessity of an intersectional framework for analyzing the experiences of African American women political elites (e.g., Smooth 2001, 2006; Stokes-Brown and Dolan 2010).[4] An intersectional approach highlights the ways in which social and political forces manipulate the overlapping and traversing inequalities both *within* and without marginal groups. Scholars who investigate the complexity of Black womanhood from the standpoint of African American women themselves offer a major conceptual framework at the convergence of African American studies and women's studies (see, e.g., hooks 1984; Guy-Sheftall 1992; Hancock 2004; Alexander-Floyd 2007; Jordan-Zachery 2007). The challenge of examining the intersections of race, gender, and class has led these scholars to reject the separability of analytical and identity categories (e.g., Davis 1981; Smith 1983; hooks 1984; Crenshaw 1989). The complexity and diversity of the Black female experience cannot be solely housed within a framework that does not address the effects of intertwined and relational dimensions of social identities. Thus, I draw on Hawkesworth's term of racing-gendering, which theorizes the process of producing distinctive groups of men and women and the political consequences of this process within legislative bodies (Hawkesworth 2003, 531). *Race/gender* identities acknowledge the simultaneous production of racialization and gendering. The term *race/gender* provides a way to portray the mutually constitutive (Fernandes 1997; Alexander-Floyd 2007) ways in which Black women experience race and gender. Thus, the move to refer to Black women state legislators' intersectional identities as *race/gender* reflects their experiences and social location within a racist and patriarchal society that renders Black women simultaneously invisible and hypervisible (Hawkesworth 2003).

Within this framework, it is not surprising that present-day African American women state legislators incorporate a raced/gendered analysis into their descriptions of their first campaigns. While conducting feminist life histories with the Black women Maryland state legislators, several volunteered stories about how being a Black woman, not a "Black" and a "woman," impacted their run for elected office. These remarks were frequently couched within three themes—perceived discrimination, "sista' networks" (Cooper 2006), and bucking the party—which illustrate the race/gender narratives of Black women legislators. I use these themes to show that Black women's experiences as candidates for state legislative office are informed by their race/gender identities—not simply their single identity categories of race or gender. The legislators' articulation of a distinct race/gender identity points to what Smooth (2006) refers to as the unique "messiness" of Black women's politics because it requires an intersectional perspective that combines both gender and racial politics. Applying an intersectional approach to how African American women experience electoral politics will necessarily be an involved undertaking, because it refuses simple explanations based on single identity categories.

This paper explores the "messy" dynamics of Black women's race/gender identities on their campaign for the Maryland statehouse. After discussing the extant literature on gender and Black women candidates, I examine how Black women frame their identities in narrating their paths to the Maryland statehouse. In doing so, I illustrate that Black women's race/gender identities provide different challenges and opportunities for their candidacies and, further, I reveal the extent to which their race/gender identities play a role in the campaigns and election of these women. I find that Black women's race/gender identities both help and detract from their ability to gain elected office and conclude that African American women state legislators use an intersectional approach in detailing their experiences as candidates. The African American women state legislators' narratives of perceived discrimination, "sista' networks" (Cooper 2006), and bucking the party illustrate that their intersectional identities, rather than a race-only or gender-only identity, impact their candidacies for seats in the state legislature.

Black Women as Political Candidates

Scholars have concluded that "when women run, women win" meaning that there is little empirical evidence illustrating that women's gender is a handicap for seeking and achieving elected office. For instance, women raise the same amounts of money as male candidates (Burrell 2005; Fox 2006), face little gender-based bias as candidates (Dolan and Kropf 2004), and are just as politically ambitious as men (Diamond 1977; Palmer and Simon 2003). Women are mentioned as just-as-likely potential candidates for open congressional seats as men (Burrell and Frederick 2006), receive more media attention than do men, and receive the same share of the vote as male candidates (Seltzer, Newman, and Leighton 1997). Additionally, there is an insignificant viability bias against women (Bystrom, Robertson, and Banwart 2001; Smith and Fox 2001). While this body of scholarship is indeed instructive to understanding how women candidates experience gender, it tends to leave out the experiences of Black women and the role of race for African American women candidates.

To understand Black women's subject positions, we need to ask a different set of questions about their experiences running for office. Feminist scholarship has presented two dominant views of Black women candidates: Githens and Prestage (1977) argue that Black women must overcome race and gender—a double disadvantage; whereas Darcy, Hadley, and Kirksey (1993) claim that Black women have fared better than their White counterparts in similar electoral environments. However, before treating this set of options as setting the terms of the conversation, we must first ask whether these two perspectives adequately portray Black women's experiences. Or, we might ask whether African American women's race/gender identities provide a more complex and nuanced understanding of how these identities impact their candidacies.

When looking at research on Black women running for political office, there are findings in support of both theories suggested above. In line with Darcy, Hadley, and Kirksey's perspective that African American women perform better than White women candidates, some research indicates that minority women candidates' race/gender identities provide them with an electoral advantage. For instance, Smooth (2006) along with Philpot and Walton (2007) argue that minority women candidates appeal to a broader range of voters, both women and communities of color. Other research has shown that beyond vote choice, women of color can be elected without substantial help from political parties. Sanbonmatsu, Carroll, and Walsh presented data on American women's political participation in the 2008 CAWP Recruitment Study. The data reported here supports both theories about Black women as candidates. Their study presents the raw data, which are used to report patterns of how women achieve elected office. As such, the Sanbonmatsu, Carroll, and Walsh study contains data that are used to support both the Darcy, Hadley, and Kirksey perspective, as well as the Githens and Prestage viewpoint of Black women candidates. For example, women of color are elected from districts where the political party is less active in recruitment (Sanbonmatsu, Carroll, and Walsh 2009). Because minority women[5] are most likely to represent majority-minority districts, which are often considered safe districts for their party, they frequently face primary competition and are less likely to gain elected office as the result of party recruitment (Sanbonmatsu, Carroll, and Walsh 2009). Sanbonmatsu, Carroll, and Walsh also show that campaign training programs that are specifically catered to Black women—such as the Center for American

Women and Politics' *Run Sister Run*—are successful in helping African American women build networks, gain access to political elites, and develop effective strategies for circumventing traditional recruitment patterns (Sanbonmatsu, Carroll, and Walsh 2009).

Despite this support for the theory that Black women are more successful than White women at seeking elected office, the majority of literature on Black women legislators adopts Githens and Prestage's (1977) view of double marginality, asserting that gender- and race-related stereotypes doubly disadvantage Black women candidates. Research by Sanbonmatsu (2006) has shown that party leaders assume that voters are unwilling to support candidates other than White males, and thus do not readily support Black women candidates. Next, Sanbonmatsu, Carroll, and Walsh (2009) found that women of color believe that it is harder for women to raise money than men. The lack of sufficient campaign resources remains a challenge for women of color. Furthermore, minority women face numerous institutional barriers. Political parties affect women's recruitment to state legislatures and, as a result, influence where women run and hold elected office (Sanbonmatsu 2002a). This is exacerbated for minority women candidates. Women of color candidates report that unlike men and White women, political parties do not recruit them (Sanbonmatsu, Carroll, and Walsh 2009).

One of the reasons that Black women may not be seen as viable candidates for political office relates to the stereotype that constructs them as being unfeminine and/or emasculators. Carroll (1994) maintains that a successful female politician must walk a fine line between balancing masculine traits and traditional feminine characteristics. However, Black women have a particularly difficult time walking this "fine line" because Black women are stereotyped as being tough or non-feminine (King 1975), an image that contrasts with that of White women as the standard-bearer of feminine archetypes (Holloway 1995). Such stereotypes, which serve to cast Black women in negative terms, are prevalent within both mainstream American society and the Black community (Alexander-Floyd 2007). The Sapphire stereotype, named after a character in "Amos 'n' Andy," is seen as loud talking, hands on the hips, always putting down her man, too strong willed to be controlled by men, and undesirable. On the professional side, women perceived as Sapphires are seen as goal-orientated, driven, intelligent, ambitious, and hardworking (Yarbrough and Bennett 2000), yet they are also seen as "ball-busting" and "wise-cracking." This masculine/emasculating stereotype is a challenge for Black women candidates, as they are stereotypically not able to walk a "fine line." Thus, as candidates, Black women may not be seen as viable options because of their "otherness" with the American polity.

Taken together, this research on Black women as political candidates presents mixed results. Some researchers support a perspective that frames Black women as doubly marginalized, while others present data that suggest Black women are more successful at achieving political office than are White women. Given these divergent perspectives on African American women's candidacies, it is possible that Black women's race/gender identities produce experiences that both challenge and provide opportunities for their candidacies. To test this hypothesis, I perform a more fine-grained analysis of Black women's narratives of their candidacies to demonstrate the varied impacts of their race/gender identities on their pursuit of elected office.

Data and Methods

This paper focuses on African American women who hold elected seats in the Maryland state legislature. As prototypical intersectional subjects—doubly marginalized by race and gender and whose narratives are used to expose the under-theorized categorization of identity[6] (Nash 2008)—Black women legislators merit careful study, particularly with respect to how they experience and manage race and gender as social processes. Further, the need to look at intragroup diversity within a single case study is guided by shortcomings within the extant literature on Black women political elites. As a result, I move beyond cross-group difference among women to look within Black women as a group to observe what makes them different and similar from themselves.

The data used for this analysis are part of a sample collected between 2009 and 2011 with members of the Maryland state legislature.[7] Maryland was selected as the case study because of the relatively large number of African American women state legislators and because of the structure of the legislature, which makes it easy to identify how race and gender influence legislative behavior.[8] The elected officials came from various backgrounds including state government, while others were community organizers, educators, union leaders, and lawyers, prior to being elected. Some were newly elected, while others had served for several years. Additionally, the age at which the women first sought elected office varies. Some women ran for office in their early thirties, while others did not begin their political career until they were in their fifties. Several of the older women are mothers and grandmothers and ran for office once their children were self-sufficient, a few sought political careers with young children, and a number of younger women were childless. All the women in this study have at least completed their bachelor's degree, while the majority have obtained advanced degrees. While the women share similar race/gender identities, their experiences and personal backgrounds differ.

Feminist life histories were conducted with eighteen of the twenty Black women Maryland state legislators between June and October 2011. Qualitative research is important here because, as Hawkesworth notes, quantitative techniques "devised to reveal uniformities of behavior are by design insensitive to difference, treating anything that deviates from the norm as an outlier or anomaly" (Hawkesworth 2003, 532). Furthermore, standard social science methodological techniques that attempt to isolate the effects of gender by controlling for race/ethnicity or by controlling for gender are at odds with efforts to trace the complex interactions of race and gender (Spellman 1988, 103). It is for these reasons that I utilize qualitative techniques to observe the nuances of how Black women's race/gender identities impact their campaign for the state legislature. The Black women state legislators I interviewed crafted their narratives by drawing on their personal experiences to represent cultural mores that are indigenous or organic to their own biographical, generational, cultural, historical/material, and geographical situations. Through these life histories, I am able to reveal a more nuanced understanding of how the legislators view and interpret their own life courses than would be possible with quantitative research, allowing me to investigate the socially defined roles and events a woman enacts over time.

Feminist life histories are a relatively new methodology in the American politics subfield of political science. Feminist theorists across several academic disciplines, including political science, have argued for the importance of locating and historicizing the lives of women (see, e.g., Collins 1990; Bell and Nkomo 2001; Berger 2004; Harris-Lacewell 2004). Feminist life histories provide women with an excellent medium within which to communicate (Jolly 2005). Thus, this method is optimal for learning about an individual's experiences, how she views the world, and how she views herself. Linking personal narrative to political behavior, I utilize feminist life histories with African American women legislators to understand how their race/gender identities and experiences influence their decision to run for office and on their campaigns.[9]

Unlike like other methodologies, using feminist life histories allows me to fully uncover how a legislator's race/gender identities have been enacted and experienced over time rather than solely relying on snapshot of a particular period in her life—her campaign. By focusing on Black women's narratives, this study yields valuable insights into the tropes of gender, race, and class that have defined the world in which these women became legislators.

In the following sections, I highlight three relevant themes that illustrate the commonalities and differences in how the women's unique race/gender identities influenced their political campaigns. It is not a goal of this essay to present each woman's complete life history, but to highlight quotes that are representative of the diversity of experiences of the women in this sample.[10] By allowing individual experience to illustrate how race/gender identities mediate the experiences of Black women candidates, the data reveal a fuller and more complicated view of Back women's paths to the statehouse. Thus, the themes that emerged in the data—perceived discrimination, "sista' networks" (Cooper 2006), and bucking the party, which tell a comprehensive story about how their race/gender identities inform Black women's experiences as candidates.

Black Women's Narratives on Their Campaigns for the Maryland State Legislature

Perceived Discrimination

Lawmaker O[11] noted that her identity was a deterrent in her senate campaign. During our meeting (over lunch in a hotel restaurant), two middle-aged White men interrupted the interview to speak with lawmaker O at length about proposed legislation that would help local businesses. Lawmaker O listened to the men's request for about ten minutes. She then pointed across the table to me and informed the men that they had interrupted both her lunch and interview. The men then apologized after she instructed me to introduce myself and my project. They then began to sing the praises of lawmaker O to me and reiterated their hope of working with her on this proposed legislation. Lawmaker O politely excused the men by asserting her desire to finish her lunch and the interview. After the men returned to their table, lawmaker O expressed her distaste for such behaviors. She was disturbed by their dismissal of me, a young Black woman whose presence she surmised that the men believed was not worthy of acknowledging from the outset and by their lack of respect for the privacy of two African American women who were engaged in a conversation while lunching. She informed me that the men were prominent businessmen in her district who had financially backed her opponent in a previous election. In reflecting on her campaign, she said, "The good ole boys were not interested in me or my campaign. But I'm not a shrinking violet. They didn't want an educated, articulate, honest, principled, and independent-thinker to win the election" (Personal Interview, July 18, 2011). Noting that the business community was now seeking to curry favor, she stated that the men had not only backed the wrong candidate, but also unknowingly insulted her, particularly as a Black woman, by assuming that she lacked the requisite knowledge to advocate on behalf of her district. Although she had proven to be an astute representative of the district, lawmaker O informed me that she still faced this challenge as lobbyists and the two men who interrupted our interview did not financially support her current campaign. According to her,

> They didn't give me money because they don't support my interests. I'm concerned about women, children, and senior citizens—the most vulnerable members of society. All they support is big business and industry, so that's all they want to see. But they don't get it. My focus is on helping Black women—"a rising tide lifts all ships" doesn't necessarily help Black women. These lobbyists just don't get it. People don't see the worth in Black women. I do. (Personal Interview, July 18, 2011)

Her assessment of the lobbyists' motivation to speak with her included a race/gender analysis. Lawmaker O added, "Black women come with a different kind of attitude, it's a motherly attitude. It's a cultural thing for Black women. It's like my mama saying 'I'll eat last once everyone has had their full'. We don't come first. People just don't respect Black women" (Personal Interview, July 18, 2011). Lawmaker O concluded that the men devalued her legislative agenda, believed that she was naïve in her understanding of economic policy, and failed to recognize Black women's significance as both voters and elected officials. We see the use of this race/gender critical lens when lawmaker O questioned whether the men would have rudely interrupted our lunch if I were not a young, Black woman. While the entire interaction lasted less than fifteen minutes, lawmaker O's candor changed and the remainder of the interview was affected by this interruption. During the last thirty minutes of the interview, lawmaker O highlighted ways in which her colleagues, legislative staff, and constituents treated Black women. Lawmaker O recounted two stories of blatant discrimination against Black women in the statehouse as well as stories from her childhood and early adulthood in which she faced gender and race-based bias. The interview ended with lawmaker O offering encouraging words, albeit couched in the language of respectability and Black middle-class norms, about her hope for a younger generation of Black women. Quoting Oprah Winfrey, lawmaker O quipped that "excellence is the best deterrent to racism or sexism" (Personal Interview, July 18, 2011).

Similar to lawmaker O's experiences with perceived discrimination, both lawmakers A and P shared that they experienced discrimination during their employment in local government prior to running for election. Both elected officials, consistent with the extant literature on women candidates (Costello, Wight, and Stone 2003; Lawless and Fox 2005; Sanbonmatsu 2006), found their way to the statehouse through the pipeline formed by holding government positions. This occupational background places these women within the "eligibility pool" of careers and professions that are part of a well-defined opportunity structure from which candidates are recruited (Darcy, Welch, and Clark 1994; Lawless and Fox 2005). Lawmaker A's prior work experiences led her to conclude that "people had difficulty working under me, a Black woman supervisor" (Personal Interview, July 25, 2011). Lawmaker P expressed a similar experience, noting that when she worked in another context, "I was more qualified than my supervisor, but because I am a Black woman I was hired as a secretary" (Personal Interview, June 22, 2011). She indicated that she left this position as a result. Both elected officials credit their prior work in private industry and government as shaping their campaigns. Unlike previous studies, which argue that minority women are discouraged from running for office because of institutional barriers, the aforementioned lawmakers noted that the discrimination they faced because of their race/gender identities in fact shaped their experiences as candidates and legislators.

Lawmaker A stated that her work in local government led to her appointment to an at-large seat on the local party committee. Her first campaign was for a newly created majority-minority district in her county. Her previous leadership positions in her county government helped her to represent this district. However, she faced criticisms from formidable foes due to her work in county government. "I established myself as a public servant who worked to improve the lives of minority X County residents," she said. "But still, I had difficulty fundraising in my district. It's difficult for women, especially Black women, to fundraise" (July 25, 2011). She noted that she had to prove to potential backers that she was capable, well-qualified, and hardworking time and again in order to receive their support. While her record of public service and leadership on the county party committee demonstrated that she diligently fought for the interests of minority residents, she nevertheless had to painstakingly provide evidence that she was worthy of financial backing from district's business leaders and prominent citizens. Lawmaker A, thus, believed that her race/gender identities caused some potential backers to question the feasibility of her state legislative campaign in spite of her proven record of leadership.

Other women in my sample expressed difficulty fundraising, which many attributed to their race/gender identities. Lawmaker O, for instance, stated "it is more difficult for Black women to fundraise. So I had little fundraisers, everyone gave a little. I never raised more than $1,500 at any one event. We just can't tap into the men's network" (Personal Interview, July 18, 2011). While lawmaker O found that it was difficult for her to fundraise as a Black woman, lawmaker B discovered that she was an innate fundraiser and did not have to follow conventional fundraising tactics to launch a successful campaign. Instead, she relied on her circle of friends to finance her first campaign, because she did not have access to big donors.

> During my first campaign . . . , I saw a political consultant who told me how much campaigns cost. I was a single mother of three boys, my husband had just left, and I didn't have that kind of money. I had $50, I bought some *hors* d'oeuvres, made punch, lit the fireplace, and invited friends over. I had a flip chart to showcase my accomplishments, I highlighted my work as a board member on several women's and Black clubs as well as healthcare organizations. I told my friends that I wanted to run for the Maryland [state legislature] and asked if they believed in me. Friends gave me checks. I raised $1500. I don't like to fundraise, but I know how to do if I have to. (Personal Interview, July 29, 2011)

This is consistent with findings that women of color report that it is more difficult for women to fundraise than men (Sanbonmatsu, Carroll, and Walsh 2009). This is a clear disadvantage for minority women as the extant literature illustrates that (White) women are able to raise and spend as much money as male candidates (Carroll and Fox 1997; Werner 1998; Burrell 2005) and that they have access to PAC money and attract large donations (Burrell 1994, 2005). Thus, the narratives of lawmakers A, B, and O demonstrate that Black women may have difficulty securing funds for their campaigns in ways that White women do not.

Further illustrating the ways in which institutional barriers add levels of difficulty for African American candidates, lawmaker P's narrative also provides an example of how her race/gender identities impacted her experiences as a city government employee and later as a candidate for the city council. Lawmaker P articulated that she worked on many political campaigns but had no previous desire to run for office herself. However, several well-known political figures recruited her to run for political office because they noticed and valued her work with city government and a community development organization. She attributed her electoral and leadership success to her hard work, tenacity, and street smarts, which is a perspective that is wholly situated within a middle-class notion of racial uplift. As Linda Williams contends, the old "adage that Black parents often tell their children, 'You've got to work twice as hard to get half as far,' seems to partially explain the puzzle of Black women's success in winning public office" (Williams 2001, 314). Williams's contention holds true for lawmaker P. She recalled plenty of family discussions about discrimination during her childhood. Her father would remind her that Blacks always had to work harder than Whites to get less than half of what Whites got. This lawmaker's strong work ethic was reinforced during her time in local government when Whites refused to give her credit for her accomplishments, acknowledge her skill level, or promote her to a position that reflected her experience or skillset. Lawmaker P believes that if she were someone other than a Black woman, her experiences in local government would have been different. However, these experiences taught her to work harder, be more proficient, present herself as a professional in spite of discriminatory circumstances, and exceed others' expectations in order to get ahead. Lawmaker P won her election because she was "not a politician; I am a person who gets things done in spite of obstacles or barriers. I work hard. I get things done. That's what I do. That's what I campaigned on" (Personal Interview, June 22, 2011). Lawmaker P concluded that she did not seek accolades and was motivated by her quest to improve constituents' lives, adding that Black women do what is necessary and do not engage in self-aggrandizement, partly because others will never fully acknowledge all the things that Black women do.

Sista' Networks

The narratives of lawmakers D, F, and G illustrate the usefulness of sista' networks, by which I mean an organization of supportive African American women who advance the political aspirations of other Black women. Coined by Tuesday Cooper, sista' networks refer to the networking and familial relationships between professional Black women which facilitate the procurement of unwritten practices and rules within various professions (2006, 4). These sista' networks, either as informal gatherings of women or organized as part of a sorority, church, or other Black women's association, are influential components of Black women's candidacies and campaigns. Building on the work of Cooper, I argue that these informal and/or formal social networks are crucial for African American women who may not have access to other forms of institutional support. These social networks provide women with advice, social support, strategic information, and mentorship (Bell and Nkomo 2001). Thus, sista' networks are useful for African American women candidates and for building the pipeline of potential candidates in the absence of strong institutional backing.

Similar to lawmakers P and A, lawmaker F's work experience with local government impacted her decision to run for political office. Lawmaker F, a young lawyer, first disclosed her intentions to run for office to a select handful of close friends and mentors. Several elements of her background seemed to stand her in good stead for such a run. Owing to her experience with real estate, legislative, and government contracts, her friends and mentors readily supported her decision to run for office. "I was toying with the idea of running and was overwhelmed with the amount of enthusiastic support I received from my friends. They thought it was a great idea because of all my work in the community. But, I really didn't have serious intentions of running" (Personal Interview, July 20, 2011). Lawmaker F's support system rallied around her to build a winning campaign apparatus. A relative served as her campaign manager. A sorority sister served as field manager. "And other Black women community leaders stepped up to help me. We raised independent money because I did not run on a ticket" (Personal Interview, July 20, 2011). Lawmaker F's campaign was almost entirely run by Black women. This group of dedicated friends, family, sorors, and mentors helped lawmaker F raise money, craft her political platform, and coordinate meetings with key groups in the district, and they emotionally supported her when necessary.

Lawmaker D's narrative also illustrates the importance of a sista' network. Lawmaker D indicated that she decided to run for office after volunteering for another delegate's campaign. "Working with Delegate F on her campaign was a great experience for me. . . I got a lot out of that experience. So when an open seat in my district appeared, I knew that I was prepared to run for that seat" (Personal Interview, July 29, 2011). The examples offered by lawmakers D and F thus illustrate the ways in which sista' networks can assist Black women in securing electoral office, either through formal organizations, such as sororities, churches, or community groups, or through informal connections such as friendships and mentoring. Such supportive networks are a necessity for Black women candidates.

Next, lawmaker G credits her supportive sista' networks with enabling her to balance family and her legislative aspirations. She is a mother of two teenagers and believes that family comes first. However, lawmaker G's political desires oftentimes are at odds with her family responsibilities. She has climbed the political ladder, serving first in her county government, then in the Maryland state legislature. Lawmaker G credited her sista' network with allowing her to reach and maintain her legislative goals.

> It's a bit easier now because my children are older. But I'm a workaholic; I have a lot of responsibility in the [state legislature] now. But even before that, I ran because I was passionate about helping children in my community succeed. My goals to improve the lives of [X County] children sometimes take me away from my own children. But I'm blessed to have two close friends who live close by; they have been surrogate mothers to my children. . . This strong network helps to support me in raising my children. My sister also lives close by and she helps with my kids. Without them, I could not even think about running for office or being as engaged in the [state legislature] as I am now. (Personal Interview, July 8, 2011)

Traditional gender socialization remains an aspect of electoral politics (see Kahn 1996; Flammang 1997; Sanbonmatsu 2002b). For example, traditional gender norms dictate that women are primarily concerned with caretaking while men are the financial providers. As a result, the household division of labor is unequal for women, which may make it more difficult for them to balance the demands of legislative duties. Some scholars find that women's family roles influence their political ambitions, and that women with young children are less likely to enter politics (Fox and Lawless 2004). Other findings show that having children living at home does not influence whether or not a woman will consider running for office (Fox, Lawless, and Feeley 2001). Yet, lawmaker G's narrative illustrates that her supportive sista' network is what enabled her to run for office as well as serve in a leadership position. Because lawmaker G's sista' network comprises former members of the state legislature, who are attuned to the needs and responsibilities faced by women office holders and their families, her support system is uniquely situated to understand her current lifestyle. While little is known about the effects of family on African American women state legislators, lawmaker G's experiences may be illustrative of the challenges faced by Black single mothers who serve in the state legislature.

Bucking the Party

The final narrative is from lawmaker L, who shared that her race/gender identities influenced her first campaign and her subsequent run for the Maryland state legislature. Lawmaker L was familiar with the inner workings of political campaigns before deciding to run for office. She had previously served as a lobbyist for a teachers union and trade union before becoming the political director of the trade union. Lawmaker L realized that she could better fight for the rights of Black working and middle-class city residents if she had a seat on the city party committee. However, she was unsuccessful in her first bid. Lawmaker L surmised that the district was not ready at that time for a Black woman candidate and that she should have waited to run in an open seat. However, in 2002, political leaders, after recognizing her skills, suggested that she run for office in that same district. Although the district was majority White, political leaders realized that the growing African American community would soon demand descriptive representation. Lawmaker L assessed the political climate of the district, the requests of the political leaders, and her family's opinion before accepting a place on the district's Democratic ticket. After agreeing to run on the Democratic ticket, lawmaker L quickly learned that she had little input into how her own campaign would be run. She explains:

> The ticket didn't even put my picture on the campaign literature! Because the district was majority White, they didn't want people to know that I was a Black woman. In the end, it turned out ok because instead of relying on the ticket, I got out and started my own grassroots campaign. I spoke to a lot of community groups; I spoke to anyone that would listen. People started to notice me. They saw how sincere I was and my desire to put working people first. People genuinely came out to my events to get to know me. I came in first in every polling place on Election Day! People voted for me because they knew me and what I stood for. So that's how I won. (Personal Interview, June 28, 2011)

The Democratic Party leadership in her district was in awe of lawmaker L's success and campaign style. While the Party first sought to hide her identity from constituents for fear that placing a Black woman candidate on ballot in a majority White district would have disastrous effects, the party soon learned that lawmaker L's race/gender identities were not a handicap. Instead, when given a chance to get to know the candidate and her stance on the issues, district residents looked past her race/gender identities and voted for the candidate they felt could best represent their issues on the city party central committee.

This poignant lesson seemed to have been lost on Maryland Governor William Schaefer. According to lawmaker L, the former mayor of Baltimore and former governor "pointed his finger in my face and told me that I wouldn't win a seat in the [in the Maryland state legislature]" (Personal Interview, June 28, 2011). Gov. Schaefer assumed that lawmaker L's election to a position in party leadership was a chance occurrence that could not be repeated in a higher visibility election such as the race for the state legislature. He also stated that she did not follow protocol by circumventing the party ticket's decision on campaign materials and procedure. As such, lawmaker L had little political etiquette, in his opinion, and had bucked the party line. However, she concluded that her election to a position in party leadership proved that she knew what was best for her political career and that White residents were ready for a Black woman representative. Political leadership was woefully behind in their assessment of race/gender relations in that district. Lawmaker L also noted that the political leadership underestimated the strength of the Black vote in that district. As the current representative for this district in the state legislature, she likes to remind party leadership of their mistake whenever her political and legislative decisions are questioned.

The lack of party support did not hinder lawmaker L's election to her party at the local level or the state legislature. Her narrative echoes the reports of other minority women who express difficulty in securing party backing (Sanbonmatsu, Carroll, and Walsh 2009). However, lawmaker L's narrative illustrates that she used her political savvy to circumvent top party leadership and, furthermore, that her race/gender identities did not deter citizens from voting her into office. Similar to lawmakers A, O, and P, who reported discrimination based on their race/gender identities, lawmaker L's narrative illustrates that Black women can maneuver past restrictive structures, such as political parties and limited access to campaign contributors, to achieve elected office. Lawmaker L's narrative indicates that parties help campaigns to be successful but are not the only avenue for political success for African American women.

Conclusion

In this research, I presented the ways in which Black women candidates experience their race/gender identities. Their individual political experiences illustrate how identity affects the success of Black women candidates running for election contests for the Maryland state legislature. From party leaders' assessments of Black women's viability as candidates to how Black women's race/gender identities influence their political agenda and consequently affect the amount of financial support from campaign donors, to African American women's sista' networks based on race/gender identities, one must consider the way in which African American women's race/gender identities affect their distinct opportunity for gaining electoral office. My findings complicate the either/or approach, prevalent in a race-only or gender-only paradigm, to understanding Black women political candidates. The "messiness" presented in the women's narratives shows that Black women report different and complicated experiences as candidates based on their race/gender identities. The data point to the heterogeneity of Black women's experiences as candidates rather than to a simplistic view presented in the two dominant perspectives of the literature, which either find that Black women are doubly disadvantaged by their race and gender or that their race/gender identities give them an electoral advantage. These narratives enable us to have a fuller and more complex view of Black women candidates, which illustrates that there is no single, overarching experience for candidates. While some women report experiencing discrimination or difficulties as candidates because of their race/gender identities, others note that their race/gender identities placed them at an advantage on the campaign trail. By exploring how race/gender identities affect Black women candidates, I have demonstrated that traditional studies of candidates for state legislatures that focus either on gender or race do not adequately capture how the intersection of these identities manifests itself for Black women.

This study constitutes only one piece of a much larger puzzle. There are many unanswered questions about the impact of race/gender on Black women's quest for electoral success. Do unsuccessful Black women candidates face similar challenges and opportunities to their victorious counterparts? Do African American women in other state legislatures share comparable experiences with their sisters in the Maryland state legislature? In what ways, if any, do Black women's race/gender experiences as candidates translate into their legislative behaviors once elected? Exploring these questions more fully should be among the avenues pursued by scholars in the future.

The current study contributes to our understanding of the role of race, gender, and electoral politics. The narratives of the Black women Maryland state legislators in this study illustrate their race/gender identities impacted their candidacies for the elected office. Repeated themes of perceived discrimination, sista' networks, and bucking the party demonstrate that Black women's intersectional identities, rather than a race-only or gender-only identity, present both challenges and opportunities in their quest for political office. Rather than evaluating the race and/or gender identities of Black women candidates, this study has presented how identity is experienced in an intersecting and mutually constitutive format.

Notes

1. This term is used throughout the paper to denote the combination of race and gender for Black woman. As such, a Black woman cannot divorce herself from either her race or gender, yet she experiences the world based on the racialized femininity of her identity. I do not wish to portray an essentialist construction of Black womanhood that purports that all African American women experience race and gender the same way, but this term represents the ways race and gender are omnipresent factors of Black women's social identities.

2. For example, the Lawless and Fox sample includes ten Black women.

3. In 2009, this number was distributed among fifteen delegates and five senators and between fourteen delegates and six senators in the 2011 session.

4. Throughout the paper, I use the terms "Black" and "African American" interchangeably.

5. This study includes African American, Latina, and Asian-American women.

6. Black feminists have long advanced the claims that multiple identities—such as race, gender, class, and sexual orientation—are mutually reinforcing and interlocking, thus calling feminist scholars to complicate the view of a "universal woman" (e.g., Davis 1981; Smith 1983; Higginbotham 1992).

7. The General Assembly includes forty-seven Senators and 141 Delegates elected from forty-seven districts. The Maryland legislature comprises part-time representatives who dedicate a ninety-day period annually to law making. Maryland's short legislative session requires a structure that facilitates lawmaking at a relatively quick pace. The state legislature is structured to enable lawmaking; therefore, legislators are given a degree of autonomy to maneuver legislation through the representative body. Maryland's political culture is regarded as individualistic, akin to that of a business, where individual legislators

broker deals and orchestrate political favors (Elazar 1972). While the party structure is highly organized, legislators have the ability to act as individuals, especially regarding policy areas in which some have specialized knowledge (Smooth 2001).

8. The multimember district structure is ideal for examining the effects of race and gender identity on Black women's legislative decision making, since a majority of the African American women represent the same constituency. As a result, I can differentiate constituent wishes from other internal factors, such as identity, that drive legislators' decision making.

9. The feminist life histories I conducted were broken into three parts; each woman answered the same set of questions. The first focused on early life experiences—childhood through young adulthood. The next set of questions focused on their work in the Maryland state legislature, and the last section focused on their current private lives—significant relationships and family. These feminist life history interviews lasted between forty-five and ninety minutes and were conducted in places convenient for legislators—their district offices, places of employment, or coffee shops (three were conducted over the telephone). My position as an insider, an African American woman interviewing African American women state legislators, fostered an environment where the women readily shared in-depth stories about their lives (see Brown 2012).

10. To examine the content of each narrative, I relied on "closed codes." By closed codes, I am referring to the process of using themes from other studies, rein order to correlate my data with the extant research, I then use a "closed code" as I read/re-read the data to thematically code the data. See Strauss and Corbin (1998).

11. While I informed the legislators that their interviews were "on the record," I have removed names from the quotations owing to the candid nature with which some legislators engaged me in conversation.

References

Alexander-Floyd, Nikol. 2007. *Gender, Race, and Nationalism in Contemporary Black Politics*. New York: Palgrave McMillan.

Bell, Edmondson Ella L. J., and Stella M. Nkomo. 2001. *Our Separate Ways: Black and White Women and the Struggle for Professional Identity*. Boston, MA: Harvard Business School Press.

Berger, M. T. 2004. *Workable Sisterhood: The Political Journey of Stigmatized Women with HIV/AIDS*. Princeton, NJ: Princeton University Press.

Bositis, David A. 2001. *Changing the Guard: Generational Differences among Black Elected Officials*. Washington, DC: Joint Center for Political and Economic Studies.

Brown, Nadia E. 2012. "Negotiating the Insider/Outsider Status: Black Feminist Ethnography and Legislative Studies." *Journal of Feminist Scholarship* 3: 19–39.

Burrell, Barbara. 1994. *A Woman's Place Is in the House: Campaigning for Congress in the Feminist*. Ann Arbor, MI: University of Michigan Press.

———. 2005. "Campaign Financing: Women's Experience in the Modern Era." In *Women and Elective Office: Past, Present, and Future*, ed. Sue Thomas and Clyde Wilcox, 2nd ed., 26–40. New York: Oxford University Press.

Burrell, Barbara, and Brian Frederick. 2006. "Windows of Opportunity: Recruitment Pools, Gender Politics, and Congressional Open Seats." Paper presented at the Southern Political Science Association meeting, New Orleans, LA, January 9–1.

Bystrom, Dianne, Terry Robertson, and Mary Christine Banwart. 2001. "Framing the Fight: An Analysis of Media Coverage of Female and Male Candidates in Primary Races for Governor and U.S. Senate in 2000." *American Behavioral Scientist* 44: 1999–2013.

Carroll, Susan. 1994. "Gender, Political Opportunity Structure, and Electoral Success." In *Women as Candidates in American Politics*, ed. Susan Carroll, 2nd ed., 93–120. Bloomington, IN: Indiana University Press.

Carroll, Susan, and Richard Fox. 1997. *Gender Dynamics in Congressional Elections*. Thousand Oaks, CA: Sage.

Center for American Women and Politics (CAWP). 2013. Women in State Legislators 2013. Fact Sheet by the Center for American Women and Politics, Eagleton Institute for Politics, Rutgers University.

Collins, Patricia Hill. 1990. *Black Feminist Thought: Knowledge, Consciousness and the Politics of Empowerment*. New York: Routledge.

Cooper, Tuesday L. 2006. *Sista' Network: African American Women Faculty Successfully Negotiating the Road to Tenure*. Boston, MA: Anker Publishing Company, Inc.

Costello, Cynthia, Vanessa R. Wight, and Anne J. Stone, eds. 2003. *The American Woman 2003–2004: Daughters of a Revolution—Young Women Today*. New York: Palgrave-Macmillan.

Crenshaw, Kimberlé. 1989. "Demarginalizing the Intersection of Race and Sex: A Black Feminist Critique of Antidiscrimination Doctrine, Feminist Theory, and Antiracist Politics." *University of Chicago Legal Forum*: 139–67.

Darcy, R., Charles D. Hadley, and Jason F. Kirksey. 1993. "Election Systems and the Representation of Black Women in American State Legislatures." *Women and Politics* 13, no. 2: 73–89.

Darcy, R., Susan Welch, and Janet Clark. 1994. *Women, Elections, and Representation.* 2nd ed. Lincoln: University of Nebraska Press.

Davis, Angela. 1981. *Women, Race and Class*. New York: Vintage Books.

Diamond, Irene. 1977. *Sex Roles in the State House*. New Haven, CT: Yale University Press.

Dolan, Julie, and Jonathan Kropf. 2004. "Credit Claiming from the U.S. House: Gendered Communications Styles?" *Harvard International Journal of Press/Politics* 9: 41–59.

Elazar, Daniel J. 1972. *Federalism: A View from the States*. 2nd ed. New York: Harper and Row.

Fernandes, Leela. 1997. *Producing Workers: The Politics of Gender, Class, and Culture in the Calcutta Jute Mills*. Philadelphia, PA: University of Pennsylvania.

Flammang, Janet. 1997. *Women's Political Voice: How Women Are Transforming the Practice and Study of Politics*. Philadelphia, PA: Temple University Press.

Fox, Richard L. 2006. "Congressional Elections: Where Are We on the Road to Gender Parity?" In *Gender and Elections: Shaping the Future of American Politics*, ed. Susan Carroll and Richard Fox, 97–116. New York: Cambridge University Press.

Fox, Richard L., and Jennifer L. Lawless. 2004. "Entering the Arena? Gender and the Decision to Run for Office." *American Journal of Political Science* 48, no. 2: 264–80.

Fox, Richard L., Jennifer L. Lawless, and Courtney Feeley. 2001. "Gender and the Decision to Run for Office." *Legislative Studies Quarterly* 26: 411–35.

Githens, Marianne, and Jewel Prestage. 1977. *Portraits of Marginality: The Political Behavior of the American Woman*. New York: David McKay.

Guy-Sheftall, Beverly. 1992. "Black Women's Studies: The Interface of Women's Studies and Black Studies." *Phylon (1960–)* 49, no. 1/2: 33–41.

Hancock, Ange-Marie. 2004. "When Multiplication Doesn't Equal Addition: Examining Intersectionality as a Research Paradigm." *Perspectives on Politics* 5, no. 1: 63–79.

Harris-Lacewell, Melissa. 2004. *Barbershops, Bibles, and B.E.T: Everyday Talk and Black Political Thought*. Princeton, NJ: Princeton University Press.

Hawkesworth, Mary. 2003. "Congressional Enactments of Race-Gender: Toward at Theory of Race-Gendered Institutions." *American Political Science Review* 97, no. 4: 529–50.

Higginbotham, Evelyn B. 1992. "African-American Women's History and the Metalanguage of Race." *Signs* 17: 251–74.

Holloway, Karla F. C. 1995. *Codes of Conduct: Race, Ethics, and the Color of Our Character*. New Brunswick, NJ: Rutgers University Press.

hooks, bell. 1984. *Feminist Theory from Margin to Center*. Boston, MA: South End Press.

Jolly, Margaretta. 2005. "Speaking Personally, Academically." *Feminist Theory* 6, no. 2: 213–20.

Jordan-Zachery, Julia. 2007. "Am I a Black Woman or a Woman Who Is Black? A Few Thoughts on the Meaning of Intersectionality." *Politics & Gender* 3, no. 2: 254–36.

Kahn, Kim Fridkin. 1996. *The Political Consequences of Being a Woman*. New York: Columbia University Press.

King, Mae C. 1975. "Oppression and Power: The Unique Status of the Black Woman in the American Political System." *Social Science Quarterly* 56, no. 1: 116–28.

Lawless, Jennifer L., and Richard L. Fox. 2005. *It Takes a Candidate: Why Don't Women Run for Office*. New York, NY: Cambridge University Press.

———. 2010. *It Still Takes a Candidate: Why Women Don't Run for Office*. New York: Cambridge University Press.

Nash, Jennifer. 2008. "Rethinking Intersectionality." *Feminist Review* 89: 1–15.

Orey, Bryon D'Andra, Wendy Smooth, Kimberly S. Adams, and Kisah Harris-Clark. 2006. "Race and Gender Matter: Refining Models of Legislative Policy Making in State Legislatures." *Journal of Women, Politics, & Policy* 28, no. 3/4: 97–119.

Palmer, Barbara, and Dennis Simon. 2003. "Political Ambition and Women in the US House of Representatives." *Political Research Quarterly* 56: 127–38.

Philpot, Tasha S., and Hanes Walton. 2007. "One of Our Own: Black Female Candidates and the Voters Who Support Them." *American Journal of Political Science* 51, no. 1: 49–62.

Sanbonmatsu, Kira. 2002a. "Gender Stereotypes and Vote Choice." *American Journal of Political Science* 46: 20–34.

————. 2002b. "Political Parties and the Recruitment of Women to State Legislatures." *Journal of Politics* 64, no. 3: 791–809.

————. 2005. "State Elections: Where Do Women Run: Where Do Women Win?" In *Gender and Elections in America: Shaping the Future of American Politics*, ed. Susan Carrol and Richard Fox, 263–87. New York: Cambridge University Press.

————. 2006. *Where Women Run: Gender and Party in the American States*. Ann Arbor, MI: University of Michigan.

Sanbonmatsu, Kira, Susan J. Carroll, and Debbie Walsh. 2009. Poised to Run: Women's Pathways to the State Legislature. Center for American Women and Politics, Eagleton Institute of Politics: Rutgers University, The University of New Jersey.

Scola, Becki. 2006. "Women of Color in State Legislatures: Gender, Race, Ethnicity and Legislative Office Holding." *Journal of Women, Politics & Policy* 28, nos. 3–4: 43–70.

Seltzer, Richard, Jody Newman, and Melissa Leighton. 1997. *Sex as a Political Variable: Women as Candidates and Voters in U.S. Elections*. Boulder, CO: Lynne Rienner.

Smith, Barbara. 1983. *Home Girls: A Black Feminist Anthology*. New York: Kitchen Table: Women of Color Press.

Smith, Eric R. A. N., and Richard L. Fox. 2001. "The Electoral Fortunes of Women Candidates for Congress." *Political Research Quarterly* 54, no. 1: 205–21.

Smooth, Wendy. 2001. African American Women State Legislators: The Impact of Gender and Race on Legislative Influence. Dissertation, University of Maryland.

————. 2006. "Intersectionality in Electoral Politics: A Mess Worth Making." *Politics & Gender* 2, no. 31: 400–14.

Spellman, Elizabeth. 1998. *Inessential Woman: Problem of Exclusion in Feminist Thought*. Boston, MA: Beacon Press.

Stokes-Brown, Atiya Kai, and Kathleen Dolan. 2010. "Race, Gender, and Symbolic Representation: African American Female Candidates as Mobilizing Agents." *Journal of Elections, Public Opinion, and Parties* 20: 473–94.

Strauss, Anselm, and Juliet Corbin. 1998. *Basics of Qualitative Research: Techniques and Procedures for Developing Grounded Theory*. Thousand Oaks, CA: Sage Publications.

Werner, Brian. 1998. "Financing the Campaigns of Women Candidates and Their Opponents: Evidence from Three States, 1982–1990." *Women & Politics* 18: 81–97.

Williams, Linda Faye. 2001. "The Civil Rights-Black Power Legacy: Black Women Elected Officials at the Local, State, and National Levels." In *Sisters in the Struggle: African American Women in the Civil Rights-Black Power Movement*, ed. Bettye Collier and V. P. Franklin, 306–32. New York: New York University Press.

Yarbrough, Marilyn, and Chrystal Bennett. 2000. "Cassandra and the 'Sistah's': The Peculiar Treatment of African American Women in the Myth of Women as Liars." *Journal of Gender, Race, and Justice* 2: 626–57.

Taking to the Airwaves: Using Content Analyses of Survey Toplines and Filmographies to Test the "Michelle Obama Image Transformation" (MOIT) Hypothesis

Ray Block Jr.
University of Wisconsin La Crosse
Christina S. Haynes
University of Wisconsin La Crosse

Introduction

In an attempt to broaden her appeal among mainstream voters, Michelle Obama took to the airwaves to transform her persona from an assertive career woman to that of an "everymom," who is more reminiscent of Jackie Onassis than Hillary Clinton (Powell and Kantor 2008; St. Clair 2009; Guerrero 2011). While it is not uncommon for First Ladies of the United States (FLOTUSes) to repackage themselves using media coverage, Michelle Obama has been on television more often than any other president's spouse (Tracey 2012; Stebner 2013). Since the 2008 presidential campaign, Mrs. Obama has graced the airwaves scores of times, (re)introducing herself to the American public, campaigning on her husband's behalf, and advancing her own agenda (Borelli 2011).[1] Conservative analyst Dan Gainor takes notice of the First Lady's busy media calendar:

> In just the last four months, viewers have seen [Michelle] Obama do push-ups with Ellen DeGeneres, play tug o' war with Jimmy Fallon, laugh along with Jay Leno and David Letterman, dance on Disney's "iCarly," work out with "The Biggest Loser" contestants at the White House, appear at the BET Honors, smile on "Sesame Street" and chat about healthy school lunches with Rachael Ray. (Excerpted from Tracey 2012)

This list of venues is as diverse as it is extensive. Presumably, one can attribute changes in the First Lady's polling numbers to her increased media exposure. In fact, the "Michelle Obama Image Transformation" (MOIT) hypothesis—that is, the idea that perceptions of Mrs. Obama have changed since the First Lady took over the airwaves—is a point of debate among journalists, survey designers, political pundits, and academics. Supporters praise the FLOTUS' decision to "go public" because they believe it enables Mrs. Obama to address any real or perceived deficiencies in her approval ratings, while anti-Obama prognosticators foretell of excessive media appearances backfiring and worsening the FLOTUS' public image (compare the viewpoints of Bryan 2009; Tulumello 2012 to those of Cohen 2008; Malkin 2012; Stebner 2013). This begs the question: does the MOIT improve or undermine Obama's popularity?

In this article, we put the MOIT hypothesis to what is thus far its most comprehensive test. A careful reading of the MOIT literature (particularly, Chapter 7 of Harris-Perry 2011) helps us to construct an aggregate-level model of Michelle Obama perceptions, one that considers the importance of both the frequency and the type of television appearances on favorability ratings. Rather than following the methods of conventional survey-based research, we use "toplines" (i.e., documents summarizing the major details of public opinion questions) as our primary source of evidence, and we collect this information from the iPOLL Databank, an online archive of questionnaires.[2] Moreover, we introduce two direct measures of Michelle Obama's media activities: an index of the number of television appearances the First Lady makes per week over the last two presidential election cycles, and a catalog of the different genres of these appearances (e.g., reality TV, news, and comedy). Using computer-assisted content analyses, our research provides a new insight into the influence of the First Lady's media activity on her public support. As such, our work extends past studies, exploring the implications of Mrs. Obama's image transformation via statistical evidence, thus documenting the impact of symbols of Black womanhood on this important public figure. The discussion of "symbols" has been a key factor in framing Black women as political actors and in public policy and culture (see King 1973; Jewell 1993; Collins 2000, 2004; Alexander-Floyd 2007, Chapters 2 and 5; Jordan-Zachery 2009; Harris 2011). This article helps readers to appreciate more fully the challenges faced by Mrs. Obama as she redefines the Office of the First Lady, while working within the narrow confines of Eurocentric and middle- to upper-class notions of femininity. As we discuss below and later demonstrate empirically, certain TV appearances are more effective than others at projecting Mrs. Obama as a "respectable" Black woman; however, excessive media exposure can foil these attempts, perhaps because they accentuate the First Lady's race and gender, and, by extension, her status as an interloper in what Carlson (1992, 31) describes as one of the most "tradition-bound and antiquated model[s] of American womanhood."

Race, Gender, Respectability, and Obama's Televisual Politics

The nation has always expected First Ladies to reflect ideals of home, family and womanhood. Even the term "lady" has connotations of middle- and upper-class *respectability* and suggests a certain kind of demeanor. These expectations illustrate the conflict all First Ladies face: As presidents' wives or host-esses, they are inevitably on the political and public stage, but as "ladies" they are expected to stay out of politics and in the background. (Mayo and Meringolo 1994, 8 [emphasis added])

The strategic use of television to manage one's political image is hardly new; politicians have been doing this for decades,[3] and so have their partners (Beasley 2005). For instance, there are numerous accounts of the media activities of Jacqueline Kennedy (Perry 2004), Betty Ford (Tobin 1990), Nancy Reagan (Benze 1990), and Hillary Clinton (Brown 1997; Parry-Giles 2000). Here, we refer to the process of appealing to voters through broadcasts as a First Lady's "televisual politics," and we discuss Mrs. Obama's image transformation as an attempt to reconcile the sometimes-competing motives of racial uplift and feminine respectability: since she holds a distinctly powerful yet non-elected or constitutionally prescribed position in America's highest political office, Mrs. Obama has the unenviable task of advocating for (and arguably epitomizing!) minority group inclusion, while simultaneously modeling White, middle to upper class, heterosexist, and patriarchal standards—hereafter referred to as "symbols"—of beauty, decorum, motherhood, domesticity, and work ethic (White 2001; Wolcott 2001; Anderson 2004; Jordan-Zachery 2009; Harris 2011).[4] Because she is the first FLOTUS of color, Mrs. Obama does not conform to the established symbols; however, she is judged, perhaps unfairly, by them. Moreover, Mrs. Obama is navigating issues of racial and gender identity on the most visible of public stages, and the Office of the First Lady provides her with little guidance. Never before has there been a non-White FLOTUS, so there is no precedent for issues of race/gender/class intersectionality entering into this public realm and, consequently, the public's imagination (Williams 2009; Guerrero 2011).

Voters tend to disparage First Ladies who contravene—or fail to master—the symbols befitting a president's spouse (Burrell, Elder, and Frederick 2011); so it is not surprising that, given her interloper status, Mrs. Obama struggles to maintain public support. In fact, the circumstances necessitating the MOIT date back to the 2008 Democratic Party presidential primaries, when opponents constructed narratives about Mrs. Obama that portrayed her as unconventional, anti-American, and/or unladylike. For instance, Mrs. Obama's undergraduate thesis (Robinson 1985)—which details, among other things, her experiences with isolation and discrimination as a woman and student of color at Princeton University—became a polarizing topic (Ressner 2008), as did the admission that her husband's success in the Iowa primary made her "very proud" of her country for the first time in her adult life (Thomas 2008; Block 2011a, 28). Moreover, Fox News contributor Juan Williams likened the First Lady's political viewpoints to those of a renowned Black Nationalist when he quipped "Michelle Obama has this Stokely-Carmichael-in-a-designer dress thing going on" (for a transcript, see Media Matters for America 2009). One of the more troubling depictions came in July of 2008, when the editors of the New Yorker (in an attempt at satire) placed on its front cover a caricature of the First Lady sporting an afro, wearing a bandolier, and toting an AK-47 assault rifle while giving her husband (clad in Islamic attire) a "fist bump" in the Oval Office as a replica of the American flag burned in a fireplace adorned with a portrait of Osama Bin Laden. This constellation of images draws on familiar myths regarding Black women as lacking femininity or etiquette, and assuming violent and even criminal dispositions (Guerrero 2011, 72–5; Harris-Perry 2011, Chapter 7).

These and related events motivated the FLOTUS to counteract negative stereotypes with public appeals. Mrs. Obama has worked particularly hard since the 2008 primaries to improve her reputation (St. Clair 2009), and recent evidence from an ABC News/Washington Post poll confirms that the First Lady's popularity continues to outpace her husband's (see Spiering 2012). More importantly, Harris-Perry (2011) shows that attitudes toward Mrs. Obama improved considerably in the summer of 2008; this boost in popularity coincides with the First Lady's decision to make cameo appearances in an unprecedented a number of television programs (Tracey 2012). Powell and Kantor (2008) and Stanley (2008) even argue that Mrs. Obama's nascent "image makeover movement" evolved into a full-on media blitz in June of 2008, when the FLOTUS starred as a guest co-host on the popular daytime talk show, "The View." The fruits of the First Lady's labor were on full display during the Democratic National Convention in September of 2012, when she impressed audiences with heartfelt and patriotic oratory, acceptably stylish clothing and accessories,[5] a playful yet self-effacing manner, and a fealty to her husband that was appropriately untiring and non-doting (Hawkins 2012). Such imagery and themes are consistent with the symbolism of the Office of the First Lady, and, given the continuing role that feminine respectability plays in conditioning Black women's political organizing and agenda setting (Wolcott 1997, 2001; White 2001), Mrs. Obama's current popularity is a testament to her skill in performing the widely cherished rituals of American womanhood.

In this sense, the rationale behind the MOIT resembles a process of racial and gender habituation. Psychologists use this term to describe the decline in a subject's sensitivity to a repeated stimulus, but more general conceptions of the word characterize a person's or group's ability to adjust to external circumstances (Berk 2007). According to research on social identity, habituation makes it possible for repeated positive interactions with members of an out group to deactivate negative out-group perceptions (Phelps et al. 2000; Wheeler and Fiske 2005). When applied to presidential politics (see Fiske et al. 2009; Block 2011b), the idea suggests that suspicions tend to wane as voters become more accustomed to seeing Mrs. Obama in positive and counter-stereotypical contexts. As the saying goes, the FLOTUS can use the airwaves to "eliminate the negative" while "accentuating the positive." But habituation does not guarantee improved Michelle Obama perceptions. Repeated television appearances, no matter how positive in intent, could also backfire, as they did during the first term of the Obama administration, when the First Lady began the "Let's Move!" campaign against childhood obesity. Some voters praised the FLOTUS' involvement in what they believed was a bipartisan initiative (Wojcicki and Heyman 2010), whereas critics questioned the logic of her efforts (Herndon 2012), rebuked her attempts to regulate exercise and eating habits (Paulson 2012), accused her of exploiting the importance of youth wellness for personal gain (Malkin 2012), or deemed her a hypocrite for not practicing the healthy lifestyle she ardently preaches.[6]

Ultimately, these televisual politics speak to broader issues of racial and gender identity. Mrs. Obama is one of the nation's most recognizable (and possibly the most influential) African American women, and studying her unique experiences moves us a step closer to understanding the complex—and ever evolving—roles of race and gender in the Oval Office (Gordon and Miller 2003). Moreover, our paper adds to the fast-growing literature on the Obama Administration by shifting the focus away from the Head of State and onto other members of the First Family.[7] Mrs. Obama never was or will ever be a "Stepford wife" (Wolfe 2007), and it goes without saying that she has achieved success on her own merits, independently of her husband. That said, conversations about the First Family often include references to both spouses, partly because, as Samuels (2008) and Henderson (2010) acknowledge, Barack's electability was influenced considerably by Michelle's support.[8] Harris-Perry (2011) articulates perhaps the strongest justification for moving the literature in a different direction: conventional research undermines not only Mrs. Obama's essential role in her husband's achievements, but also the importance of First Ladies more generally (see also Gutin 1989; Anthony 1993).

Modeling the MOIT Hypotheses

In the seventh chapter of her recent book, *Sister Citizen*, Harris-Perry (2011) lays the groundwork for analyzing the influence of the First Lady's image transformation on Michelle Obama perceptions, and, to our knowledge, she is one of the few authors (if not the first one) to draw an empirical connection between Mrs. Obama's television appearances and her favorability ratings (commonly measured as the percentage of survey participants who have a "generally favorable" opinion of the First Lady). We extend Harris-Perry's reasoning by arguing that the MOIT hypothesis entails two sets of expectations: one pertaining to the influence of the frequency of TV appearances on Michelle Obama perceptions, and another regarding the impact of the type of such media activity on favorability ratings. We test both sets of expectations using heteroskedastic regression models (Harvey 1976; Greene 1993). These models take the following general form: $Y_i = \mu_i + \sigma_i + \varepsilon_i$, where the dependent variable (Y_i) is polling item i's favorability percentage for Michelle Obama, and we examine the effect of our independent variables on the overall mean of the favorability percentages (μ_i), as well as the variability in these percentages across polling items (σ_i). Rather than simply being a "nuisance parameter," the error term (ε_i) is an essential component of the models: we use it to predict fluctuations in the discrepancy between predicted and actual favorability percentages.

Data for our dependent variable comes from the iPOLL Databank and other resources provided by the Roper Center for Public Opinion Research. We used iPOLL's search engine to find survey questions that included the keywords "Michelle Obama" in the text and derivations of the term "favorable" in the response options. At the time of this article's writing, there were 128 results (dating from September 27, 2007 to January 18, 2013) matching our search criteria. Each keyword match connects to a webpage displaying a "topline" summary of the polling results. These toplines contain details about a single survey question, including a polling item's raw text, a graph illustrating the survey responses, and "metadata"—that is, iPOLL's indexing information, as well as information about the organization (or "survey house," to borrow a term popularized by Smith [1978]) conducting the poll, dates of the survey, mode(s) of interviewing, sample characteristics, and, when available, questionnaire from which the item originates. We hand-coded each topline, taking percent "favorable" for items with nominal response categories, collapsing ordinal responses (e.g., percent "somewhat favorable" + percent "strongly favorable"), and computing the average percentage for Mrs. Obama feeling thermometer questions (which are measured at the interval level).[9] The overall distribution of our dependent variable, along with favorability results sorted by date and survey houses, appears in Figure 1. The patterns within the scatter plots of Figure 1 confirm that the First Lady's popularity has improved over time. With the exception of one polling organization (the McClatchy-Marist College Institute for Public Opinion), all the correlations between the survey dates and favorability percentages are positive,[10] and the overall relationship between these variables is statistically significant ($r = 0.47$, $p < 0.05$). Put in substantive terms, the average favorability percentage nearly doubles, rising from roughly 32 percent to approximately 61 percent, over the five-year period covered in our analyses.

Figure 1.
Trends in the Percentage of Respondents Expressing Favorable Opinions about Michelle Obama

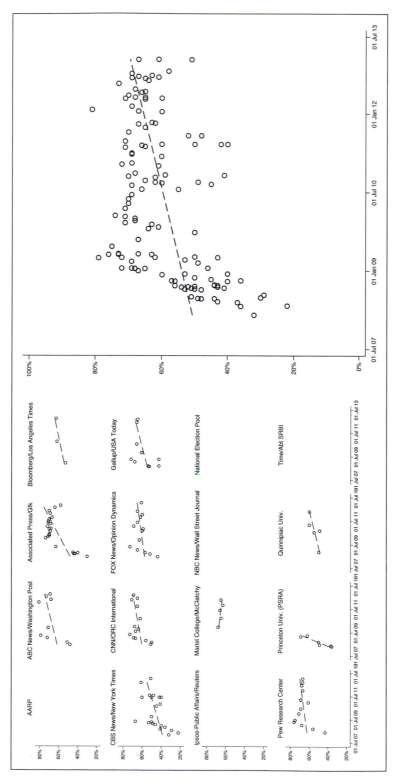

Source: The FLOTUS Project: Obama (September 27, 2007 to January 18, 2013). Polling results obtained from the iPOLL Databank. http://www.ropercenter.uconn.edu/data_access/ipoll/ipoll.html.

Notes: Scatter plots illustrate changes in the percentage of survey respondents who express favorable attitudes about Michelle Obama over time. The left half of the figure records the trends for each survey house separately, while the right half combines the results into an overall trend. When enough data are available (some survey houses had too few observations), we add regression lines to show the linear relationship between survey date and favorability percentages. All graphs were created using Stata 12.1.

To explore the influence of media activity on FLOTUS favorability, our models include the following system of equations:

$$\mu_i = E(Y_i) = \beta_0 + \beta_i X_i \qquad (1.1)$$
$$\sigma_i = VAR(\varepsilon_i) = exp(\gamma_0 + \gamma_i Z_i) \qquad (1.2)$$

where X_i and Z_i are collections of independent variables. For data-collection purposes, it helps to view the FLOTUS as a celebrity (see Hennessey and Skiba 2012), and we search through entertainment-related websites to uncover information about her television appearances (these variables appear in X_i in Equation [1.1]). The Internet Movie Database (IMDb), a digital resource for information on films, video games, television programs, etc., archives each celebrity with an interactive "filmography" page from which viewers can download chronological lists of past performances (Michelle Obama's filmography is available at http://www.imdb.com/name/nm2349292/). To merge the filmography data with our survey toplines, we tally up the number of cameo appearances the First Lady makes during the week in which an iPOLL survey is conducted.[11] We combine these tallies into an additive index that ranges from zero to five (the First Lady never made more than five appearances in a single week). The rationale for our additive index is simple: the more times in a week that the First Lady appears on the airwaves, the greater the likelihood that Mrs. Obama's messages have made it into a voter's "information environment" (Jerit, Barabas, and Bolsen 2006; Jerit and Barabas 2012). This increased level of TV exposure raises the probability that voters will be influenced one way or another by the First Lady's media activity. The index is skewed left (mean = 0.461), because there were many weeks when the FLOTUS did not hit the airways.

Recall that the MOIT hypothesis assumes that Mrs. Obama's favorability varies by the level as well as the type of media activity. IMDb keeps track of the genres of the performances in Mrs. Obama's filmography (see Figure 2 for a timeline of her media activities). We create separate dummy variables for the genres, each recording whether Mrs. Obama appeared in a particular type of television show during the week that a survey entered the field. We discovered eight genres: award ceremonies, comedies, documentaries, family/children's programs, musicals, newscasts, reality TV, and talk shows.[12] The first cameo role in our timeline took place on October 26, 2007 (when Mrs. Obama attended a panel discussion on "To the Contrary" with Erbe 2009); the last one happened in September 17, 2012 ("The Rachel Ray Show"). A closer look at Figure 2 reveals that news programs, talk shows, and comedy sketches are the most common media events, comprising approximately 15, 14, and 10 percent, respectively, of Mrs. Obama's television appearances. Figure 2 also shows that the First Lady's press office schedules Mrs. Obama's television events in waves: the busiest months correspond with the major periods of the last two presidential election cycles (from fall 2008 to winter 2009, and from winter 2011 to fall 2012), with the quietest months taking place between campaigns (from the spring to the fall of 2010).

In addition to allowing for multiple measures of media activity, our model accommodates divergent sets of predictions. On the one hand, the MOIT posits that television appearances, the First Lady's instrument of choice for transforming her reputation, enabled Mrs. Obama to generate the positive media coverage needed to make her image more

Figure 2.
A Timeline of Michelle Obama's Television Appearances

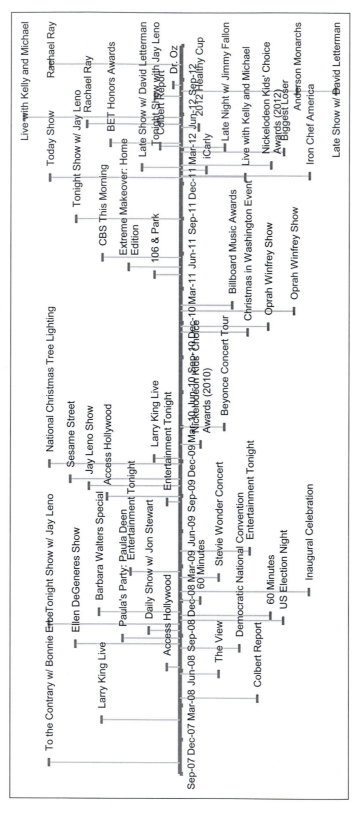

Source: Michelle Obama filmography (September 27, 2007 to December 26, 2012). Information obtained from the Internet Movie Database (IMDb): http://www.imdb.com/name/nm2349292/.

Notes: We arrange television appearances chronologically and in accordance with the timing of iPOLL survey items. For example, any media event that takes place within one week (seven days) of a survey being conducted gets counted as being relevant to that polling item's "information environment." We created this timeline using Microsoft Office Excel 2007.

favorable. On the other hand, the MOIT hypothesis also suggests that cameo roles can backfire and drive down the FLOTUS' approval ratings. We apply these predictions to both the level and genre of media activity, for some TV shows are more effective than others at influencing Michelle Obama perceptions. This means that the First Lady must be selective when gracing the airwaves. For example, by choosing entertainment (rather than journalistic) television shows, the FLOTUS minimizes the need to address uncomfortable questions about her husband's decisions regarding healthcare reform and the financial crisis, thus freeing her up to focus on less controversial topics, such as assisting military families and fighting childhood obesity (Tracey 2012). On the basis of this line of reasoning, we anticipate that media activity, however measured, will have either a positive or negative impact on favorability percentages. Stated formally: we predict that $\beta_i \neq 0$.[13]

It is possible that FLOTUS perceptions do not vary because of media activity per se and are instead shaped by broadcasting/programming-related factors specific to those TV shows. To rule out the possibly spurious relationship between media appearances and favorability percentages, we include predictors that assess the target audiences of the television shows Mrs. Obama attends. "Dayparting" is the practice of dividing airtimes into several intervals, during each of which a different type of television programming appropriate to that time slot is aired (see Vane and Gross 1994 for details). Television viewing days typically divide into the eight blocs: late fringe (12:00 a.m.), post late fringe (1:00 to 1:30 a.m.), early morning (6:00 to 9:00 a.m.), daytime (10:00 a.m. to 4:30 p.m.), early fringe (5:00 to 7:00 p.m.), prime access (7:30 to 8:00 p.m.), prime time (8:00 to 10:00 p.m.), and late news (11:00 p.m. to midnight). Since they are geared toward specific audiences and tend to attract different numbers of viewers, we include dummy variables representing the "dayparts" of Mrs. Obama's TV appearances.

Next, we control for the sample composition of the surveys. For example, Harris-Perry (2011, Table 13) uncovers racial differences in FLOTUS support. We may not be able to obtain information about specific respondents, but we can identify which polls conduct additional "oversamples" of African Americans and Hispanics. It is common for pollsters to include this information in their topline summaries, and we believe that a survey's overall demographic makeup can serve as a crude, but serviceable, proxy for respondents' race or ethnicity.[14] We also include control variables that record whether the survey targets registered voters, the idea being that registered voters are arguably more interested in politics than their non-registered counterparts, and might therefore express different Michelle Obama perceptions. In addition, we keep track of the percentage of survey respondents who are self-reported Democrats to check for variation in FLOTUS support stemming from differences in political orientation.

Finally, the literature on "polling artifacts" examines the degree to which survey design (particularly, question wording, question order, response category labeling, etc.) biases survey responses (see Bishop 2004). In view of this, the remaining predictors in our model control for the potential influence of survey artifacts on Michelle Obama perceptions. These control variables include dichotomous indicators of a polling item's level of measurement (nominal = 1, else = 0) and a survey's mode of interviewing (1= phone, 0 = otherwise), as well as two within-item measures of "survey fatigue" (see Saris and Gallhofer 2007), that is, the number of words a survey question has and the number of responses categories offered. Finally, we record sample sizes because of their strong connection to a survey's "margin of error" (Fowler 2009).[15] Past research (e.g., Schaeffer and Presser 2003) shows that these artifacts make polling results less predictable (i.e., more inconsistent), so we add these control variables to Equation (1.2) as predictors of the variance ($VAR(\varepsilon_i)$), rather than the mean levels ($E(Y_i)$) of Mrs. Obama's favorability percentages. Accordingly, we anticipate that survey artifacts can either increase or decrease the variability of FLOTUS perceptions, or, put differently: $\gamma_i \neq 0$.[16]

Findings and Discussion

Figure 3 illustrates some results from the heteroskedastic regression model of the impact of TV appearances on Michelle Obama perceptions.[17] As noted, the dependent variable is the percentage of respondents in a survey topline that expresses favorable attitudes toward the First Lady. The parameter estimates (displayed as dots) represent the change in FLOTUS favorability percentages associated with a one-unit increase in that independent variable, holding all other predictors constant. The horizontal lines extending from each dot are 95 percent confidence intervals (CIs), and estimates with intervals that overlap with zero are statistically insignificant. We control for broadcasting/programming factors, survey sample characteristics, and polling artifacts; however, to conserve space, we interpret only the theoretically central determinants of FLOTUS perceptions.[18] Figure 3 offers qualified support for the MOIT hypotheses. Overall, favorability tends to decrease as the number of Obama's TV appearances per-week increase (coefficient estimate is –2.83; CI is [–4.82, –0.84]). Using King's CLARIFY package (King, Tomz, and Wittenberg 2000; Tomz, Wittenberg, and King 2001), this decrease translates to a 15.05 percent drop in favorability (from roughly 60.53 percent to approximately 45.48 percent) when the TV appearance index moves from its minimum to its maximum value. The results are mixed for the genre indicators. Mrs. Obama's expected favorability level shrinks by 11.27 percent (from 59.61 percent to 48.34 percent) during weeks in which she appears in award ceremonies (estimate = –7.61; CI = [–14.69, –0.53]). They are higher, conversely, when the First Lady appears in comedies (5.67; [0.25, 11.09], which raises favorability from 58.75 percent to 62.03 percent), children's shows (7.57; [1.31, 13.84], a jump of 12.49 percent, from 58.59 percent to 71.08 percent), musicals (6.09; [1.48, 10.70], a 7.44 percent increase, from 58.79 percent to 66.23 percent), and reality TV episodes (8.39; [1.63, 15.14], a boost in favorability of 12.07 percent, from 58.70 percent to 70.77 percent). Documentaries, newscasts, and talk shows are statistically insignificant predictors: the confidence intervals for these TV-show genres include the null hypothesis that the impact of this type of media activity on FLOTUS perceptions is indistinguishable from zero.

In addition to presenting evidence from these "main effects," we also provide estimates from a series of models that include interaction terms for each TV genre predictor and the additive index (number of TV appearances per week). Specifically, we use Brambor, Clark, and Golder's (2006) statistical program to plot the conditional influence of media genre on favorability percentages across the frequency of those types of TV appearances.[19] The *y* axes in Figure 4 represent the effect of that particular TV genre on Mrs. Obama's favorability percentages (holding other independent variables constant), and the *x* axes illustrate how this conditional effect increases, decreases, or holds steady as the number

Figure 3.
The Influence of Michelle Obama's Television Appearances on Her Favorability Ratings

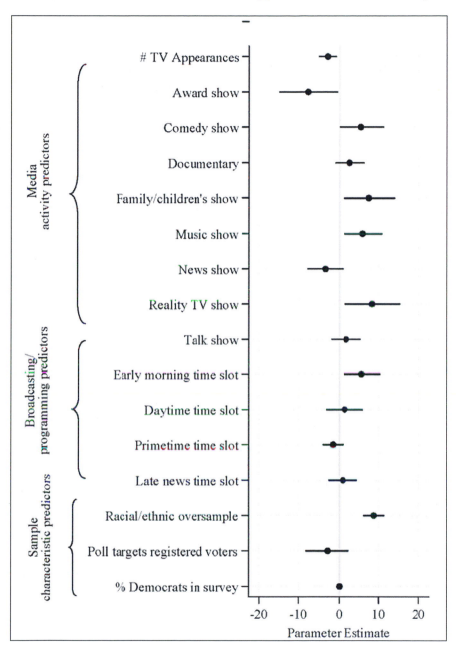

Source: The FLOTUS Project: Obama (September 27, 2007 to January 18, 2013). Polling results obtained from the iPOLL Databank. Filmography data compiled from the Internet Movie Database (IMDb).

Notes: Estimates (shown as dots) are *heteroskedastic* regression coefficients, with horizontal lines denoting 95 percent CIs. We suppress the estimates for the model's *y*-intercept (constant), and we do not show the results for the control variables presumed to affect the variance in Michelle Obama's favorability levels. The sample size for the full model is 128 survey toplines, and the model fit statistic (in this case, the variance-weighted least squares [VWLS] R^2) is 0.27. We created this graph in Stata 12.1 by customizing Kastellec and Leoni's (2007) computer code (http://www.ats.ucla.edu/stat/stata/paperexamples/Kastellec_Leoni/default.htm).

Figure 4.

The Conditional Impact of TV Genre on Michelle Obama Favorability, Estimated across the Number of Media Appearances

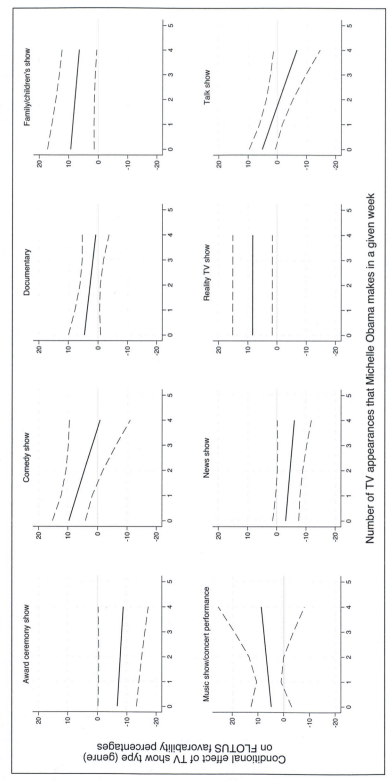

Source: The FLOTUS Project: Obama (September 27, 2007 to January 18, 2013). Polling results obtained from the iPOLL Databank. Filmography data compiled from the Internet Movie Database (IMDb).

Notes: We calculated the conditional effect estimates (solid lines) and 95 percent CIs (dashed lines) using the computer code developed by Brambor, Clark, and Golder (2006) (https://files.nyu.edu/mrg217/public/interaction.html). All the results are based on regression models including interaction terms for each particular TV genre variable and the frequency of media activity predictor, and they represent simulated values that we calculated while holding the influence of other variables constant. All the graphs above were created using Stata 12.1.

of those types of media appearances moves from its lowest to its highest values (in this case, from zero to four [rather than five] because of data limitations). The dashed lines in this figure show the 95 percent CIs for these conditional effects, which allow readers to determine the statistical significance of the impact of genre on FLOTUS perceptions at a particular number of TV appearances. The results reveal that the positive impact of the television genre tends to decrease as the number of media events per week rises, while the negative effects of media activity tend to become even more pronounced as the number of TV shows increases. Taken together, the evidence in Figure 4 suggests that "less is more" when it comes to the First Lady's commitment to taking over the airwaves. Clearly, certain TV appearances benefit the First Lady and should therefore remain on her event calendar. That said, Mrs. Obama must take care to avoid overexposure. Scheduling multiple media appearances in the same week adds little to her popularity levels, and doing so might actually decrease her favorability quotient and, potentially, cost her some support among constituents.

Conclusion

What do these results teach us about Black women in politics and First Ladies as public figures? We address this question by examining the First Lady's media activities from the perspectives of race/gender intersectionality and the politics of respectability. Using a novel dataset and a mixed-methods research approach, we subject the Michelle Obama Image Transformation (MOIT) hypothesis to what is hitherto its most stringent test. This hypothesis suggests that Mrs. Obama's media activities may either help or hurt her public image, and we find support for both sets of predictions. Depending on the genre of the television show, cameo appearances can have a positive or negative impact on the First Lady's popularity. Beyond these conceptual and empirical contributions, our research informs the debate over the success rate of the MOIT and related image-make-over campaigns. Critics can take solace in the findings of Figure 3, for they imply that the American public might grow weary of Mrs. Obama's media blitz. For some voters, this weariness stems from concerns about the FLOTUS behaving too much like a prima donna and not enough like a public servant. Others, however, may disapprove of Mrs. Obama taking over the airwaves because they question the legitimacy of the Obama administration and/or perceive Mrs. Obama as unfit for the title of First Lady. On the other hand, the results in Figure 4 might excite the First Lady's press office because they suggest the possibility of streamlining Mrs. Obama's overbooked media calendar to focus on fewer but better-placed public appeals. More broadly, our analyses speak to the importance of Black women in politics reclaiming control over the framing of their personas. To fight against racial and gender stereotypes, and to balance the dual pressures of uplift and respectability, these women must be particularly strategic in the selection of their political agendas, the manner in which they embrace their public roles, and their method of communicating with constituents.

According to Kuhn (1962), "normal science" is the cumulative enterprise of bringing further evidence to pre-existing arguments. The claims we test here are not uniquely ours; however, no study to date evaluates the MOIT hypothesis more systematically, and, as noted above, our work adds to the scholarship of First Ladies and African American women in politics. Specifically, the results lend further credence to the impact of symbols on Black women's political environment, for they suggest that Mrs. Obama, as the first Black FLOTUS, can only enter into the traditional role of affirming gender norms and definitions of womanhood by utilizing carefully chosen narratives of respectability. The First Lady's political success depends on her ability to deploy these narratives, and the challenges she faces are both the cause and the consequence of her journey to (re)define this important political office. Our focus on normal science should not be dismissed, for our attention to measurement detail (we offer the first direct indicators of media activity), the extensive data collection (doubling the time period and number of polls typically considered), and its analytical complexity (we examine the relationship impact of the frequency and the genre of TV appearances on the strength as well as the stability of FLO-TUS support) set this study apart from previous research on the MOIT. Future work will hopefully benefit from our efforts. For example, we chose to examine aggregate patterns in survey responses instead of exploring individuals' attitudes regarding the FLOTUS' media activities. The ideas expressed in this paper might inspire micro-level research to complement these macro-level arguments.

Acknowledgments

We thank Jeremy Arney, Jo Arney, Tim Dale, Grace Deason, Vince Hutchings, John Kovari, Steve McDougal, Betsy Morgan, Wendy Smooth, Atiya Stokes-Brown, Adam Van Liere, the representatives at iPOLL and IMDb (particularly, Lois Timmsferrara and Giancarlo Cairella, respectively), and the editors and anonymous reviewers at the *National Political Science Review* for their assistance and encouragement. Financial support for this research comes from a University of Wisconsin, La Crosse College of Liberal Studies (CLS) start-up grant that funds the "FLOTUS Project," a relational database of public perceptions of contemporary First Ladies.

Notes

1. POLITICO.com created a video mashup of some of Obama's more recent cameo appearances: http://www.politico.com/multimedia/video/2012/05/michelle-obamas-many-tv-appearances.html.
2. iPOLL is the world's oldest and most extensive web-based clearinghouse of survey data. Maintained by the Roper Center for Public Opinion Research and headquartered at the University of Connecticut, iPOLL enables users to sift through (and, when available, download) thousands of polls. More information about iPOLL is available at their website: http://www.ropercenter.uconn.edu/data_access/ipoll/ipoll.html. Please note that the views expressed in this paper are ours alone and do not reflect those of the Roper Center or any survey organization affiliated with iPOLL.
3. See Iyengar and Simon (2000), Graber (2003), and Goldstein and Ridout (2004) for reviews of the vast literature on the role of the media in political campaigns.
4. Wolcott (1997) refers to these symbols when she recounts the history of the National Training School, a trade- and professional-education institution for African American women founded in 1909 by religious leader and feminist activist Nannie Helen Burroughs. The author notes that Burroughs adopted the motto of the "three Bs" ("Bible, Bath, and Broom") when arguing that the ideal curriculum for Black women emphasized Judeo-Christian morality, cleanliness with the outward appearance of gentility, and housekeeping skills, respectively.
5. Recent controversies over the First Lady's sartorial choices stem from the nation's preoccupation with her height, skin complexion, and fuller, athletic figure (Guerrero 2011, 75). This fixation reflects enduring anxieties regarding African American female sexuality (Jewell 1993; White 2001; Collins 2004).
6. Conservative commentator Rush Limbaugh is particularly outspoken in his criticism of the First Lady's figure, as evidenced in the February 21st edition of his radio show. For an audio recording of his comments, see http://mediamatters.org/video/2011/02/21/rush-dare-i-say-this-it-doesnt-look-like-michel/176687.

7.   This is not an exhaustive list, but recent contributors to the field of First Family studies more generally, and Obama research in particular, include Williams (2009), Smooth (2010), and the entire September 2009 edition of the *Communication and Critical/Cultural Studies* journal. We hope that our work will join ongoing dialogues about Obama as a political figure.

8.   This is, perhaps, what Guerrero (2011) had in mind when she mentions Obama and the "ideal of Republican womanhood," a gender paradigm that merges notions of civic activism with traditional conceptions of domesticity by recommending that women work behind the scenes to sway their fathers/sons/spouses, and, ultimately, the outcomes of politics (see also Mayo and Meringolo 1994).

9.   We saved screenshots of each topline as image files that we imported into NVivo, a popular content-processing program for categorizing, analyzing, and interpreting non-numeric or unstructured data (Bazeley 2007). Next, a team of three coders read each screenshot, looking for themes. NVivo provides Cohen's Kappa as a measure of inter-coder reliability. Cohen's Kappa is expressed as a proportion, with higher values indicating greater agreement between coders. As a decision rule, we consider Kappa statistics of 0.70 or higher as representing satisfactory agreement. We achieved a Kappa estimate of 0.92 for the favorability variable.

10. Because of the uniformity of these results, all analyses that follow are based on the entire sample of survey toplines (rather than specific polling organizations), and the coefficients in our heteroskedastic regression models include robust standard errors that cluster toplines by polling house.

11. For example, the June 20, 2008 Princeton Survey Research Associates (PSRA) poll went into the field within days of Mrs. Obama's cameo appearance on "The View," and this was the only media event that the First Lady scheduled that week.

12. Some media events have overlapping genres (e.g., "The Colbert Report" is both a news show and a comedy show), and our measurement strategy allows us to account for these special cases.

13. These expectations assume a null hypothesis of no influence of TV appearances on the magnitude of Obama favorability (i.e., $\gamma i = 0$).

14. Because racial and ethnic minorities make up small segments of the American population, oversampling from these subgroups yields higher numbers of these respondents than would typically appear in nationally representative surveys. To get around the issue of Blacks and Hispanics being "over-represented," researchers apply sample weights to their analyses of surveys that include oversamples. Mathematically, these sample weights ensure that, despite their larger numbers, the relative presence of racial and ethnic minorities reflects current population proportions (for a technical discussion of oversampling, see Saris and Gallhofer 2007). Polling organizations make these sample weights available for users who wish to download the raw data of surveys with oversamples. However, because sample weights are not always applied to topline summaries, the results from these documents may represent the unmodified opinions of racially and ethnically diverse groups of respondents, and we demonstrate that aggregated opinions across these types of surveys (oversample versus no oversample) not only can differ, but often do.

15. A team of three researchers hand-coded each control variable and achieved individual kappa estimates of 0.92 (level of measurement), 0.84 (number of response categories), 0.88 (interview method), 0.89 (word count), and 0.96 (sample size). The average reliability score (across all content codes) is 0.90.

16. Again, these expectations assume a null hypothesis of no impact of survey artifacts on the variability of Obama favorability (i.e., $\gamma_1 = 0$).

17. Kastellec and Leoni (2007) offer recommendations for converting tables of regression coefficients into figures. For details, see http://statistics.ats.ucla.edu/stat/stata/paperexamples/Kastellec_Leoni/default.htm.

18. The only other independent variables to reach statistical significance in the mean portion of the heteroskedastic regression model are "early morning time slot" (a broadcasting/programming predictor) and "racial/ethnic oversample" (a sample characteristic predictor). Compared to other "dayparts," Mrs. Obama tends to get higher favorability percentages when she appears in early morning broadcasts like "CBS This Morning" or "Good Morning America" (coefficient estimate = 5.83; 95 percent CI = [1.36, 10.29]). Likewise, the expected percentage of Obama's favorability is the greatest in surveys with oversamples of racial and ethnic minorities (estimate = 8.85; CI = [6.42, 11.28]). Neither of these results is surprising, for it makes sense that the First Lady would enjoy greater popularity levels among women—who are the target audience of early morning TV shows (see Vane and Gross 1994) and Blacks and Latinos—who are widely documented to express greater support for the Obama administration than their White counterparts do (see Hutchings 2009). Overall, the "survey artifact" predictors in the variance portion of the model behave as expected: survey date (−0.01; [0.00, 0.02]), sample size (−0.02; [0.00, 0.03]), and the number of response categories (−0.86; [0.05, 1.67]) have small but statistically significant effects, and a one-unit shift in each of these predictors corresponds with a decrease in the variability

of Obama's favorability, holding the influence of other predictors constant. Likewise, moving from a nominally measured polling item to a more precise response scale contributes to a significant decrease in the variance in FLOTUS support (−1.25; [0.43, 2.92]). These results are consistent with those of existing studies examining the influence of polling artifacts on the predictability of survey responses (see Schaeffer and Presser 2003; Bishop 2004).

19. Computer code for this program is available from the research page of Matt Golder's website: https://files.nyu.edu/mrg217/public/interaction.

References

Alexander-Floyd, Nikol G. 2007. *Gender, Race, and Nationalism in Contemporary Black Politics*. New York, NY: Palgrave Macmillan.

Anderson, Karrin Vasby. 2004. "The First Lady: A Site of 'American Womanhood.'" In *Inventing Voice: The Rhetoric of American First Ladies of the Twentieth Century*, ed. Molly Meijer Wertheimer, 17–31. Lanham, MD: Rowan and Littlefield.

Anthony, Carl Sferrazza. 1993. *First Ladies: The Saga of Presidents' Wives and Their Power Vol II*. New York, NY: Harper Perennial.

Bazeley, Patricia. 2007. *Qualitative Data Analysis with NVivo*. Thousand Oaks, CA: Sage.

Beasley, Maurine Hoffman. 2005. *First Ladies and the Press: The Unfinished Partnership of the Media Age*. Evanston, IL: Northwestern University Press.

Benze, James G. Jr. 1990. "Nancy Reagan: China Doll or Dragon Lady?" *Presidential Studies Quarterly* 20: 777–90.

Berk, Laura E. 2007. *Habituation: Development through the Lifespan*. 4th ed. New York, NY: Pearson Education, Inc.

Bishop, George F. 2004. *The Illusion of Public Opinion: Fact and Artifact in American Public Opinion Polls*. Lanham, MD: Rowan and Littlefield.

Block, Ray Jr. 2011a. "What about Disillusionment? Exploring the Pathways to Black Nationalism." *Political Behavior* 33: 27–51.

———. 2011b. "Backing Barack Because He's Black: Racially Motivated Voting in the 2008 Election." *Social Science Quarterly* 92: 423–46.

Borelli, Mary Anne. 2011. *The Politics of the President's Wife*. College Station, TX: Texas A&M University Press.

Brambor, Thomas, William Roberts Clark, and Matt Golder. 2006. "Understanding Interaction Models: Improving Empirical Analyses." *Political Analysis* 14: 63–82.

Brown, Mary Ellen. 1997. "Feminism and Cultural Politics: Television Audiences and Hillary Rodham Clinton." *Political Communication* 14: 255–70.

Bryan, Clifford. 2009. "Michelle Obama's Image Softened: Hats off to Catherine (Katie) McCormick Lelyveld's Think Tank." Examiner.com, October 9, 2009. http://www.examiner.com/michelle-obama-in-national/michelle-obama-s-image-softened-hats-off-to-catherine-katie-mccormick-lelyveld-s-think-tank (accessed March 8, 2011).

Burrell, Barbara, Laura Elder, and Brian Frederick. 2011. "From Hillary to Michelle: Public Opinion Polls and the Spouses of Presidential Candidates." *Presidential Studies Quarterly* 41: 156–76.

Carlson, Margaret. 1992. "All Eyes on Hillary." *Time Magazine*, September 14: 1–4.

Cohen, Richard. 2008. "Michelle Obama's Sad Transformation." *The Washington Post*, August 26. http://logcabinkitbuilder.com/blog/2008/08/26/michelle-obamas-sad-transformation-washington-post/ (accessed February 12, 2011).

Collins, Patricia Hill. 2000. *Black Feminist Thought: Knowledge, Consciousness, and the Politics of Empowerment*. Revised 10th Anniversary Edition. New York, NY: Routledge.

———. 2004. *Black Sexual Politics: African Americans, Gender, and the New Racism*. New York, NY: Routledge.

Erbe, Bonnie. 2009. "Michelle Obama's Mom-In-Chief Image Is a Cave to Politics and Stereotypes." *U.S. News & World Report*, May 12–14.

Fiske, Susan T., Hilary B. Bergsieker, Anne Marie Russell, and Lyle Williams. 2009. "Images of Black Americans: Then, 'Them,' and Now, 'Obama.'" *Du Bois Review* 6: 83–101.

Fowler, Floyd J. 2009. *Survey Research Methods*. 4th ed. Thousand Oaks, CA: Sage.

Goldstein, Kenneth, and Travis N. Ridout. 2004. "Measuring the Effects of Televised Political Advertising in the United States." Annual Review of Political Science 7: 205–26.

Gordon, Ann, and Jerry Miller. 2003. "Gender, Race and the Oval Office." In *Anticipating Madam President*, ed. Robert P. Watson and Ann Gordon, 145–55. Boulder, CO: Lynne Rienner.

Graber, Doris. 2003. "The Media and Democracy: Beyond Myths and Stereotypes." *Annual Review of Political Science* 6: 139–60.

Greene, W. H. 1993. *Econometric Analysis*. 2nd ed. New York, NY: Macmillan.

Guerrero, Lisa. 2011. "(M)Other-In-Chief: Michelle Obama and the Ideal of Republican Womanhood." In *New Femininities: Postfeminism, Neolibralism and Identity*, ed. Rosalind Gill and Christina Scharff, 68–82. New York, NY: Palgrave Macmillan.

Gutin, Myra G. 1989. *The President's Partner: The First Lady in the Twentieth Century*. Westport, CT: Praeger/Greenwood Press.

Harris, Duchess. 2011. *Black Feminist Politics from Kennedy to Obama*. New York, NY: Palgrave Macmillan.

Harris-Perry, Melissa V. 2011. *Sister Citizen: Shame, Stereotypes, and Black Women in America*. Cambridge, MA: Yale University Press.

Harvey, A. C. 1976. "Estimating Regression Models with Multiplicative Heteroscedasticity." *Econometrica* 44: 461–65.

Hawkins, Arielle. 2012. "Michelle Obama Convention Speech Dress Dazzles, Scores." CNN.com, September 5. http://politicalticker.blogs.cnn.com/2012/09/05/michelle-obama-convention-speech-dress-dazzles-scores/ (accessed March 1, 2013).

Henderson, Nia-Malika. 2010. "Michelle Obama Speaks Frankly about Race." *Politico*, February 19. http://www.politico.com/news/stories/0210/33162.html (accessed January 1, 2013).

Hennessey, Kathleen, and Katherine Skiba. 2012. "Relishing the Role of First Celebrity." *Los Angeles Times*, September 4. http://articles.latimes.com/2012/sep/04/nation/la-na-michelle-obama-20120904 (accessed January 7, 2013).

Herndon, April. 2012. My Beef with Michelle Obama's Let's Move! Campaign: What Every Child Deserves Regardless of Weight. Dry Land Fish, Perspectives from the Misplaced, April 25. http://www.psychologytoday.com/blog/dry-land-fish/201204/my-beef-michelle-obamas-lets-move-campaign (accessed November 15, 2013).

Hutchings, Vincent. 2009. "Change or More of the Same: Evaluating Racial Attitudes in the Obama Era." *Public Opinion Quarterly* 73: 917–42.

Iyengar, Shanto, and Adam F. Simon. 2000. "New Perspectives and Evidence on Political Communication and Campaign Effects." *Annual Review of Psychology* 51: 149–69.

Jerit, Jennifer, and Jason Barabas. 2012. "Partisan Perceptual Bias and the Information Environment." *Journal of Politics* 74: 672–84.

Jerit, Jennifer, Jason Barabas, and Toby Bolsen. 2006. "Citizens, Knowledge, and the Information Environment." *American Journal of Political Science* 50: 672–84.

Jewell, K. Sue. 1993. *From Mammy to Miss America and Beyond: Cultural Images and the Shaping of US Social Policy*. New York, NY: Routledge.

Jordan-Zachery, Julia S. 2009. *Black Women, Cultural Images, and Social Policy*. London: Routledge.

Kastellec, Jonathan P., and Eduardo L. Leoni. 2007. "Using Graphs Instead of Tables in Political Science." *Perspectives on Politics* 4: 755–71.

King, Gary, Michael Tomz, and Jason Wittenberg. 2000. "Making the Most of Statistical Analyses: Improving Interpretation and Presentation." *American Journal of Political Science* 44: 347–61.

King, Mae C. 1973. "The Politics of Sexual Stereotypes." *The Black Scholar* 4: 12–23.

Kuhn, Thomas S. 1962. *The Structure of Scientific Revolutions*. Chicago, IL: University of Chicago Press.

Malkin, Michelle. 2012. "Michelle Obama's 'Civilian' Act Is Hard to Swallow." Creators Syndicate, May 30. http://michellemalkin.com/2012/05/30/yes-michelle-obama-is-fair-game/ (accessed June 21, 2012).

Mayo, Edith P., and Denise D. Meringolo. 1994. *First Ladies: Political Roles and Public Image*. Washington, DC: National Museum of American History, Smithsonian Institute.

Media Matters for America. 2009. "Juan Williams Again Baselessly Attacked Michelle Obama, Claiming 'Her Instinct Is to Start with This 'Blame America' . . . Stuff,'" January 27. http://www.blogher.com/frame.phpurl=http://mediamatters.org/items/200901270002 (accessed March 8, 2011).

Parry-Giles, Shawn J. 2000. "Mediating Hillary Rodham Clinton: Television News Practices and Image-Making in the Postmodern Age." *Critical Studies in Media Communication* 17: 205–26.

Paulson, Scott. 2012. "Opinion: Stop Michelle Obama! The Children Are Hungry." *CBS Baltimore*, September 26. http://baltimore.cbslocal.com/2012/09/26/stop-michelle-obama-the-children-are-hungry/ (accessed November 25, 2013).

Perry, Barbara A. 2004. *Jacqueline Kennedy, First Lady of the New Frontier*. Lawrence, KS, University of Kansas Press.

Phelps, Elizabeth A., Kevin J. O'Connor, William A. Cunningham, E. Sumi Funayama, J. Christopher Gatenby, John C. Gore, and Mahzarin R. Banaji. 2000. "Performance on Indirect Measures of Race Evaluation Predicts Amygdala Activation." *Journal of Cognitive Neuroscience* 12: 729–38.

POLITICO.com. 2012. Video: Michelle Obama's Many Political Appearances. POLITICO.com, May 11. http://www.politico.com/multimedia/video/2012/05/michelle-obamas-many-tv-appearances.html (accessed August 22, 2012).

Powell, Michael, and Jodi Kantor. 2008. "After Attacks, Michelle Obama Looks for a New Introduction." *New York Times*, June 18: A1.

Ressner, Jeffrey. 2008. "Michelle Obama Thesis Was on Racial Divide." POLITICO, February 22. http://www.politico.com/news/stories/0208/8642.html (accessed April 6, 2012).

Robinson, Michelle LaVaughn. 1985. Princeton-Educated Blacks and the Black Community. Senior Thesis, Princeton University.

Samuels, Allison. 2008. "Daring to Touch the Third Rail: Barack Obama Avoids Talking about the 'Race Issue,' but His Wife Doesn't. How Michelle Is Becoming the Point Person for African-American Votes." *Newsweek*, January 19: 4.

Saris, Wilem E., and Irmtraud N. Gallhofer. 2007. *Design, Evaluation, and Analysis of Questionnaires for Survey Research*. New York, NY: Wiley-Interscience.

Schaeffer, Nore Cate, and Stanley Presser. 2003. "The Science of Asking Questions." *Annual Review of Psychology* 29: 65–88.

Smith, Tom W. 1978. "In Search of House Effects: A Comparison of Responses to Various Questions by Different Survey Organizations." *Public Opinion Quarterly* 42: 446–63.

Smooth, Wendy. 2010. "African American Women and Electoral Politics: A Challenge to the Post-Race Rhetoric of the Obama Moment." In *Gender and Elections: Shaping the Future of American Politics*, ed. Susan Carroll and Richard Logan Fox, 165–86. New York, NY: Cambridge University Press.

Spiering, Charlie. 2012. "Michelle Obama: I Am More Popular than President." *The Examiner*, April 11. http://washingtonexaminer.com/michelle-obama-i-am-more-popular-than-president/article/1224966 (accessed March 20, 2012).

St. Clair, Stacy. 2009. "Michelle Obama Image Makeover: First Lady's Approval Ratings Soar as She Embraces Traditional Role—with a Modern Twist (Michelle Obama Adopts 'Everymom' Persona and Sidesteps Controversies)." *The Chicago Tribune*, April 28: C3–C5.

Stanley, Alesandra. 2008. "Michelle Obama Shows Her Warmer Side on 'The View.'" *The New York Times*, June 19: B1.

Stebner, Beth. 2013. "First Lady of Publicity? Outcry over Michelle Obama's FIVE Television Appearances in Past Two Weeks (And She'll Be on LIVE with Kelly and Michael on Monday)" *MailOnline*, February 26. http://www.dailymail.co.uk/news/article-2285074/First-lady-publicity-Outcry-Michelle-Obamas-FIVE-television-appearances-past-weeks.html#ixzz2ML44gQ5L (accessed March 1, 2013).

Thomas, Evan. 2008. "Alienated in the USA." *Newsweek*, March 13: 12–13.

Tobin, Leesa E. 1990. "Betty Ford as First Lady: A Woman for Women." *Presidential Studies Quarterly* 20: 761–67.

Tomz, Michael, Jason Wittenberg, and Gary King. 2001. *CLARIFY: Software for Interpreting and Presenting Statistical Results, Version 2.0*. Cambridge, MA: Harvard University, June 1. http://gking.harvard.edu (accessed May 18, 2011).

Tracey, Bree. 2012. "Michelle Obama Becoming the Most Televised First Lady." Fox News.com, April 22. http://www.foxnews.com/politics/2012/04/22/michelle-obama-becoming-most-televised-first-lady/ (accessed January 1, 2013).

Tulumello, Jennifer Skalka. 2012. "Michelle Obama's Transformation to First Lady Powerhouse." *The Alaska Dispatch*, September 4: A6–A7.

Vane, Edwin T., and Lynne S. Gross. 1994. *Programming for TV, Radio, and Cable*. Woburn, MA: Butterworth-Heinermann.

Wheeler, Mary E., and Susan T. Fiske. 2005. "Controlling Racial Prejudice: Social-Cognitive Goals Affect Amygdala and Stereotype Activation." *Psychological Science* 16: 56–63.

White, E. Frances. 2001. *Dark Continent of Our Bodies: Black Feminism and the Politics of Respectability*. Philadelphia, PA: Temple University Press.

Williams, Verna L. 2009. "The First (Black) Lady." *Denver Law Review* 86: 833–50.

Wojcicki, Janet, and Melvin B. Heyman. 2010. "Let's Move: Childhood Obesity Prevention from Pregnancy and Infancy Onward." *The New England Journal of Medicine* 362: 1457–59.

Wolcott, Victoria W. 2001. *Remaking Respectability: African American Women in Interwar Detroit*. Chapel Hill, NC: The University of North Carolina Press.

———. 1997. "'Bible, Bath, and Broom': Nannie Helen Burroughs's National Training School and African-American Racial Uplift." *Journal of Women's History* 9: 88–110.

Wolfe, Richard. 2007. "Barack's Rock: She's The One Who Keeps Him Real, The One Who Makes Sure Running for Leader of The Free World Doesn't Go To His Head. Michelle's Story." *Newsweek*, August 28: 12–18.

Research Article: Black Urban Leadership

Black Mayoral Leadership in New Orleans: Minority Incorporation Revisited

Stefanie Chambers
Trinity College
William E. Nelson, Jr.
The Ohio State University

Introduction

For over thirty years, the tradition of Black mayoral leadership was a characteristic of the political and cultural landscape of the Crescent City. As in many other urban areas, Black mayors in New Orleans became a centerpiece of municipal politics. From the election of the first Black mayor, Ernest "Dutch" Morial in 1979, through the tenure of Clarence Ray Nagin (2002–2010), Black mayors employed different leadership styles to advance their agendas and address the political, social, and economic needs of residents. With some exceptions (e.g., Stone 1989), studies of Black mayors and the politics manifested in their cities generally treat them as identical expressions of strong liberalism. In this paper, we analyze the performance of New Orleans' Black mayors in terms of the substantive benefits they offered their Black constituents. The question driving this study is whether different Black-led mayoral administrations responded to socially disadvantaged segments in their city differently depending on their governing ideologies.

The classic minority incorporation literature provides a theoretical roadmap for marginalized groups to find a seat at the policymaking table (Browning, Marshall, and Tabb 1984). There have been many criticisms of this theoretical framework for failing to present a realistic view of the challenges faced by Blacks and Latinos in urban America (Hero 1992; Persons 1993). In general, scholars contend that the social capital of Blacks is very much connected to their political status in the city (Orr 1999). However, the seminal study of Black Atlanta by Stone (1989) presents a city where liberal Black leaders ultimately became aligned with business interests and middle class Blacks, leaving the larger Black community with few tangible benefits. Stone's regime theory places all mayors generally in a framework that favors conservative political interests. The different leadership and governing styles of mayors, and notably minority mayors, is not seen as especially crucial under this approach. However, we argue that there is an important connection between Black social capital and leadership style. Both are important, but analyzing leadership style in New Orleans provides a unique opportunity to understand variations in leadership and how this variable affects the Black community.

In this study, Black interests are defined as policies aimed at eliminating the structural barriers that produce racial inequalities in the provision of public goods and services. Radical politicians best address the policy concerns of poor, urban minorities because they take on these issues as a central concern in their electoral and governing coalitions. In simple terms, radical leaders seek change that responds to the needs of the most politically neglected groups. Moderate mayors, however, bypass inequalities, often rooted in structural conditions and are thus significantly less responsive to the needs of inner-city poor minority groups. In practical terms, these leaders favor the status quo. Dawson (2001) makes a distinction between Black liberalism and Black liberal radicalism. These terms also explain the variation in the leadership style of New Orleans' Black mayors apart from the racialized versus deracialized categories. The differences between radical and moderate leaders have implications for the larger theoretical notion of minority political leadership.

Our conclusions are based on an application of multiple research methods. Because the electoral coalition of mayors is an important determinant of his or her leadership style, we analyzed the electoral coalitions of New Orleans' four Black mayors. This analysis was complemented by examining historical and political scholarship on Black leadership in New Orleans. We also conducted forty in-depth interviews with elected officials and community leaders from 2006 to 2010. We sought out respondents who had lived in the city during the period under investigation (1970–2010), or had a deep understanding of mayoral regimes during this period. These individuals included past and present city council members, former mayors, mayoral candidates, religious leaders, academicians, and community organizers. Respondents were asked to evaluate the different mayors in terms of their responsiveness to Black interests. We interviewed twenty-four community activists, seven elected officials, four ministers, four academics, and one journalist. Ninety percent of our respondents were Black.

We find that the impact of radical versus moderate Black mayors is of significant consequence in a racially unequal city such as New Orleans. Less radical Black leadership is believed to be the consequence of generational change among Black leaders in a "post-racialized" era (Gillespie 2009, 2012). Recent work by Andra Gillespie indicates that there is a growing political moderation among the most recent wave of Black leaders (2010). Studying the legacy of Black mayoral leadership in New Orleans is important for urban and Black politics scholars. It provides a rare opportunity to evaluate how Black mayoral leadership can influence the political empowerment of a large Black community.

We classify Mayors Dutch Morial (1978–1985) and Marc Morial (1994–2002) as radical leaders, and Mayors Barthelemy (1986–1994) and Nagin (2002–2010) as political moderates. While generational change plays a role in these distinctions, the emergence of different Black leaders, we contend, depends on factors such as the candidates' electoral coalitions and the broader political environments at the times of their elections. Radical leaders are less likely to promote policies that accommodate business interests, and more likely to respond to the needs and interests of Black constituents. In contrast, moderate Black mayors are more likely to accommodate business interests at the same time that they downplay the radical racial interests of the Black community. Our findings suggest that the emergence of another radical Black leader in New Orleans is a possibility, though much depends on the political environment and the electoral coalition behind such a leader. Given the impact of Hurricane Katrina on the Black community, rebounding from that catastrophe is of vital importance to the rise of another radical leader.

New Orleans in the Minority Political Incorporation Literature

The recent election of a Democratic White mayor in New Orleans aligns with a pattern seen in cities like Philadelphia, Baltimore, and Chicago. In New Orleans, Black voters overwhelmingly favored the White mayoral candidate in the 2010 election, something unthinkable only a few years earlier. Did the decades of Black mayoral leadership in New Orleans or Black political incorporation make this election uncontested or uncontroversial?

The minority incorporation literature suggests that incorporation in the political system, through trends such as the election of Black mayors, leads to policies that can address the concerns of the minority community. In other words, minority incorporation can contribute to minority political empowerment (Karnig and Welch 1980; Browning, Marshall, and Tabb 1984, 1997; Button 1989). In New Orleans, the deplorable position of the Black poor in the city, despite the political incorporation of Black mayors, challenges the idea that minority incorporation leads to minority empowerment. The stagnation of this community, despite its electoral power, left it essentially powerless when Katrina hit and during the post-Katrina recovery period (Dawson 2011). The continuing crisis that Blacks experience leads us to question the current conception of minority incorporation and subsequent empowerment.

While this scholarship, and especially the work of Browning, Marshall, and Tabb in *Protest is Not Enough* (1984), presents a compelling model that includes mobilization, incorporation, and ultimately the political empowerment of minority communities, it fails to capture the complex role of Black leadership style in the incorporation and empowerment process. Understanding this relationship offers a revised model of minority incorporation. The broader implication is that the Black underclass is less empowered, as its interests are not on the national political radar.

There have been two types of Black mayoral leadership in New Orleans: moderate and radical. Radical Black politicians have a vision more in line with Black power arguments, as shown by their focus on policy and reform, which benefit the Black community. Institutional racism, identified as the major barrier to the advancement of Blacks in the Black power framework, is targeted by radical minority leaders in their politics and policy objectives. In contrast, moderate Black leaders trust leadership within the Democratic Party, often pursue coalition politics, and favor instrumentalism as appropriate ways to solve urban problems. For our purposes, leaders who confront racial stratification and inequality are radical, whereas those who shy away from these racial issues are moderate.

Black mayors in New Orleans fall on this radical to moderate continuum, whereas the city's White mayors have been moderates and conservatives. Studies of Black members of Congress use a moderate to radical framework to evaluate leadership style and the policy repercussions of these different approaches (Cannon 1999; Tate 2010). This scholarship is very useful in evaluating Black mayors in New Orleans and elsewhere in the United States. Understanding the style of Black mayoral leadership—either moderate or radical—sheds light on the persistent economic, political, and social subordination of the Black underclass. It is also helpful in framing the history of a Black radical tradition as distinct from those of periods of White political liberalism (Dawson 2001).

The limits of urban policymaking for advancing the political, social, and economic position of minorities has not been systematically examined in the minority incorporation literature despite four decades since the first wave of Black mayors was elected. One reason for this omission is that it is very difficult to systematically examine policy outcomes across different mayoral administrations. When the minority incorporation literature emerged in the 1980s, it demonstrated the significance of minority office holding without integrating the existing literature on the limits of policy making in urban governments. Hero's theory of two-tiered pluralism made a very important contribution in this regard (1992). Addressing the unique situation of Latinos in the US political system, Hero demonstrates that procedural equality does not necessarily equate with substantive equality. In other words, minorities might be equal in a formal or legal sense, but it is a marginalized equality. Black mayors in New Orleans have largely been trapped in a governmental embodiment of this marginalization, which contributes to their inability to meet the needs of the Black poor. For some of New Orleans' Black mayors, this compromised position led to more moderate policy positions. Unfortunately, pursuing this leadership model diminishes the political power of the Black poor who might have power at the ballot box, but remain at the bottom of the governing coalition.

Ernest "Dutch" Morial: The First Black Mayor

Of all New Orleans Black mayors, Ernest "Dutch" Morial is renowned for achieving many "firsts" as an African American leader. Morial's roots as a Creole, a light-skinned African American of French Roman Catholic descent, influenced his political experience. Morial attended the city's first college preparatory high school for students of color, graduated from Xavier University in New Orleans, and was the first Black student to earn a law degree from Louisiana State University in 1954 (Lewis 2009). One of his five children would later follow in his footsteps and become mayor of New Orleans.

Any discussion of Dutch Morial's initial victory must be presented in light of the changing demographics of the city and the history in terms of racially moderate leadership style, which still generated Black voter support. Piliawsky's (1985) research documents the electoral coalition of the racially moderate mayor, deLepsseps "Chep" Morrison, who served from 1947 to 1963. During his administration, Morrison provided financial support to Black political organizations in exchange for their electoral support. In fact, this arrangement gave him over 90 percent of the Black vote (Liu and Vanderleeuw 2007, 55). However, it is worth noting that these early Black political organizations were not progressive or independent from the city's White political organizations. It was not until the passage of the Voting Rights Act in 1965 that strong and independent Black political organizations such as the Southern Organization for United Leadership (SOUL) and the Community Organization for Urban Politics (COUP) would emerge (Liu and Vanderleeuw 2007, 55).

Mayor Moon Landrieu (1970–1978) was the city's "first racially liberal mayor" (Piliawsky and Stekler 1991, 115). He appealed to Black leaders and organizations for support (Schexnider 1982). The Black political organizations COUP and SOUL supported Landrieu (Perkins 2002, 8). Unlike Morrison, who exercised a level of control over Black political organizations, Landrieu made his appeals to the established and independent leadership as an outsider. In return, he pursued policies that would help the Black community (Piliawsky and Stekler 1991, 115; Liu and Vanderleeuw 2007, 57). Liu and Vanderleeuw point out that during Landrieu's administration, Black city employment increased from 10 to 40 percent of all city jobs (2007, 57). Although some of the city's earlier White mayors made appeals to the Black electorate, especially when Black participation increased after the Supreme Court outlawed the White primary in 1944, Landrieu received the highest level of Black electoral support to that point. Landrieu's 1969 victory marked the first time a candidate received more support from Black voters than White voters (Liu and Vanderleeuw 2007, 57). By garnering about 40 percent of the White vote and over 90 percent of the Black vote, Landrieu's election shaped the campaign of Dutch Morial (Piliawsky and Stekler 1991, 115).

By the time of the 1978 election, Blacks were 42 percent of the city's voters (Piliawsky and Stekler 1991, 115). Dutch Morial made his first bid for mayor under these circumstances and campaigned heavily in the Black community, but also appealed to educated and wealthy Whites (Schexnider 1982). Because he was a Creole, the Black electorate found it hard to relate to Morial and he received only 58 percent of the Black vote in the primary. Even without total Black support, Morial had the largest percentage of primary votes, 26.6 percent. In the runoff election, he won 51.8 percent of the votes, including 95 percent of the Black vote and 20 percent of the White vote, to defeat a conservative White councilman, Joseph V. DiRosa (Liu and Vanderleeuw 2007, 60).

Although Dutch Morial was able to win the election with a majority of Black support, he was not a product of the Black political organization network (Liu and Vanderleeuw 2007, 60). Morial vocalized his position that these organizations were for sale to the candidate willing to give them the most money (Piliawsky and Stekler 1991). In fact, in the 1987 primary, the major Black political organizations (SOUL, COUP, OPPVL, and ROOTS) endorsed Morial's White opponents (Piliawsky 1985, 9). Despite the opposition of these organizations, Morial appealed directly to the Black electorate through radical policy positions. As one community respondent indicated:

> Dutch had a saying when he was running for the first time. "I'm going to promise meagerly, and deliver extravagantly." He understood that if you let it, the hopes of the Black community would exceed your ability to perform. I think some of the people who came after Dutch didn't realize or didn't care and promised Black voters the moon and stars with no intention of delivering. (Community Member Interview 2009a)

Morial managed to win the runoff election with 97 percent of the Black vote (53.4 percent of the total votes) (Liu and Vanderleeuw 2007, 61).

Once elected, Morial remained committed to the radical leadership style that appealed to his Black constituency. However, the city was experiencing staggering unemployment, gross misdistribution of income, and low educational attainment (Schexnider 1982). One community respondent explained:

Dutch got into office and inherited a cash strapped city with an enormous need for services. That created a problem. He proposed the earnings tax to be implemented for everyone who worked in New Orleans. It was perfectly legal in the state constitution, but the suburban legislators fought it tooth and nail. Dutch was committed to helping the underclass of New Orleans, but it was never an easy thing to do. (Community Member Interview 2008)

According to James R. Bobo, the New Orleans economy was plagued from the mid and late 1950s because of inadequate economic development. Due to the severe economic stagnation beginning in 1966, there were inadequate employment opportunities for a growing labor force (Bobo 1975). To complicate matters, Morial was not on good terms with some business leaders due to disagreements about the city's role in business affairs. Morial claimed he only wanted to ensure that the city benefited from the economic development and he criticized the press for blowing the disagreement out of proportion (Perry 2003, 233). It was not uncommon for the local press to characterize Morial as confrontational and combative, traits often ascribed to radical leaders. According to several of the respondents in this study, the media's ability to frame Dutch in a negative light limited some of his initiatives. One respondent noted:

Dutch didn't hold back if he was upset. That sometimes hurt him, especially in terms of helping the people who elected him in the first place.....White business leaders didn't like seeing an angry Black politician calling people out. Dutch's personality clashed with these people. Blacks had city hall, but Whites still controlled the economy. This was a small part of the problem Dutch had. (Community Member Interview 2006b)

Morial also faced considerable opposition to his economic plans from the City Council, specifically Council President Sidney Barthelemy, a powerful Black politician who later became mayor of New Orleans. Barthelemy's opposition weakened Morial's support in the Black community, and made it easier for the city council to oppose the mayor's agenda. Because Morial had not served on the council prior to becoming mayor, he was somewhat of a political outsider. Of the seven members of the council, five were Black and two White. Morial claimed that council members "expected his support for traditional patronage politics" in return for their vote for his policies (Perry 2003, 234). Morial's inability to gain the support of more than two council members severely undermined his effectiveness as mayor. As Perry articulated, "these competing forces in Black politics in New Orleans have severely limited the ability of Black political participation to produce public resources for African Americans" (2003, 234). Interestingly, Morial and Barthelemy were on opposite spectrums of the moderate versus radical leadership scale. Barthelemy's moderate position limited Morial's power to address the policy concerns of poor Blacks.

Not only did Morial lack the support of the council and business leaders, but federal aid to New Orleans was cut dramatically during the Reagan administration from $123 million in 1980 to $65 million in 1982 (Piliawsky 1985, 10). During Morial's eight years in city hall the Louisiana economy went from a $400 million surplus to a $500 million deficit. Consequently, New Orleans lost 155,000 jobs and witnessed a 10 percent drop in employment (Liu and Vanderleeuw 2007, 63). Morial tried enacting a number of programs including a progressive property tax based upon the size of a house and an earnings tax to generate revenue from persons who worked in New Orleans but lived elsewhere (Piliawsky 1985, 10). Morial lacked the necessary support and consequently a regressive sales tax hike was the only mechanism available to keep vital city services available to city residents. In 1983, Morial proposed *The Mayor's Job Equity Plan*, which mandated that all city funded construction jobs hire at least 25 percent minority and 10 percent female workers (Piliawsky 1985, 15). This program is one of the best examples of the substantive benefits Morial delivered to the middle-class Black community.

New Orleans faced a $60 million deficit in 1985. Despite Morial's efforts to create a progressive tax system and to cut nonessential services, his efforts largely failed and he was forced to rely again on regressive sales tax increases to fund the government. As Piliawsky has noted:

> The result is that the poor, predominantly Black population of New Orleans is now saddled with the nation's highest sales tax of 9 cents—the burden of which falls heaviest on the poor and near-poor, but with no improvement in public services or public schools, both of which are among the nation's worst. (Piliawsky 1985, 11)

Morial's plan for economic improvement centered on expanding the private sector so the poor could find new jobs and avoid dependence on low-wage government service jobs. In 1980, *Black Enterprise* magazine reported that, "No Black mayor in the country is more committed to Black economic ambitions through alliance with corporate capital than Ernest Morial in New Orleans" (Piliawsky 1985, 12). During Morial's administration, two billion dollars from state oil revenue was spent on construction in the central business district. The economic boom immediately helped the White business community, but the Black underclass reaped few benefits (Piliawsky 1985, 13). One Black resident lamented:

> The city skyline changed, but there's nothing in it for us in terms of ownership. The principal beneficiaries of his economic development programs were in the White—as opposed to the Black—business community. (Liu and Vanderleeuw 2007, 61)

Dutch Morial's Legacy: Radical Leadership and Limited Black Advancement

Although Morial tried twice to change the mayoral two-term limit, voters opposed it on both occasions (Perry 2003, 248). Assessments of Morial's effectiveness in elevating the position of Blacks remains mixed. Like so many other Black mayors, Morial was limited by the political and economic situation of the times—federal retrenchment, unwillingness of state officials to substantially help a majority Black city, White and middle class flight to outlying areas, and general economic stagnation. Opposition by a moderate Black leader also diminished Morial's power in terms of elevating the position of Blacks. In addition, Morial presided over a city with a failing school system and a police department with a reputation for corruption and brutality against the Black population. Despite these limitations, Morial was able to create important symbolic and substantive benefits for Blacks. One community respondent commented:

> He was elected mayor and appointed African Americans to key boards and commissions, and jobs in city hall. African Americans had friends in city hall. They could call about getting the streets done, or getting the grass cut, or the parks serviced for their children. That was a significant improvement because even though these things improved (with?) Landreau, it was different with Dutch. You went to church with these people, they were your neighbors, you went to school with them growing up. You could just pick up the phone and call them. We couldn't do that when Whites were in there. (Community Member Interview 2009b)

During Dutch Morial's tenure, the number of Black municipal department heads increased by 58 percent (Perry 2003, 241). The Black middle class also expanded from 10 percent in 1970 to 31 percent in 1985 (Perry 2003, 245). Unfortunately, while he was able to help the Black middle class through jobs and minority set-aside programs, the Black underclass experienced few gains in the areas of its greatest needs: employment, education, and police services (Piliawsky 1985, 18). Still, many respondents identified specific examples of attempts by Morial to elevate issues that mattered to lower class Blacks. One academic respondent commented that:

> Dutch was aggressive in terms of economic development for poor Black residents, something I don't think he got credit for. The media focused on his delivery, not the substance of his message. And, although the middle class and educated Blacks benefitted more under Dutch in terms of jobs and contracts, he tried to help others too. (Academic interview 8 January 2008)

Sidney Barthelemy: A Moderate Black Leader

A New Orleans Native, Sidney Barthelemy was educated in the city's parochial schools and earned a degree in philosophy at St. Joseph Seminary. After receiving a Master's of Social Work at Tulane University, Barthelemy worked in the nonprofit sector before joining the Landrieu Administration as Director of the Department of Welfare from 1972 to 1974. In 1974, he was elected to the Louisiana State Legislature, an experience that would later help him work with the state when he became mayor of New Orleans. After four years in the legislature, Barthelemy was elected to an at-large seat on the New Orleans City Council, a position he held until his election as mayor in 1986.

With Dutch Morial's departure from the mayor's office through term limits, Barthelemy saw an opportunity to pursue the seat held by his political nemesis. Not surprisingly, Barthelemy's policy positions and electoral coalition differed sharply from those of Morial. Barthelemy avoided the racial issues associated with Morial's tenure in favor of policies supported by the White community, such as a city lottery, a French Quarter gaming casino, and a theme park. Respondents in this study were agreed that Barthelemy was the candidate recruited by the White business establishment for the position. As one former city council member noted:

"I think what happens in New Orleans is that the White community seeks a Black candidate they perceive as less aggressive and with a less redistributive agenda. That's what happened with Sidney [Barthelemy] and Nagin" (Elite Interview 2007).

For Whites who felt "left out" during the Morial years, the new direction taken by this Black mayor was embraced (Piliawsky and Stekler 1991). One respondent noted:

> Sydney engendered a relationship with the White community. He basically became their pawn and they basically got everything they wanted that had been taken from them by Dutch Morial. (Community Member Interview 2007)

Whereas Dutch Morial was seen by Whites as an abrasive Black politician, Barthelemy capitalized on his image as a congenial and racially conciliatory Black alternative.

Barthelemy built an electoral coalition dominated by Whites. His policy positions, opposition to Morial while on the city council, and his deracialized campaign were all reassuring to White voters. Barthelemy, unlike Morial, was able to secure the endorsement of the city's Black political organizations. Barthelemy was one of the founders of COUP and used his organizational ties to land his political appointment in Moon Landrieu's administration. However, the endorsement of Black organizations was not a guarantee that the rank and file Black vote would be delivered. One community respondent noted:

> Black organizations, particularly COUP, were really undercut when Dutch was reelected. The patronage that went to these people dried up during his term in office. Barthelemy's election resurrected Black political organizations or at least gave a certain segment of the Black middle class some influence again. (Community Member Interview 2006b)

Ultimately, Barthelemy's core coalition was composed of Black political organizations, White voters, fairly conservative White legislators, and members of the city council (Piliawsky and Stekler 1991).

Leading up to the 1990 mayoral race, approval of Mayor Barthelemy among both Blacks and Whites reached record lows. A poll in late 1987 showed Barthelemy with a 76 percent approval rate. By 1988, his approval rate had fallen below 50 percent—50 percent among Blacks and 48 percent among Whites (Perkins 2002, 27). For Blacks, the inability of the mayor to address the skyrocketing crime and murder rates was a driving force in their dissatisfaction (Perkins 2002). For Whites, the mayor's inability to deliver on his economic promises led to a drop in their approval.

Still, Barthelemy carried the election with 55 percent of the vote to his liberal White challenger, Donald Mintz. However, the racial composition of Barthelemy's electoral coalition completely shifted in this election. Whereas his first victory was primarily due to White support, in 1990, he captured 86 percent of the Black vote and 23 percent of White votes (Perry 1990). The challenger, Mintz, received 75 percent of the White vote and 14 percent of the Black vote. While Barthelemy depended on Black political organizations in his first mayoral bid, he was more beholden to Black ministers for delivering the Black vote in the 1990 race. However, in 1990 there was a dramatic decline in Black turnout despite having a viable Black incumbent with a White opponent (Perry and Stokes 1987). A respondent in this study commented:

> Sidney's reelection was more about the tradition of Black mayors in New Orleans. He was supported by Blacks because the thought of losing the mayor's office was unthinkable . . . so, even hanging onto a Black mayor who didn't have a great record in terms of delivering to the Black community was better than the alternative, but this was not an election where you could claim that the Black community was happy with Sidney's first term. (Academic interview 9 January 2008)

Sidney Barthelemy's Legacy: Moderate Leadership and Black Stagnation

Barthelemy's moderate leadership style appears to have helped him win reelection, but not in terms of addressing the policy concerns of the Black underclass. Much of Barthelemy's agenda centered on business development. Some of the highlights under his stewardship include: the Aquarium of the Americas, the Riverfront Streetcar, and legalization of riverboat gambling. At the same time, he was also concerned about granting city contracts to Black-owned businesses. However, while he was sensitive to issues that affected the Black middle class, he was primarily concerned with overall economic development for the city. Whereas Whites initially supported Barthelemy in the hope that he would reverse some of the trends associated with the Morial years, he was unable to deliver on those promises. For example, under Morial, the White unemployment rate increased from 6.09 to 10.36 percent (Liu and Vanderleeuw 2007, 63). Barthelemy's inability to meaningfully improve this situation was probably one of the reasons the White community opposed him during his second election.

New Orleans also continued to be affected by the decline in federal grants during the Reagan administration. Barthelemy decided to raise money for the city by expanding tourism and improving the New Orleans International Airport:

> When you compare New Orleans to other cities, you have to look at the revenue generators—Chicago's income tax and Atlanta's airport. We need a major economic project to see economic progress and Black business involvement. If we go back and check the history books, there were some Black business [sic] in Atlanta, but it wasn't until the airport development that a significant turnaround emerged. (Liu and Vanderleeuw 2007, 63)

An economic glimmer of hope occurred during Barthelemy's second term. With the city on the verge of a fiscal disaster, the mayor was able to refinance $165 million of the city's bonded debt. Through refinancing, Barthelemy boosted the city's operating budget by $35 million and kept the juvenile justice system functioning (Perkins 2002, 34). In addition, the state legislature gave the city $145 million for several projects such as the expansion of the convention center and improvements to Charity Hospital. Observers credit Barthelemy's experience in the state legislature and the relationships he developed there for some of the economic support the city received. Barthelemy spent the bulk of his final years in office trying to work with the governor to create a casino in New Orleans that would benefit the city economically. Although the casino would not materialize until the next mayor was in office, Barthelemy laid the groundwork. The federal government also came through during Barthelemy's second term with money for the University of New Orleans ($10 million), local housing ($17 million), and Lake Pontchartrain Basin projects ($21.4 million) (Perkins 2002, 35).

Despite the financial assistance from the state and federal governments during Barthelemy's second term, the increase in violent crimes during his tenure received national attention. In 1992, the US Justice Department ranked New Orleans first in reports of police brutality between 1985 and 1990 (Perkins 2002, 37). Murders and criminal offenses increased dramatically. Furthermore, Barthelemy's propensity toward cronyism would follow him throughout his term as mayor. In addition to reports that he received free trips in exchange for city contracts, he offered his son one of the city's coveted municipal scholarships for full tuition at Tulane University. Meanwhile, the unemployment rate among Blacks remained staggering and the Black underclass continued to struggle. The bottom line was that the moderate leadership style of Barthelemy did not advance policies that could reduce the racial inequalities in the city.

Marc Morial: Radical Leadership and "The Most Popular Black Mayor"

Marc Morial, the son of Dutch Morial, followed in his father's footsteps in terms of his career path as an attorney in New Orleans, and as mayor of their hometown. Before running for mayor, Morial cut his political teeth through involvement with politics at the national and state levels. Morial worked as a key player in Jesse Jackson's New Orleans satellite campaign during the 1988 presidential race. In 1990, Morial mounted an unsuccessful bid for an open seat in the U.S. House of Representatives against then Louisiana State Senator William Jefferson. Despite Morial's loss in the congressional race, he was elected as Jefferson's successor in the state senate in 1991 (Perry 1990). In 1994, at the age of thirty-six, Morial was elected mayor of New Orleans in one of the most racially polarized races in the city (Liu and Vanderleeuw 2007).

By the 1994 election, Blacks comprised 65 percent of the city population and were 54.4 percent of registered voters. Violence in the city rose to record levels, with the murder rate reaching 396 a year. According to a study conducted by Howell and Marshall, the crime and drug epidemic in New Orleans caused Black confidence in local Black leadership to decline (1998). In the 1994 election, Morial faced off against nine other opponents, five of whom were White. Morial was the most formidable Black candidate and was endorsed by New Orleans' Black newspaper, *The New Orleans Tribune.* The paper acknowledged the lingering problems plaguing the Black community despite the two Black mayors, but said:

> To those who say that Blacks have occupied city hall since 1978 and perhaps it is the time to give it up, we say 16 years of governance by African Americans is a very short time in the 275 year history of our city, we also contend that those problems now facing us are not of 16-years' making, but the result of the 200 years of real violence of slavery, poverty, miseducation and economic deprivation. (Liu and Vanderleeuw 2007, 67)

Marc Morial used the lack of Black empowerment in the city as the centerpiece of his radical leadership campaign.

Black political organizations played a minor role in both the 1994 and 1998 elections. By this time, there were a number of ward-based Black political organizations. Louisiana Independent Federation of Electors (LIFE) was the primary backer of Morial, but this organization, like the others, functioned in a unique way. Rather than taking contributions, these groups started endorsing candidates who paid the organization to hire staff and organize publicity for the particular campaign. So, while these groups helped some Blacks vote, they operated more as "insurance policies" for candidates who paid them for electoral support (DuBos and Johnson 1997).

Among the field of White mayoral candidates in 1998 was Mitch Landrieu, the son of the former mayor, Moon Landrieu. However, Landrieu was not the most formidable opponent for Morial. That designation belonged to Donald Mintz who launched a second consecutive run for mayor. Mintz's electoral strategy centered on deracialized appeals to the voters. One of his campaign brochures stated: "he believes in a New Orleans where we set aside our differences and focus instead on what we have in common." In this same brochure, he included photos of himself surrounded by Black residents. Thus, while his rhetoric was deracialized, he was also sending a message to Black voters that he was their candidate. Mintz won the primary with 39.6 percent to Morial's 32.5 percent of the vote (Liu and Vanderleeuw 2007, 67).

In the end, Mintz was entangled in an outrageous scandal that led to his defeat. Fake anti-Semitic pamphlets aimed at mobilizing the Jewish vote and contributors were created by his campaign staff, unbeknown to Mintz. According to most assessments, had this scandal not come to light, Mintz might have won, not Morial who took 54.5 percent of the vote in the runoff.

Morial did not have any Black challengers in 1998. He faced two unknown White candidates, lawyer Kathleen Cresson and arts store manager Paul Borrello (Perry 2003, 247). He easily won the primary with 79 percent of votes cast (37.5 percent of the White vote) (Liu and Vanderleeuw 2007, 68). Since he won a majority of the votes, there was no need for a runoff election. The attention Marc Morial brought to racial inequality in the city places him in the radical leadership category. His overwhelming support in the Black community and his rhetorical and policy pronouncements about elevating the position of the Black community contributed to his broad popularity among New Orleans' Blacks. He was now also popular with many White voters.

Despite Morial's popularity, the city remained in dire economic straits. Burns and Thomas thoroughly document the economic problems of the city between the 1960s through 2000. The loss of businesses and declining federal aid put New Orleans in an impossible position. The population decreased by 20 percent between 1960 and 1990. This decline reflected the continuing exodus of middle-class taxpayers from the city. The city also experienced a 3.3 percent decline in employment in the 1990s. This drop in employment was in sharp contrast to the tremendous job growth in cities such as Atlanta and Orlando during the same period (Burns and Thomas 2004, 795).

Morial ultimately worked with the Governor to create a land-based casino on the edge of the French Quarter and brought an NBA franchise to the city as revenue generators. Like so many big-city mayoral projects, these economic enticements often reflect a desperate move to stabilize the local economy and to attract people to the area. More often than not, they do not fulfill their objectives.

Despite his popularity in the Black community, at the end of his second term, he was unable to convince voters, even Blacks, that the term limit statute should be revised. Like many Louisiana politicians, at the end of his term, he also faced corruption charges.

Marc Morial's Legacy: Radical Leadership Style and Black Support

Although there were symbolic improvements for Blacks in New Orleans, some said the greatest beneficiaries were his friends and not the community as a whole. The limits of Black political advancement have more to do with the structural hurdles Morial faced than a failure of his radical leadership style. In fact, it was his commitment to police reform, a routine concern for New Orleans' Blacks, which resulted in significant improvements in crime statistics. One minister noted:

> Marc was a phenomenal coalition builder. He had a personality that made you respect him. He was the mayor out of all four who actually got a handle on crime and brought it down based upon selection of a very good police chief and alliance with the community. I think he was one of the brightest and most energetic leaders our city ever saw. (Minister Interview 2008)

Yet, these improvements did not mean that Blacks were empowered, as the minority incorporation literature would lead us to believe.

Nagin: Moderate Leadership with a Twist

Clarence Ray Nagin Jr. was born in New Orleans in 1956. He received a BA from Tuskegee and an MBA from Tulane University. Before entering political office, Nagin had a successful career as the vice president and general manager of Cox Communication. Although Barthelemy and Nagin differ in terms of their occupational background prior to their election to mayor, they gained distinction by garnering a majority of White support in their first elections, and relying on Black support in their reelection campaigns. Like Barthelemy, Nagin pursued racially moderate policies with the exception of the post-Katrina period where he used radical tactics to draw attention to the racial inequalities in the city. With the exception of this period, Nagin's leadership reflects the trend of racial moderation that has become more common in the United States today.

Economic development was the primary issue of the 2002 mayoral election. Nagin campaigned as a political outsider who could turn the city around economically because he was free from the political baggage of his predecessors. Originally a Republican, Nagin became a Democrat when he ran for mayor. Nagin's biggest opponent was Richard Pennington, the highly regarded African American police chief under Marc Morial. Pennington was favored in the election due to his record of cleaning up crime and corruption in the police department. Nagin beat Pennington in the primary by 6 percent. In the runoff, Nagin won a decisive majority. Even though the city's Black ministers supported Pennington (Carr, Nolan, and Young 2004), Nagin created a majority White electoral coalition that was 50 percent White in the primary and 86 percent White in the runoff. One respondent noted:

> I think he [Nagin] came across as a Black man who could work with White people on their agenda. He had obvious ties to the Republican Party and that helped a whole lot with crossover voters. He just seemed the kind of guy a lot of White people could say "are there any more like him you can bring around." (Community Member Interview 2006a)

Nagin received just enough crossover from Blacks to solidify his victory—40 percent in the runoff (Liu and Vanderleeuw 2007, 70). Nagin appealed to Whites because of his business background, entrepreneurial skills, pledges to increase tourism, root out corruption, and reform education (Liu and Vanderleeuw 2007, 102).

According to the 2000 Census, the Black population of New Orleans before the storm hit was approximately 68 percent. After the storm, it was estimated that the city had a slight White majority. Even a year after the storm, the Black population was estimated at only 53.7 percent, indicating that a substantial number of residents had not returned to the city (Liu and Vanderleeuw 2007, 4). Nagin's crisis mismanagement led to a massive change in his electoral strategy and coalition. Whites were no longer convinced that he could effectively lead the city. Once Nagin assumed a public presence after the storm, his rhetoric focused on the lack of support from the federal and state government. As time went on, he expressed frustration with the lack of influence he exercised over federal relief efforts (Connolly and Roig-Franzia 2005). However, many White voters interpreted Nagin's criticism of the federal government as a tactic to avoid criticism that he was under-qualified to handle a large-scale natural disaster.

Sensing the revolt against him in the White community, Nagin started a massive appeal to Blacks leading up to the election. In addition to the outreach to displaced Black voters, Nagin received national attention for his 2006 Martin Luther King Day speech's "chocolate city" remarks. This period marks Nagin's brief experimentation with a radical leadership style. During interviews, Black respondents often commented that Nagin's ability to articulate their concerns gave them hope that their policy priorities would become a national priority.

The 2006 election occurred in a city that was a dramatically different place. The mayoral primary consisted of twenty-two candidates, ten of whom were Black. However, with the exception of Nagin, no Black candidate received over 1 percent of the primary vote. Nagin's top challenger was Mitch Landrieu, Lieutenant Governor and former member of the state legislature. Landrieu challenged Marc Morial in the 1998 election, was the son of former mayor Moon Landrieu, and brother to Louisiana Senator Mary Landrieu.

The displacement of so many Black voters due to Katrina meant that racial politics would be different in this election. In an effort to make sure the displaced did not become disenfranchised, the NAACP, ACORN, and the Grassroots Legal Network filed a federal lawsuit to allow physical polling places in cities such as Houston and Atlanta where over 200,000 New Orleans families had relocated (Liu and Vanderleeuw 2007, 9). Although they lost the case, the organizations mounted a movement to urge evacuees to vote. Ultimately, more than six times more absentee ballots were requested in this election, 70 percent from Black voters (Liu and Vanderleeuw 2007, 10). Nagin also traveled to the cities where potential Black voters temporarily resided to urge them to vote. In addition, busloads of displaced Blacks were brought in to vote by the NAACP.

In the 2006 primary, Nagin received 72.9 percent of the votes cast by Black voters, but only 5.7 percent from Whites. In contrast to Nagin's majority Black coalition, Landrieu's primary vote was more racially balanced with 32.9 percent White and 21.9 percent Black support (Liu and Vanderleeuw 2007, 10). As Liu and Vanderleeuw explain, "the 2006 New Orleans mayoral runoff election shows that Black voters voted as a bloc at even a greater level than did White voters. The end result was that the 2006 New Orleans election continued that city's pattern of racially divided mayoral elections" (2007, 11). After the primary, Black registration surged by 21.1 percent compared to 2.1 percent among Whites. Nagin won reelection with 52.9 percent of the vote—83.3 percent of the Black vote and 20.5 percent of the White vote. Landrieu received almost 80 percent of the White vote and 17 percent of the Black vote. Blacks accounted for 55.6 percent of the total vote in the election (Liu and Vanderleeuw 2007, 11).

During our interviews, respondents were almost unanimous in their assessment that, before the hurricane, Nagin's focus was his pro-business agenda, which accomplished little in the wake of Katrina. His original electoral coalition selected him because he was a political outsider with extensive business experience. In the end, Nagin's limited political experience and his acrimonious relationship with the city council contributed to his inability to lead effectively after the hurricane.

Post-Katrina, many of Nagin's White supporters were able to evacuate the city. In contrast, Black constituents were vulnerable and without the necessary resources to deal with the effects of the storm. Nagin's neglect of these constituents during his first term made his strategic metamorphosis and direct appeals to Blacks quite ironic. Judging from his record during his second term and interviews with respondents for this study, this new populist front was merely an electoral strategy to retain his position as mayor. Because the Black community suffered such devastating losses in the hurricane, the symbolic value of the mayor's office was one thing they wanted to retain. Thus, Nagin was able to capitalize on these circumstances and secure a second term despite his inability to manage a disaster that further eroded the political, social, and economic resources in the Black community.

Legacy: Moderate Leadership and Catastrophic Failures

Like his predecessors, Mayor Nagin was limited to two terms. By the end of his second term, his approval had plummeted to the lowest levels ever seen in the city. Among White voters, Nagin's approval was about 5 percent in 2009. For Blacks, Nagin's approval fell during his last two years in office from 50 to 35 percent (Schwartz 2009).

The Nagin administration is reminiscent of the Barthelemy administration in several ways. First, the shift in strategy from a majority White electoral coalition to a majority Black coalition in the second term is strikingly similar. Both mayors realized that their political futures were tied to the electoral support of the Black community for their second election and, accordingly, appealed directly to this electorate. In both cases, the prospect of electing a White liberal mayor and losing the symbolic value of a Black mayor caused Blacks to support the incumbent. The main difference is that Nagin encountered a surge in electoral support from the Black community in his reelection, whereas Barthelemy experienced a relatively unenthusiastic Black voter base. Nagin's win can be attributed to his radical leadership style in the immediate post-Katrina period. One of the great disappointments of Nagin's tenure was his inability to translate the Black support he received in his second election into a permanent source of political strength for that community. The legacy of Nagin centers on poor crisis management, an inability to forge useful political coalitions, and a failure to deliver on his promise of economic development in the city. His legacy is currently evolving because of an indictment in January 2013 based on allegations of corruption during his time in office.[1] Our research indicates that the broken promises from his re-election campaign played an important role in the minds of Black voters who favored substantive politics over symbolic representation in the 2010 election.

Conclusion: Have New Orleans' Black Mayors Made a Difference?

The central question addressed in this paper is whether Black mayoral leadership style can influence the political incorporation and empowerment of the Black community. Through 40 in-depth interviews with community leaders and elected officials, we find clear evidence that radical leaders are more responsive to the interests of impoverished Black city residents. The findings from our interviews support our careful examination of electoral coalitions and analysis of the political legacies of New Orleans' Black mayors. Although there were clear limits in the ability of radical mayors like Dutch and Marc Morial to actually advance the situation of the Black poor, they were far more important to that community in terms of raising awareness of their plight and advocating public policies that responded to the needs of this community than Mayors Barthelemy and Nagin.

Incorporation has undeniably brought minorities into the political process. The electoral mobilization of minorities has been an important step in making our system more democratic, and it has led to greater minority incorporation in municipal governments. The symbolic value of Black elected officials remains extremely important in urban politics today. Black respondents in this study clearly believe that Black representation in government remains important in New Orleans. Our research helps to explain why: Radical

Black leaders prioritize policies that target racial inequality in New Orleans. This aspect of Black mayoral leadership is valuable because the leadership styles associated with most Black mayors brings greater attention to structural barriers that create racial inequality.

In some respects, a strong case can be made that Black mayoral leadership made little difference in terms of the economic, political, and social situation of New Orleans' Black underclass. Their vulnerability when Hurricane Katrina ravaged the city is one piece of evidence to support this argument. And, like Stone (1989), one could argue that Black leadership in New Orleans was closely linked to interests of White economic elites and only really helped the Black middle class. However, this assessment overlooks the significance of Black leadership style in a city like New Orleans. The forty interviews we conducted in the city indicate that there were noteworthy differences between radical and moderate leaders that mattered to the Black electorate. In fact, the endorsement of the Black electorate symbolizes the hope of this community that their candidate would engage in redistributive public policies. Radical leaders such as Dutch and Marc Morial did give voice to the Black population and delivered in some noteworthy ways. However, neither of the Morials was able to elevate the position of the Black underclass. Still, the overwhelming sentiment among the Black respondents in this study was that these mayors elevated the interests of the Black underclass; it is a group that remains off the political radar in New Orleans and at the national level.

Moderate leaders like Sydney Barthelemy and Nagin provide a more complex model of moderate Black leadership. Both mayors had majority White electoral coalitions in their first term, followed by Black majorities in the second. Although they appealed to Black voters the second time around, and in the case of Mayor Nagin, used radical rhetoric to appeal to Black voters, neither mayor was viewed by respondents as a leader with a significant interested in elevating Blacks in the city. Perhaps, this has something to do with their initial mayoral victories reliance on White business leaders' support. It could also be the case that they were limited to two terms and their first term centered on pleasing those who elected them to office. In Nagin's case, his rhetorical shift was clearly a post-Katrina response, as rising voices across the nation sympathized with New Orleans' poor in the aftermath of that disaster. The moderate leadership style of Barthelemy and Nagin were noteworthy in our interviews and led us to realize that at least in New Orleans, leadership style is significant.

While there is greater political responsiveness to minority interests in general, not all segments of such groups are empowered. In fact, empowerment of the least advantaged segments of communities may not be a natural byproduct of minority incorporation. As Hero's (1992) theory of two-tiered pluralism demonstrates, formal equality in urban American has opened the door for greater substantive equality through events like the election of minority officials in urban areas. However, these officials have faced structural limitations such as fiscal instability, the limited role of big-city mayors in national political debates, decades of federal retrenchment from urban issues, unresponsive suburban dominated state legislatures, and residents in need of many redistributive services. Addressing the policy needs of minority communities has been an uphill struggle that yields limited minority empowerment. When a mayor has a radical leadership style, there is a better chance that the policy priorities of minority communities will receive attention. Moderate politicians mostly shy away from these issues in favor of deracialized policies.

The result is a failure to fully realize minority empowerment. In fairness, the structural challenges faced by Black elected officials also limits their ability to address the needs of the minority community, even in the case of radical Black leaders. This situation is not dissimilar to Erie's findings in his study of machine politics and the position of new immigrant groups (1988). The proverbial economic bootstraps are fraying as cities can no longer provide upward mobility to newly incorporated groups. In New Orleans, the rise of Black mayors has provided a stepping-stone for some Blacks, but has not led to upward mobility and political empowerment for the community as a whole.

The path to greater minority empowerment in urban America is very much tied to the structural barriers that maintain a system of racial inequality in our cities. Because state legislatures heavily favor the issues of suburban residents, the prospects for progress rest with the federal government to create policies designed to level the playing field. Since many of these federal policies are framed in racially moderate terms, the role of radical leaders and electorally mobilized minorities is central to policy advancement for communities of color. Determining the exact path and prescription for minority empowerment remains an important priority for scholars. This study is a significant step in that direction.

Note

1.   These charges include bribery, wire fraud, falsified tax returns, and money laundering.

References

Bobo, James R. 1975. *The New Orleans Economy: Pro Bono Publico?* New Orleans: College of Business Administration, University of New Orleans.

Browning, Rufus P., Dale Rogers Marshall, and David H. Tabb. 1984. *Protest Is Not Enough*. Berkeley and Los Angeles, CA: University of California Press.

———. 1997. *Racial Politics in American Cities*. New York: Longman, Inc.

Burns, Peter, and Matthew O. Thomas. 2004. "State Government and the Development Regime in New Orleans." *Urban Affairs Review* 39, no. 6: 718–812.

Button, James W. 1989. *Blacks and Social Change*. Princeton, NJ: Princeton University Press.

Cannon, David T. 1999. *Race, Redistricting, and Representation: The Unintended Consequences of Black Majority Districts*. Chicago: The University of Chicago Press.

Carr, Martha, Bruce Nolan, and Tara Young. 2004. "Blessings and Condemnations." *The Times-Picayune*, March 28.

Community Member Interview. 2006a. Interview by Authors, July 19.

———. 2006b. Interview by Authors, July 20.

———. 2007. Interview by Authors, October 9.

———. 2008. Interview by Authors, January 8.

———. 2009a. Interview by Authors, July 7.

———. 2009b. Interview by Authors, August 12.

Connolly, Ceci, and Manuel Roig-Franzia. 2005. "A Shrinking New Orleans; Mayor Says Infrastructure Can't Support Previous Population." *The Washington Post*, October 26.

Dawson, Michael. 2001. *Black Visions: The Roots of Contemporary African-American Political Ideologies*. Chicago: University of Chicago Press.

———. 2011. *Not in Our Lifetimes: The Future of Black Politics*. Chicago: University of Chicago.

DuBos, Clancy, and Allen Johnson. 1997. "Street Politics in the Big Easy." *Campaigns & Elections*, September 9.

Elite Interview. 2007. Interview by Authors, July 7.

Erie, Steven P. 1988. *Rainbow's End: Irish Americans and the Dilemmas of Urban Machine Politics 1840– 1985*. Berkeley, CA: University of California Press.

Gillespie, Andra. 2009. "The Third Wave: A Theoretical Introduction to the Post-Civil Rights Cohort of Black Elected Leadership." *National Political Science Review* 12: 139–61.

———, ed. 2010. *Whose Black Politics?: Cases in Post-Racial Black Leadership*. New York: Routledge Press.

———. 2012. *The New Black Politician: Cory Booker, Newark and Post-Racial America.* New York: NYU Press.

Hero, Rodney. 1992. *Latinos and the US Political System: Two-Tiered Pluralism.* Philadelphia, PA: Temple University Press.

Howell, Susan E., and Brent K. Marshall. 1998. "Crime and Trust in Local Government: Revisiting a Black Empowerment Area." *Urban Affairs Review* 33, no. 3: 361–81.

Karnig, Albert K., and Susan Welch. 1980. *Black Representation and Urban Policy.* Chicago: University of Chicago Press.

Lewis, Edmund W., ed. 2009. "Morial Family Reflects on Dutch's Legacy and the Challenges Facing Barack Obama." *Louisiana Weekly*, February 2.

Liu, Baodong, and James M. Vanderleeuw. 2007. *Race Rules: Electoral Politics in New Orleans, 1965–2006.* New York: Lexington Books.

Minister Interview. 2008. Interview by Authors, January 9.

Orr, Marion. 1999. *Black Social Capital: The Politics of School Reform in Baltimore, 1986–1998.* Lawrence, KS: University of Kansas Press.

Perkins, Lyle Kenneth. 2002. "Failing the Race: A Historical Assessment of New Orleans Mayor Sidney Barthelemy, 1986–1994." History Master's Thesis, Louisiana State University.

Perry, Huey L. 1990. "The Reelection of Sidney Barthelemy as Mayor of New Orleans." *PS: Political Science and Politics* 23: 156–57.

———. 2003. "The Evolution and Impact of Biracial Coalitions and Black Mayors in Birmingham and New Orleans." In *Racial Politics in American Cities*, ed. Rufus P. Browning, Dale Rogers Marshall, and David H. Tabb. New York: Longman, Inc., 227–254.

Perry, Huey L., and Alfred Stokes. 1987. "Politics and Power in the Sunbelt: Mayor of New Orleans." In *The New Black Politics: The Search for Political Power*, ed. Michael B. Preston and Lenneal J. Henderson, Jr. New York: Longman, Inc., 222–255

Persons, Georgia A. 1993. *Dilemmas of Black Politics: Issues of Leadership and Strategy.* New York: Harper Collins Publishers.

Piliawsky, Monte. 1985. "The Impact of Black Mayors on the Black Community: The Case of New Orleans' Ernest Morial." *The Review of Black Political Economy* 13, no. 4: 5–23.

Piliawsky, Monte, and Paul Stekler. 1991. "From Black Politics to Blacks in the Mainstream: The 1968 New Orleans Mayoral Election." *The Western Journal of Black Studies* 15: 114–21.

Schexnider, Alvin J. 1982. "Political Mobilization in the South: The Election of a Black Mayor in New Orleans." In *The New Black Politics: The Search for Political Power*. Eds. Michael B. Preston and Lenneal J. Henderson, Jr. New York: Longman, Inc. New York: Longman, Inc., 221–238.

Schwartz, John. 2009. "Term Limits Say New Orleans Mayor Can't Return; Residents Say They Don't Mind." *New York Times*, May 3.

Stone, Clarence N. 1989. *Regime Politics: Governing Atlanta, 1946–1988.* Lawrence, KS: University of Kansas Press.

Tate, Katherine. 2010. "Black Radical Voices and Policy Effectiveness in the US Congress." *The Forum* 8, no. 2: 1346.

Current Issue Analysis: The Supreme Court's *Shelby County v. Holder* Decision

Reflections on *Shelby v. Holder*

Christina Rivers
DePaul University

The Supreme Court's decision to strike down Section 4 of the Voting Rights Act in *Shelby County v. Holder* (2013) demonstrates how, to borrow from Tyson King-Meadows, the judiciary has employed the letter of the Voting Rights Act (VRA) to betray its spirit.[1]

In 1965, Congress passed the VRA to enforce and enhance the Fifteenth Amendment. Obstacles to voter registration still existed at that time, and included insufficient availability of registrars and registration sites and times, and disproportionate purges of minorities from voter registration rolls. Other obstacles such as insufficient polling places, hours, and staff, last-minute relocation or closures of polling places, insufficient notice of such changes, and inadequate enforcement of fair election procedures also impeded the act of voting.

Due to the severity and pervasiveness of such problems in the former Confederate states, Section 5 of the VRA initially targeted those areas for federal scrutiny in order to eradicate existing and to prevent further racial discrimination at the polls. Over time, Congress has added other regions under this provision. Section 5 compels covered areas to submit any changes of electoral plans to the Department of Justice for preclearance before those plans could go into effect. Section 5 scrutiny is triggered by two provisions. Section 4 identifies areas with a sustained history of discrimination and it "bails in," or adds, those regions to undergo the Section 5 preclearance process. Section 4 also allows covered regions that can demonstrate nondiscriminatory electoral procedures for ten years to "bail out" of federal scrutiny. Section 3 "bails" in regions demonstrating recent or recurring evidence of racially discriminatory electoral procedures.

Taken together, and typically referred to as Section 5, Congress intended all three provisions as measures to prevent states and localities from engaging in discriminatory electoral practices based on the arguable premise of a states' rights or dual federalism principle. Not surprisingly, Section 5 has been highly controversial since its initial passage. Given the tenacity of such discrimination, however, Congress has extended Section 5 three times; the last two extensions were for unusually long periods of twenty-five years.

As I have argued elsewhere, since 1993 in *Shaw v. Reno*, the Supreme Court has rendered decisions that reveal the majority's constricted and ahistorical reading of the VRA and its relevant constitutional provisions.[2] That majority has also reinterpreted or dismissed Congress' remedial intent for those laws. This is how in *Shelby County*, the Court nullified Section 5 by invalidating Section 4. According to the majority's rationale, the Fifteenth Amendment "is not designed to punish for the past; its purpose is to ensure a better future." Regarding the 2007 reauthorization of Section 5, it contended that Congress essentially ignored itself in that "it did not use the record it compiled to shape a coverage formula grounded in current conditions. It instead reenacted a formula based on forty-year-old facts having no logical relation to the present day."[3]

A number of justices have vigorously dissented against the *Shaw v. Reno* and the *Shelby County* decisions. In particular, Justice Ginsburg's approach to minority voting rights demonstrates an historical and nuanced understanding of the legislative intent for the VRA as well as the post-Civil War Fourteenth and Fifteenth Amendments. In her *Shelby County* dissent, she asserted that the Court majority, not Congress, ignored the legislative record that the latter brought forth in 2007: "hardly showing the respect ordinarily paid when Congress acts to implement the Civil War Amendments . . . the Court does not even deign to grapple with the legislative record." The result, according to Ginsburg, is the "sad irony" that the Court would strike down a key provision of the VRA as unnecessary while "utter[ly] fail[ing] to grasp" why that provision has made the VRA so effective.[4]

The *Shelby County* decision does not simply exemplify the Supreme Court's narrow voting rights jurisprudence. It also weakens the VRA and federal protection of minority voting rights in the South and other problematic regions. It is easily among the most serious judicial erosions of the Second Reconstruction to date. Yet, it is important to note here that neither the original nor the Second Reconstruction were completed *and* sustained. The First Reconstruction was successful, especially electorally, until national political and judicial institutions allowed southern states to dismantle it. The Reconstruction of the 1960s, on the other hand, has been more durable and better enforced for a longer period than in the previous era. The Supreme Court was instrumental in enforcing the VRA until the 1990s. The progress toward racial equality that the Second Reconstruction had brought about cannot be completed or sustained without a strong and enforced VRA.

Congress must, thus, restore Section 4. The Fourteenth and Fifteenth Amendments of the Constitution clearly grant it the authority to do so. And Congress reauthorized the VRA in 2007, precisely to reassert its intent and authority to negate what it saw as state and judicial erosions of the VRA in *Shaw v. Reno*, *Miller v. Johnson*, *Bossier Parish*, and *Georgia v. Ashcroft*. In that instance as well as in the 1975 and 1982 reauthorizations of Section 5, there was significant bipartisan cooperation. Key figures in the Republican Party also joined an *amicus curiae* brief supporting the respondents and endorsing Section 5 in *Shelby County*.[5] Unfortunately, it is highly unlikely that legislators can restore Section 4 amid the partisan and ideological tensions that currently grip Congress.

Even if Congress did manage to pull that off, doing so may amount to little more than another salvo in the ongoing battle between the legislative branch on the one hand and a judicial branch on the other that is clearly hostile to Sections 3–5 and the remedial purposes behind them. For example, in 2009, the Court upheld Section 5 in *Northwest Austin v. Holder*. The 8-1 decision (unusual for its voting rights verdicts) nonetheless belied its disdain for Section 5. Implicitly, it threatened Congress to repeal that provision. Congress did not respond, effectively calling the Court's bluff. In *Shelby County*, the Court majority made good on its threat by invalidating Section 4 instead of Section 5. Throughout these developments, minority political power is caught between institutional crossfires.[6]

For now, the Justice Department is more aggressively enforcing Section 3 of the VRA. The Attorney General and civil rights organizations are currently seeking to bail in Texas based on recent electoral changes that are potentially racially and ethnically discriminatory. If they succeed, Texas would again be under federal scrutiny for at least ten years.[7] Additional efforts to mitigate *Shelby* must include expanding ongoing voter education, registration, and turnout drives. This includes sustaining the high Black turnout seen in recent presidential elections, and increasing it in mid-term and primary elections. Efforts must also be made to remedy the intertwined problems of disproportionately high incarceration rates among African Americans, pervasive felon disenfranchisement laws, and prison-based gerrymandering practices that, taken together, suppress an alarming number of potential Black voters. This includes exerting far more pressure on the forty-eight states that disenfranchise prisoners to ensure that ex-felons who re-enter civil society do so with full citizenship rights. Here, coalitions between African American and Latino voting rights advocates are key. The political power of both groups is diluted by electoral discrimination, mass incarceration, and felon disenfranchisement. Restored voters among both groups would be inclined to reform those laws. Thus, the political fates of Black and Latino voters are more tightly linked than public opinion tends to acknowledge.[8]

Ultimately, however, the Supreme Court majority must reconsider its narrow interpretation of the VRA, along with its reliance on the unrealistic, ahistorical, and retrogressive aspects of color-blind constitutionalism. Absent such reconsideration, Black voting and political power will remain constrained by institutional and ideological battles over the role of race in the American democratic experiment.

Notes

1. Tyson King-Meadows, *When the Letter Betrays the Spirit: Voting Rights Enforcement and African American Participation from Lyndon B. Johnson to Barack Obama* (Lanham, MD: Lexington Books, 2011), ix–xx, 72–73, 121–58.
2. Christina Rivers, *The Congressional Black Caucus, Minority Voting Rights, and the U.S. Supreme Court* (Ann Arbor, MI: University of Michigan Press, 2012), 126–49.
3. *Shelby County v. Holder*, 557 US 193, 20–21.
4. Justice Ginsburg dissenting in *Shelby County v. Holder*, 557 US 193, 1–8, 13–23, 36.
5. Rivers (2012, 87–98). Brief of Rep. F. James Sensenbrenner Jr., John Conyers Jr., Steve Chabot, Jerrold Nadler, Melvin L. Watt, and Robert C. Scott as Amici Curiae in Support of Respondents in *Shelby County v. Holder*, http://www.americanbar.org/content/dam/aba/publications/supreme_court_preview/briefs-v2/12-96_resp_amcu_reps.authcheckdam.pdf (accessed October 31, 2103).
6. Rivers (2012, 64–101, 143–46, 167).
7. Lyle Denniston, "Key Date for Test of Voting Law's Preclearance Requirement," *SCOTUSblog*, July 18, 2013, http://www.scotusblog.com/2013/07/key-date-for-test-of-voting-laws-preclearance-requirement/ (accessed October 31, 2013); Lyle Denniston, "Texas Fights New Voting Supervision," *SCOTUSblog*, August 6, 2013, http://www.scotusblog.com/2013/08/texas-fights-new-voting-supervision/ (accessed October 31, 2013).
8. Michael Dawson, *Behind the Mule: Race and Class in African-American Politics* (NJ: Princeton, 1995), 76, (internal citations omitted). I am using a broad interpretation of Dawson's thesis that linked fate "explicitly links perceptions of self-interest to perceptions of racial group interests."

Trends

Black Women State Legislators—Electoral Trend Data 1995–2011

B. D'Andra Orey
Jackson State University
Nadia E. Brown
Purdue University

Arguably, the Voting Rights Act (VRA) of 1965 is the most effective piece of civil rights legislation passed by Congress. It was designed to prohibit the discrimination of voting based on race or color. Since the passage of the VRA, minority voting research has evolved over "four generations" (Davidson and Grofman 1994). In their study of voting rights from 1965 to 1990, Davidson and Grofman (1994) indicate that first-generation research questions evaluate minority enfranchisement; second-generation questions deal with vote dilution and the election of minority candidates; third- and fourth-generation research questions examine whether or not the success of electing minority officials translates into substantive gains for the masses. The first- and second-generation research examines "descriptive" representation, while third- and fourth-generation research examines "substantive" representation. Descriptive representation is when the representative resembles those he or she represents (Pitkin 1967). In other words, what are the physical characteristics of those elected? Are they members of underrepresented groups? Substantive representation focuses on whether those who are elected to political office represent their constituents (Pitkin 1967).

Once in office, scholars argue that Black women are positioned to be aware of and respond to the demands of diverse interests of racial/ethnic and gender representation (Brown 2014). This finding illustrates that Black women legislators are more likely to view race/ethnicity and gender as intersectional forms of representation (Barrett 1995, 1997; Carroll 2002; Lisa, Tate, and Wong 2005; Bratton, Haynie, and Reingold 2007). While it is clear that the VRA has been instrumental in vastly increasing the number of people of color who are elected to office, this has not been the case for the election of women. Indeed, the VRA does include a provision that is designed to improve women's representation, unless of course they are women of color.[1]

Using state legislatures, the purpose of this study is to investigate a variety of trends associated with the election of African American women, when compared to their male counterparts. The current data, derived from the Joint Center for Political and Economic Studies, track the number of African Americans elected to the state legislature from 1995 to 2011. The data reveal that African American men and women remain underrepresented in state legislatures in proportion to their presence in the US population. However, data from the Center for American Women and Politics (2013) indicate that African American women state legislators are at an all-time high.

In 2013, out of 7,776 female state legislators serving nationwide, 364 are women of color; of these, 239 are African American women. Currently, women of color only comprise 4.9 percent of all state legislators (Center for American Women and Politics 2013). African American women are central to African American political representation. Namely, African American women have achieved elective offices more than African American men since 1990 (Orey et al. 2006). Bositis finds (2001) that the increase in the number of African American elected officials can be attributed to African American women. While overall women's election to state legislatures has begun to languish (Sanbonmatsu 2006), African American women elected to state legislatures is on the rise—this population constitutes 13.5 percent of all women in state legislatures (CAWP Fact Sheet 2013). Since 1992, African American women and Latinas have outpaced African American and Latino men (Bositis 2001; Tate 2003; Lisa, Tate, and Wong 2005; Fraga et al., 2006; Smooth 2006). As a result, female legislators have become more racially and ethnically diverse. Gender diversity is higher between African American and Latinos than it is among White congressional and state legislators (Montoya, Hardy-Fanta, and Garcia 2000; Tate 2003; Lisa, Tate, and Wong 2005; Fraga et al. 2006; Smooth 2006; Bratton, Haynie, and Reingold 2007). These findings have been attributed to the creation of majority-minority districts (Smooth 2006; Carroll and Sanbonmatsu 2013).

According to Figure 1, there was a vast increase in the election of African American women to state legislatures ranging from 170 in 1995 to 241 in 2011. The number of men in comparison, however, remains stagnant over time. In fact, while the average number of African American male legislators is roughly 391, the numbers decline from 387 in 1995 to 381 in 2011. These numbers are consistent with the work of Smooth (2010) who concludes that, over the last ten years, all of the growth in the number of African American elected officials is attributed to the trends documenting the growth in African American women's representation. The pattern revealed in Figure 2 roughly duplicates that of Figure 1. Figure 2 illustrates that African American women's election to state legislatures has continued to grow. During that same period, Black men's election to state legislatures has remained the same. Figure 3 is the most illuminating among those presented here. According to these data, African American women state legislators appear to have made their greatest gains, when compared to their male counterparts in the upper chamber of the Senate. There has been a decline from ninety-three to eighty-five in the number of African American male state legislators, compared to a steep increase from forty-four to sixty-seven in the number of African American women.

The research here documents the concerns expressed in an earlier essay by Smooth (2012), whereby she examines the dearth of research conducted on African American women in politics despite the various gains made by this group over time. In her essay, Smooth notes how scholars and pundits alike failed to mention the gender gap in the African American community that helped to enhance Obama's victory in the 2012 presidential election. As per her assessment, women supported President Obama with 96 percent of their vote, compared to only 87 percent by African American men, a nine-point

Figure 1.
African-American State Legislators from 1995 to 2011

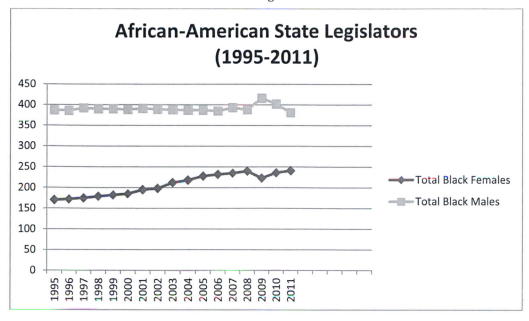

Source: Joint Center for Political and Economic Studies.

Figure 2.
African American State Legislators in the House from 1995 to 2011

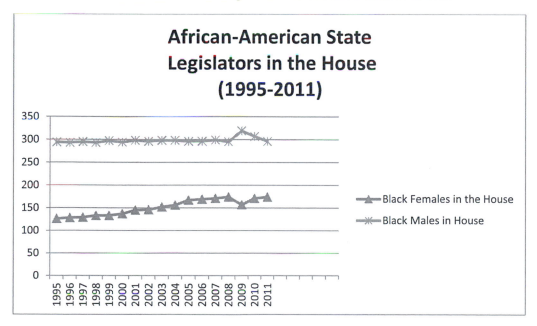

Source: Joint Center for Political and Economic Studies.

Figure 3.
African American State Legislators in the Senate from 1995 to 2011

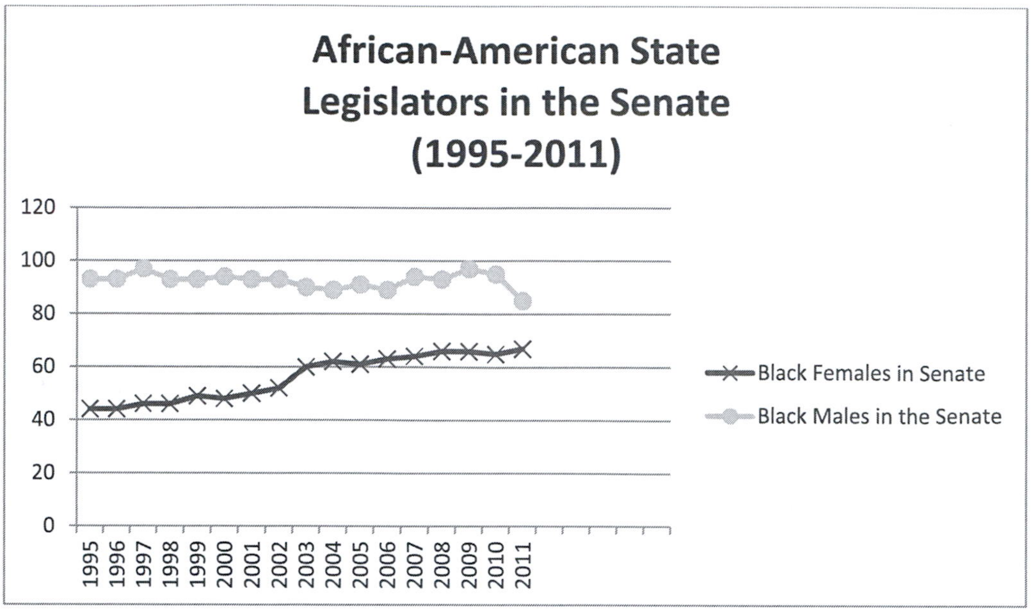

Source: Joint Center for Political and Economic Studies.

differential. She continues by stating that when scholars disaggregate the 13 percent of the electorate that consisted of African Americans during the 2012 election, roughly 8 percent were women. Smooth also recognizes that despite the dismal performances of the congressional candidates in the 2010 mid-term elections, all four of the Democratic newcomers to Congress were African American women. The sheer growing number of African American women elected officials speaks to the continued need to study this population. This trend suggests that women and politics scholars as well as Black politics scholars must begin to employ an intersectional analysis of identity. No longer can studies of political representation solely include discussions of race and not include gender and vice versa.

Note

1.   This assumes that the women are elected on the basis of their race in majority-minority districts where polarized voting occurs.

References

Barrett, Edith J. 1995. "The Policy Priorities of African American Women in State Legislatures." *Legislative Studies Quarterly* 20, no. 2: 223–47.
———. 1997. "Gender and Race in the State House: The Legislative Experience." *Social Science Journal* 34, no. 2: 131–44.
Bositis, David A. 2001. *Changing the Guard: Generational Differences among Black Elected Officials.* Washington, DC: Joint Center for Political and Economic Studies.
Bratton, Kathleen A., Kerry L. Haynie, and Beth Reingold. 2007. "Agenda Setting and African American Women in State Legislatures." *Women, Politics, and Public Policy* 28 (Summer/Fall): 71–96.

Brown, Nadia E. 2014. *Sisters in the Statehouse: Black Women and Legislative Decision Making*. New York, NY: Oxford University Press.

Carroll, Susan J. 2002. "Representing Women: Congresswomen's Perceptions of Their Representational Roles." In *Women Transforming Congress*, ed. Cindy Simon Rosenthal, 50–68. Norman: University of Oklahoma Press.

Carroll, Susan J., and Kira Sanbonmatsu. 2013. *More Women Can Run: Gender and Pathways to the State Legislatures*. New York, NY: Oxford University Press.

Center for American Women and Politics (CAWP). 2013. Women in State Legislatures 2013, *CAWP factsheet* New Brunswick, NJ: Eagleton Institute of Politics, Rutgers University.

Davidson, Chandler, and Bernard Grofman, eds. 1994. *Quiet Revolution in the South: The Impact of the Voting Rights Act, 1965–1990*. Princeton, NJ: Princeton University Press.

Fraga, Luis Ricardo, Linda Lopez, Valerie Martinez-Ebers, and Ricardo Ramírez. 2007. "Gender and ethnicity: Patterns of electoral success and legislative advocacy among Latina and Latino state officials in four states." Journal of Women, Politics & Policy 28, no. 3–4: 121–145.

García Bedolla, Lisa, K. Tate, and J. Wong. 2005. "Indelible Effects: The Impact of Women of Color in the U.S. Congress." In *Women in Elective Office, Past Present and Future*, ed. S. Thomas and C. Wilcox, 2nd ed., 152–75. New York: Oxford University Press.

Montoya, Lisa J., Carol Hardy-Fanta, and Sonia Garcia. 2000. "Latina Politics: Gender, Participation, and Leadership." *PS: Political Science and Politics* 33: 555–61.

Orey, Bryon D'Andra, Wendy Smooth, Kimberly S. Adams, and Kisah Harris-Clark. 2006. "Race and Gender Matter: Refining Models of Legislative Policy Making in State Legislatures." *Journal of Women, Politics, & Policy* 28, no. 3/4: 97–119.

Pitkin, H. F. 1967. *The Concept of Representation*. Berkeley, CA: University of California.

Sanbonmatsu, Kira. 2006. "State Elections: Where Do Women Run: Where Do Women Win?" In *Gender and Elections in America: Shaping the Future of American Politics*, ed. Susan Carroll and Richard Fox, 189–214. New York: Cambridge University Press.

Smooth, Wendy. 2006. "Intersectionality in Electoral Politics: A Mess Worth Making." *Politics & Gender* 2, no. 31: 400–14.

———. 2010. "African American Women in Electoral Politics: A Challenge to the Post-Race Rhetoric of the Obama Moment." In *Gender and Elections*, ed. Susan J. Carroll and Richard Fox, 2nd ed.,165–86. New York: Cambridge University Press.

———. 2012. "As if Black Women Mattered." *National Political Science Review* 15: 79–83.

Tate, Katherine. 2003. *Black Faces in the Mirror: African Americans and Their Representatives in the U.S. Congress*. Princeton, NJ: Princeton University Press.

Book Reviews

Book Reviews: Special Issue on
Black Women in Politics

While our colleagues in history continue to outstrip us in terms of sustained scholarly productivity in Black Women's Studies—a quick sample includes *Shirley Chisholm: Catalyst for Change* (Westview Press 2013) by Barbara Winslow; *Radicalism at the Cross-roads: African American Women Activists in the Cold War* (New York University Press 2011) by Dayo Gore; *Sojourning for Freedom: Black Women, American Communism, and the Making of Black Left Feminism* (Duke 2011) by Erik McDuffie; *Want to Start a Revolution? Radical Women in the Black Freedom Struggle* (New York University Press 2009) edited by Dayo Gore, Jeanne Theoharis, and Komozi Woodard; and *Women in South African History, Basus'iimbokodo, Bawel'imilambo/They Remove Boulders and Cross Rivers* (Human Sciences Research Council 2007) edited by Nomboniso Gasa—there has been an explosion of extraordinary works by Black women in politics scholars making important inroads into the study of the nature and lineage of power as well.

Wendy Smooth examines silence and violence in her review of Rachel Swarns's *American Tapestry: The Story of the Black, White, and Multiracial Ancestors of Michelle Obama*, a book concerned with the genealogy of the Obama Administration and its roots in enslavement. Brittany Lewis's review of *Still Brave: The Evolution of Black Women's Studies* edited by Frances Smith Foster, Beverly Guy-Sheftall, and Stanlie M. James explains that Black Women's Studies have contributed to the "academies most robust contemporary intellectual debates." Maylei Blackwell's *¡Chicana Power! Contested Histories of Feminism in the Chicano Movement* reviewed by T. Jackie Cuevas echoes this by noting that "women of color political subjectivities have gone largely unhistoricized because they often occurred *between* various and distinct social movements" (Blackwell 21). Stephanie Mitchem reviews the 2012 W. E. B. DuBois Distinguished Book Award winner *The Black Megachurch: Theology, Gender, and the Politics of Public Engagement* by Tammelyn Tucker-Worgs and its contribution to Black religious thought. Increasingly, the labors of love and solidarity of our colleagues in Race and Ethnic Politics and Gender Politics scholarship are beginning to coalesce around the interdisciplinary work, which has been a mainstay in Black Women's Studies.

We owe incredible debts to the historians of political movements, the historians of dry-longso practices of critical Black feminist consciousness, and those rare exemplars whose scholarship moves with ease between social movement history and the study of political consciousness and cultural production. Nadia E. Brown reviews *Sister Citizen: Shame, Stereotypes, and Black Women in America* by Melissa Harris-Perry with an eye toward the institutionalization of "misrecognition" and "public myths about black womanhood."

Zenzele Isoke reminds us of these critical Black feminist reading practices in her review of Katherine McKittrick's *Demonic Grounds: Black Women and the Cartographies of Struggle*. Such interdisciplinary texts model the capacity to listen to, amplify, theorize about, and expect Black women's "uncertain," "unpredictable," and unbowed political action. As the late Dr. Hanes Walton observed in reviewing Lisa Nikol Nealy's *African American Women Voters: Racializing Religiosity, Political Consciousness and Progressive Political Action in U.S. Presidential Elections from 1964 through 2008*, "the fact that African American women simply out-protested, out-participated, out-organized, out-mobilized, out-registered and out-voted African American males" goes under-examined in order to reproduce a set of power relations that normalize violence and silence historical memory. Ofelia Cuevas considers this in her review of three important texts on the prison industrial complex: *Arrested Justice: Black Women, Violence and America's Prison Nation* by Beth Richie; *Inside this Place, Not of It: Narratives From Women's Prisons* edited by Robin Levi and Ayelet Waldman; and *Visions of Abolition: From Critical Resistance to a New Way of Life* directed and produced by Setsu Shigematsu, Cameron Granadino, and Jolie Chea. Indeed, the role of Black women in the republic and the significance of the reproductive capacity of Black women as political metaphors and central figures in the material and economic architecture of the society shows up in the range of national conversations about the lives of people like Hadiya Pendleton, Sybrina Fulton, Renisha McBride, Susan Burton, and all the sisters shackled while bearing Black children in somebody's prison house. Several books reviewed here consider reproduction and "social reproduction" that dimension of parenting, which focuses on intergenerational ties that rear politically astute "sister citizens" among the next generations. These include: Mignon Moore's *Invisible Families: Gay Identities, Relationships, and Motherhood among Black Women* reviewed by E. Patrick Johnson; Andreana Clay's *The Hip-Hop Generation Fights Back: Youth, Activism, and Post-Civil Rights Politics* reviewed by H. L. T. Quan; and Cathy Cohen's *Democracy Remixed: Black Youth and the Future of American Politics* reviewed by Melina Abdullah. Taken together, they find that Black women's politics animate incredible levels of legislative and advocacy behavior as well as everyday politics of transformation and community building, even among people who have been most forcefully disabused of mythic notions about what citizenship and state inclusion can guarantee.

From the bevy of texts on Black feminist internationalists to those engaged with questions of Black women in defense of ourselves to the women of color scholars who are producing new analytics that further enable Black feminist histories of economic justice and social movements, the research agenda of Black Women's Studies continues to make impressive and long-lasting contributions.

Tiffany Willoughby-Herard
University of California, Irvine

Swarns, Rachel L. *American Tapestry: The Story of the Black, White, and Multiracial Ancestors of Michelle Obama* (New York: Amistad/Harper Collins, 2012), $16.99, 391 pp. ISBN: 978-0-06-199987-1 (trade paperback).

American Tapestry: The Story of the Black, White, and Multiracial Ancestors of Michelle Obama traces the roots of First Lady Michelle Obama starting with the DNA testing of a distant African American cousin who discovers through Rachel Swarns's investigation that she shares blood lines with the First Lady. The centrality of racial entanglements among Blacks and Whites becomes clear when Swarns repeats the same DNA test with a White woman who is also found to share blood lines with Mrs. Obama also as a distant cousin. With these two pieces of information in place, the tale then begins tracing the shared genealogical roots between the Black and White ancestors to weave together multiple generations of Mrs. Obama's family legacy. For many readers, this is a shocking tale of cross-racial, historically forbidden sexual entanglements that result in generations of Black and White families sharing blood lines without publicly acknowledging one another's existence. Though some will be shocked by the nature of these family ties, Swarns reveals through her investigation that Mrs. Obama's genealogical story is not at all unique. Many African Americans understand this reality as one of the key, even if unspoken, features of America's history. The precarious conditions of slavery, particularly for Black enslaved women, produced sexual vulnerabilities, further complicating the many other perils they faced under the ownership of their masters. This book is a stark reminder of that past and is another piece of evidence that encourages America to embrace the extensive intertwining of Blacks and Whites in this country. While Rachel Swarns provides more evidence of this reality, she allows her readers to do more romanticizing and fantacizing surrounding the typical relationships Black women endured with White men during slavery. Rather than straightforwardly facing the gravity of the brutalities of Black women's sexual victimization under slavery, she allows readers the option to cast Black women's relationships with White men during this time period as romances among equals invoking the unusual liaison between Sally Hemings and Thomas Jefferson.

In telling Mrs. Obama's family story, Swarns is able to trace the First Lady's roots to her great great great great grandmother who as Melvinia was born into slavery and lived under those conditions through Emancipation. Melvinia gives birth to a biracial son, Dolphus Shields, and his life constitutes much of the book's focus. Dolphus Shields is the great great grandfather of Mrs. Obama who was born into slavery in 1859. Through his descendants, Swarns is able to establish connections between Mrs. Obama and her roots in slavery, as well as the Black and White bloodlines that construct her family's story. Swarns tells much of this story by uncovering the mysterious secrets and family whispers surrounding the race and actual identity of Dolphus Shields's father. Swarns establishes that Dolphus Shields is the son of a Black, enslaved mother and White father, but we are left with only strong suggestions as to the actual identity of his White father. Swarns settles on the White slave owner Henry Shields or one of his sons as the father of the biracial child Dolphus. This claim is far from a certain paternity given the evidence she presents, yet this does not deter her claim. This is one of many points in which Swarns relies on inference and conjecture to tell this story rather than on soundly supported evidence.

Using the many census records, property declarations, land titles, and church records among other historical artifacts, Swarns is able to extract the historical roots of Mrs. Obama's family across several generations and tells an enthralling story in the process. It is a story that many Americans can connect to and as a teaching tool, it allows us to explore many commonalities between African American experiences and broader American history. However, even with extensive attempts to pin down the evidence, Swarns is faced with the realities that historical records for African American families are spotty and incomplete. She also makes us keenly aware of the many silences that haunt the pages of history for African American families that are further compounded by family silence that often attempts to shield us from the painful realities of oppressive conditions family members faced in this country.

While *American Tapestry* centers on Mrs. Obama's family legacy, it is really an American tale of enslavement, endurance, perseverance, migration, freedom, and confronting the impossible. So much of the story centers on the intimate relationships that occurred between Black enslaved women and White men with speculations as to whether these sexual liaisons emanated from mutual desire or violent rape. Swarns explores both scenarios as possibilities and makes much of the silence that surrounded these connections between Blacks and Whites. It is in these silences that go from one generation to the next that so much of history and individuals' identities are lost. Given the unspeakable, forbidden nature of these ties, Swarns and others doing such research are robbed of the luxuries of birth certificates, and other records that establish identities for the children of these liaisons. It is in these silences that so much of American history dwells. As Swarns states, "It is in so many ways the story of America, in which racial intermingling lingers in the bloodlines of many African Americans, and slavery was the crucible through which many contemporary family lines were forged." Swarns offers us an understanding of the African American spirit for survival, perseverance, and resilience. From one generation's experience to the next, Swarns offers a clearly constructed "striver's mentality" focused on self-uplift and she links these attributes across generations leading to Mrs. Obama's own personal story of perseverance and generational betterment.

In several of the stories, as Swarns weaves through her narrative of Mrs. Obama's ancestral roots, we are reminded of the broader quests for freedom and inclusion that is a universal story applying to those who have been marked as outsiders in some way. These stories offer us new ways to conceptualize contemporary quests for inclusion that we see playing out in today's headlines. In one story, Swarns illustrates the impact of emancipation on both previously enslaved couples and those who had always lived as free Blacks. With the realities of emancipation, for the first time some African Americans could have their marriages recognized by law. Swarns captures the moment by sharing a story of Blacks both previously free and newly freed who stood in lines at an Illinois courthouse to have their marriages recognized by the state. With that moment, we are reminded of the current desires to be recognized and legitimized by the state that same-sex couples today seek. Swarns's account is reminiscent of same-sex couples who lined the sidewalks of cities from Washington, DC, and New York City to states like California, Maine, and Vermont who awaited opportunities to register their marriages with the state and be recognized and recorded in history as married couples. The book reminds us that changes in public policy can impact multiple populations, just as emancipation changed the lives of free and previously enslaved Blacks alike, though we seldom think of its impact on free men and women of color.

Readers will find that there are many parallels to Swarns's book and Isabel Wilkerson's *Warmth of Other Suns*, especially noting that both authors mark the migration patterns of African Americans from the American south to points north. Swarns is certainly aware of these early migrants citing Mrs. Obama's ancestor, Phoebe Moten, who started migrating north as early as 1899. Perhaps, more historical texts will take this long historical view of Black migration realizing the longevity of this phenomenon.

With regard to teaching, this book offers a stimulating hook for students by offering its readers a glimpse into the private life of First Lady Obama's family, and may serve as a sufficient draw to interest students in its broader stories. However, there are many more elements that make this book less desirable as a teaching tool and relegate it more toward casual as opposed to scholarly reading. As a text, it does not provide enough substantiating evidence to offer students a rigorous example of scholarship at its best. In fact, there are some places in the book where the author is so heavily relying on extrapolation from one piece of historical evidence that it is uncomfortable to read as she moves from genealogical study to a very different genre, historical fiction. Swarns's efforts to root out family secrets, whispers, and speculation in the historical record are admirable, but they do not rise to the level of appropriate classroom material, as they vacillate between historical accuracy and conjecture in ways that leave the reader uncertain of the reliability of the text.

Wendy G. Smooth
The Ohio State University

Foster, Frances Smith, Beverly Guy-Sheftall, and Stanlie M. James, eds. *Still Brave: The Evolution of Black Women's Studies* (New York: Feminist Press at City University of New York, 2009), $18.36, 400 pp. ISBN: 978-1-55861-611-0 (paper).

Still Brave (2009) is an anthology that provides a nuanced genealogical perspective on the state of Black Women's Studies since the publication of Gloria Hull, Patricia Bell Scott, and Barbara Smith's groundbreaking text *But Some of Us Are Brave* (1982). This historic volume laid the framework for a burgeoning field of study whose main purpose was to ensure the survival of Black women in the United States using five key problematics. These include: employing a pro-Black-feminist frame as central to Black liberation rather than as an affront to Black masculinity, confronting racism as a critical first step toward gaining a critical consciousness, dispelling the myths of racialized sexuality that deny Black women humanity, acknowledging multiple modes of survival developed by Black women, and praising early Black female literary interventions as a counter frame to dominant erasure. By bringing the embattled lives of Black women from the margins to the center of activism and scholarship, this volume and its five key problematics would later foster some of the academies most robust contemporary intellectual debates.

Still Brave is a "praise song" not a sequel to this earlier work of resistance that uses the aforementioned five key problematics as an organizational tool in exploring how Black Women's Studies has developed into a multidisciplinary field of study. Focusing primarily on the major intellectual ruptures and debates that have ensued within these five distinct areas of inquiry *Still Brave* deviates from the publication *But Some of Us Are Brave* by not providing actual syllabi, descriptions of classroom activities, or sample handouts. In *Still Brave*, readers gain a general sense of the field's origins, direction, and most pressing contemporary questions. Relying on what formative scholarship has taught the field about the political position of Black women, these phenomenal texts continually redefine the meaning of "politics" to mean more than political parties and voting, but an act charged with exposing the ways that differential power affects the lives of Black women and compels them to resist. There are a number of notable contemporary Black Women's Studies scholars such as Ruth Nicole Brown, Dayo Gore, T. Denean Sharpley-Whiting, Joy James, and Kimberly Springer that continue to expand the field using these foundational problematics to frame their sources of inquiry and enable one to understand the complexity and diversity of the Black female experience in the United States.

Still Brave is broken up into five sections that highlight critical turning points in Black Women's Studies. In Section 1, "The Way We Were," the reader is prompted by early Black feminists such as the Combahee River Collective, Cheryl Clark, and Audre Lorde to remember that Black women's politics is a shared struggle that must be made visible within and outside their own organizational and political networks. Developing the foundational concept of "identity politics" early Black feminist activists publically exposed the distinct forms of oppression they experienced within the Feminist and Black Liberation movement to refute the dominant scripts that continue to render them marginal subjects. "The mere naming of the pejorative stereotypes attributed to black women (e.g., mammy, matriarch, Sapphire, whore, and bulldagger), let alone cataloguing the cruel, often murderous, treatment we receive, indicates how little value has been placed upon our lives during four centuries of bondage in the Western Hemisphere."[1] By remembering the resistant voices of early Black feminists as they named their distinct forms of oppression the nation bore witness to the political realization that comes from "the seemingly personal experiences of individual black women's lives" (Combahee, 4).[2] This section aims to orient the reader to a time when Black female activists and scholars were no longer willing to accept an absence of critical attention to Black women's lives as was reflected in scholarship, teaching, and activism at the time.

In the second section, "I Call My Name," Black feminist scholars explore the importance of naming and redefining oneself as the field of Black Women's Studies becomes institutionalized and at times co-opted. I was particularly struck by Nikol Alexander-Floyd and Evelyn Simien's piece, which argued that the development of Africana Womanist Thought served a disciplinary function for Black Studies and was, in fact, an accommodationist politics that neglects sexism for racism. This aforementioned piece is coupled well with Patricia Hill Collins exploration of the contradictions of Afrocentrism in the United States. Collins argues that although "Afrocentrism offers an affirmation of Blackness, a love ethic directed toward Black people,"[3] it presumes some level of group homogeneity and refuses to adequately address questions of gender, class, and sexuality. These essays are critical of the ways that disciplines such as Women's Studies and Black Studies render the study of women of color invisible while simultaneously acknowledging that these are the only intellectual spaces where their work is respected. Monica Coleman goes further to argue that she feels conflicted by being encouraged to name herself a womanist religious scholar when there are no current womanist religious scholars addressing questions of homosexuality. Coleman suggests that womanism has not paid tribute to its revolutionary Black feminist roots propelled by early Black lesbian activists placing terms such as "feminism" and "womanism" into question. In this section, the reader gets a snapshot of the many ways that Black feminist teachings are read, misread, and co-opted by the academic spaces these Black female intellectuals call home.

The third section focuses on the inseparable nature of identity for Black women in the pursuit of naming and reclaiming their "Body and Soul." Paula Giddings and Ann duCille argue that Black women who are willing to challenge Black male sexism are too often accused of putting their feminist agenda before "their black family." Black women who aim to reclaim their own humanity by naming their sources of oppression, even if it implicates those within the Black community, find themselves labeled race traitors and thus marginalized and named an enemy to the Black Nationalist agenda. Adrienne Davis provides a critical re-reading of the sexual economy of American slavery and states that, "the failure of language to document and archive the sexual abuse of reproductive exploitation of enslaved women is the origin of the absence of language to articulate for contemporary black women sexual identities that are empowering, fulfilling, and joyous" (216). Highlighting the ways that Black women today still continue to suffer from the silences of White pleasure and profit, Davis insists that we must first confront our histories of exploitation to then seek personal reconciliation. This is coupled well with Evelynn Hammonds's piece where she exposes the silence, secrets, suffering, and shame of the AIDS epidemic for Black women. The essays in this section compel the reader to recognize how the policing of the Black female body in the public and private sphere have come to limit her ability to seek self-determination.

The fourth section "To Be Young, Gifted, and Black" features essays that challenge various disciplines to acknowledge and take seriously the critique of intersectionality, which states that identity characteristics do not act independently of one another but are codependent variables producing multiple forms of oppression at any given moment. Elsa Barkley Brown writes an excellent piece that argues that acknowledging the difference between scholarship on women's history and politics does not "leave us [women] void of common ground on which to build a collective struggle" (294), but it recognizes the relational nature of different women's lives. Brown challenges scholars to dispel the idea that the political community of women is homogeneous, and illustrates how these communities are in dialogue and simultaneously constituting one another. Farah Jasmine Griffin argues that the use of literature to theorize the lives of Black women would later result in the emergence of many new fields that rely on the reading practices developed by Black feminist critics. Josephine Beoku-Betts and Wairimu Ngaruiya Njambi prompt us to consider how African women scholars encounter and negotiate heterosexist, ethno-centric, and class-biased institutional spaces. These authors dispel the myth that all women professors share similar experiences in the academy. Calling upon the collective memory of Black feminist pioneers to inform our ways of knowing, contemporary Black feminist scholars continue to challenge various disciplines to reimagine their institutional politics.

The fifth section "From This Moment On . . ." aims to honor the past legacies of resistant Black Women within and outside the academy as they continue to influence scholarship across multiple disciplines. This section begins with the *Black Men for the Eradication of Sexism* (1994) mission statement and turns to Black feminist internationalism. Joy James highlights the legacy of Black female activists such as Ida B. Wells and Angela Davis whose attention to ideological diversity beyond US borders has led contemporary Black feminist organizing to reflect on the oppressive conditions of people around the world while acknowledging their own will to survive and continue to seek purpose. June Jordan's "Some of Us Did Not Die" is a testament to the founders of Black Women's Studies for having the political courage to insist that the survival of Black women was a battle worth waging within and outside the borders of the academy as well as within and outside the borders of the US nation-state. Lastly, Carole Boyce Davies's piece on the neocolonial politics of Condoleezza Rice and the practices of Black women in power and political leadership provided an excellent framework for the development of future scholarship. This piece is critical of the ways that Black leaders who have reaped the rewards of social movement era gains make political decisions. This section does an excellent job illustrat-ing how Black Women's Studies continues to influence the ideological development of multiple communities committed to intellectual struggle inside and outside the academy while making gestures toward critical inquiry across the globe.

Still Brave is a well thought out introductory text for any audience looking to gain a broad interdisciplinary understanding of the development and direction of Black Women's

Studies. However, this text narrowly focuses on the United States and does not explore with any depth how Black Women's Studies have transcended US borders. Despite the text's limitations, the editors chose essays that were jargon free, thus making this volume accessible to all audiences. Lastly, the decision not to republish essays that have been heavily anthologized is a testament to the editors' commitment to invite contemporary scholars to provide fresh new perspectives on past intellectual debates.

Still Brave is a phenomenal study of the development and direction of Black Women's Studies. The reader is prompted to remember the important interventions of past Black women writers, activists, and intellectuals and analyze how their work continues to influence scholarship within and beyond Black Women's Studies today. By theorizing the lives of Black women a new way of understanding "politics" has emerged. The politics of Black women's lives and the knowledge that has developed from its exploration have pushed multiple disciplines to rethink how they ask questions, re-imagine their own purposes, and reengage with marginalized voices. As such, politics becomes more about questions of power, influence, and survival rather than political parties and voting. Black Women's Studies has challenged the academy to reflect on its intellectual and political practices for the purposes of social transformation, which is undoubtedly political.

Brittany Lewis
University of Minnesota

Notes

1. The Combahee River Collective, "A Black Feminist Statement," in *Still Brave: The Evolution of Black Women's Studies,* ed. Stanlie M. James, Frances Smith Foster, and Beverly Guy-Sheftall (New York: The City University of New York, 2009), 5.
2. Combahee, "Black Feminist Statement," 4.
3. Collins, Patricia Hill, "When Fighting Words Are Not Enough: The Gendered Content of Afrocentrism," in *Still Brave: The Evolution of Black Women's Studies*, ed. Stanlie M. James, Frances Smith Foster, and Beverly Guy-Sheftall (New York: The City University of New York, 2009), 151.

Blackwell, Maylei. *¡Chicana Power! Contested Histories of Feminism in the Chicano Movement* (Austin: University of Texas Press, 2011), $24.95, 312 pp. ISBN: 978-0-292-72690-1 (paper).

A political cartoon from an unpublished 1971 issue of *Hijas de Cuauhtémoc*, a short-lived Chicana feminist newspaper, shows two men dressed in Brown Beret gear ogling a woman while telling her, ". . . You might get to be *movimiento* [movement] princess" (75). The cartoon's caption reads "The 'Heavies' of Aztlán recruiting *bodies* for the *movimiento*." The struggle against the blatant sexism captured in the cartoon is just one of many dilemmas navigated by the Mexican American women activists featured in Maylei Blackwell's *¡Chicana Power! Contested Histories of Feminism in the Chicano Movement.*

Over a period of twenty years, Blackwell archived documents, collected stories, and conducted interviews of Chicanas involved in groups such as the *Hijas de Cuauhtémoc* (Daughters of *Cuauhtémoc*), one of the first Chicana or Latina feminist organizations in the United States. Through oral histories and examination of print materials, Blackwell weaves a narrative of how Chicana and Latina activists of the 1960s and 1970s contributed to the civil rights movements that shifted the sociopolitical terrain of the United States, especially around race and gender. Blackwell documents how these groups made a tremendous impact on disseminating feminist knowledge among Mexican American women across the US Southwest, often referred to in the Chicano Movement as Aztlán.

Blackwell introduces the book with a familiar but necessary discussion of how "The Telling is Political" (1). This section of the book focuses on how the dominant discourse of civil rights movement history, including the Chicano Movement history, largely overlooks Chicana and Latina contributions. Through her historical scholarship, Blackwell seeks to redress this by demonstrating how various strands of Chicana feminist organizing took hold across many communities, especially in California and Texas, among other places.

In particular, Blackwell interrogates how the women she interviewed contended with the pervasive masculinist attitudes embedded in the Chicano Movement's dominant form of cultural nationalism. The women's stories chronicle how they vied for leadership positions in male-dominated Chicano organizations, where women were typically relegated to service positions to support the male leaders. In one poignant example, Blackwell describes how Anna Nieto Gómez, a former student leader at *Movimiento Estudiantil Chicano de Aztlán* (MEChA) and a cofounder of *Hijas de Cuauhtémoc*, experienced organized harassment from male colleagues several times in her career, from her days as a student activist to her time as a professor. Male colleagues staged a mock burial of several Chicana feminist activists and hung an effigy of Nieto Gómez in an attempt to censure their public feminist critiques of the national Chicano Movement's lack of a gender analysis. Later,

Nieto Gómez was denied tenure at California State University Northridge despite an intense battle in which she was backed by hundreds of students and colleagues, but not the male leadership of the Chicano Studies department. Through Blackwell's in-depth, longitudinal research, a narrative of targeted harassment of outspoken Chicana feminists in the academy, among other spaces, emerges.

Blackwell dialogs with Nieto Gómez and other Chicanas, several of whom became activist-scholars in the academy, who weathered such battles in attempts to shift the Chicano Movement's dialog from a nationalist myopia toward a multifarious, internationalist women of color feminist approach. By compiling and connecting the women's stories to find convergences, Blackwell interrupts the dominant discourse of singular male heroes of civil rights movements, favoring a more collective narrative that posits women as central agents of movement organizing during this pivotal era. In describing her method, Blackwell likens herself as oral historian to a DJ spinning records, engaged in ". . . the intergenerational sampling of oldies into new rhymes in which the layering of memory and time helps each generation make meaning and claim their place in narrative grooves that have been passed down" (42). Blackwell advocates revealing her ". . . role as oral historian in cutting, mixing, and sampling the narratives" (42), thereby making the method more transparent.

Blackwell not only samples the women's narratives, but also theorizes how their stories have been largely overlooked as contributors to a major political upheaval. Although there have been other studies of women involved in the Chicano Movement, this book develops a critical genealogy of how Chicana feminism coalesced and works to apprehend the multiple historical nodes that have informed and emanated from it. As Blackwell observes, "Women of color political subjectivities have gone largely unhistoricized because they often occurred *between* various and distinct social movements" (21). Building on the scholarship of Chicana historians Emma Pérez and Vicki Ruiz, Blackwell situates Chicana feminism within a larger transnational context that includes feminist solidarity work with Mexican and Latin American feminists. By showing how Chicana feminist leaders dialoged with their Mexican and Latin American counterparts, Blackwell traces how they participated in a larger network of third world women of color feminisms. In positioning Chicana feminism within a transnational feminist framework, Blackwell's oral history project expands the archive of what she terms "the multiple feminist insurgencies of women of color" (21).

Blackwell's book offers a valuable contribution in its description of the complex analyses and lived praxis of these Chicana feminists. Their political work not only incorporated race, class, gender, and sexuality, it also bridged multiple efforts across youth movements, student movements, and labor movements. Blackwell demonstrates how documenting their efforts to build multi-issue organizations and political platforms magnifies the contemporary understanding of ". . . the parallel development of various women of color feminisms" (26). Blackwell calls this process constructing "retrofitted memory," in which multiple layers of minoritized histories are brought to the fore. Blackwell claims that, for the oral historian of suppressed knowledge, the practice of retrofitting memory involves looking "within the gaps, interstices, silences, and crevices of the uneven narratives of domination" as a means of "fracturing dominant narratives and creating new spaces for new historical subjects to emerge" (2).

Blackwell remains vigilant to avoid applying dominant logics of mainstream feminist historiography that might misinterpret Chicana feminism's struggles. Blackwell stresses that the Chicana feminist strategies deployed by her interviewees defy neat categorization into common feminist typologies such as liberal, radical, and so forth. Because of the regional and ideological nuances that attached different values to different forms of activism and gender justice, and because of the complex tactical maneuvers required of Chicanas occupying multiple subjectivities, what might be interpreted as radical feminism in one context might seem reformist in another political arena. Blackwell draws on Chicana feminist scholars such as Chela Sandoval, citing Sandoval's notion of a "differential consciousness" as an apt descriptor for the many forms of feminism expressed by the interviewees, all of whom in their varying ways were enacting oppositional stances to White—and Chicano—heteropatriarchy.

An especially powerful chapter examines the role of small publications and feminist presses in circulating Chicana feminist materials. Blackwell tracks how Chicana organizers used the printed word to spread information about events such as public rallies and to engage in the latest political debates impacting them. Throughout the book, Blackwell pieces together a complicated history by drawing on newsletters, political essays, and correspondence. By distributing their literature, the women forged new channels of representation and contestation. Blackwell describes the women's strategic use of print as a way for them to construct Chicana feminist counterpublics. This occurred through homegrown, localized pamphlets and ephemeral zines as well as larger projects, including anthologies such as *This Bridge Called My Back* (Moraga and Anzaldúa 1981) and *Encuentro Femenil* (1973), the first academic journal for Chicana scholarship.

In the Chicano Movement, as in many liberation movements, political gatherings became historical flashpoints. *¡Chicana Power!* devotes a chapter to providing a deep context for the 1971 *Conferencia de Mujeres por la Raza*, the first national conference to bring together Chicana feminists. This conference, contends Blackwell, continues to serve as a symbol of promise and failure. Blackwell collected multiple, sometimes contradictory, stories of this five hundred-person Houston conference that provided a space for Chicanas to connect at a mass level but surfaced fissures in the movement. On the basis of the many stories researched by Blackwell, some participants viewed the conference as a White women's event because of the involvement of Young Women's Christian Association (YWCA); others cited regional and ideological differences around political strategy. The seeming irresolvability of tensions, argues Blackwell, undermined the Chicanas' ability to forge a cohesive national organization.

One of the pleasures of this book is the strength of the interviewees' voices, which come through with emotion, working-class dialects, and polemics intact. Blackwell folds many voices into the book, allowing the women to retell, through their own memories and thoughtful analyses, their experiences in an emerging landscape of women of color feminisms that included Chicana feminism.

Blackwell's book undoubtedly lends critical insight into the emergence of Chicana feminism in the 1960s and 1970s. The book brings together a rich collection of stories of Chicana voices to amplify the historical record of Chicana/o civil rights movement experiences. The book's appendix includes brief biographical data on the key voices represented, those of activists such as Elizabeth "Betita" Martinez, Keta Miranda, Anna

Nieto Gómez, and many who remain active in activist and academic circles. At times, the book, even in its resistance of a singular civil rights narrative, risks relying on a "great individuals" slant to telling history. This may be partly due to the author's attempt to provide thick descriptions of some of the stories told by the activists, leading to a focus on selected individuals. Blackwell herself acknowledges the limitations of conducting a study of such a complex social movement while relying on a methodology that pieces together a wide array of archival documents, oral interviews, and contested memories.

In terms of the civil rights groundswell in the 1960s and 1970s, Blackwell's work urges the reexamination of social movements through a lens of the multiple insurgencies within them, resisting the historicizing of movements as monolithic forms of political mobilization. Blackwell also takes into account how Chicana feminisms developed in tandem with Black feminisms, Latin American feminisms, and third world women of color feminisms more broadly. Blackwell's book would read well alongside a text such as Alma M. García's *Chicana Feminist Thought: The Basic Historical Writings* (1997), a collection of Chicana/o Movement primary documents, some of which Blackwell references in her important study. For those interested in learning more on the topic of feminist organizing in the Chicana/o Movement, Maylei Blackwell's book proves indispensible.

T. Jackie Cuevas
University of Texas at San Antonio

Tucker-Worgs, Tamelyn. *The Black Megachurch: Theology, Gender, and the Politics of Public Engagement* (Baylor University Press, 2011), $39.95, 275 pp. ISBN: 978-1-6025-8422-8 (cloth). Winner of the 2012 W. E. B. DuBois Distinguished Book Award—Presented by the National Conference of Black Political Scientists.

The Black Megachurch is a good work in political science that offers many arenas for further research by more interdisciplinary-oriented researchers. Megachurches are generally accepted as those with at least two thousand members. Tucker-Worgs states that her work is the only "comprehensive study of the Black megachurch to date" and her central argument revolves around how these churches "fulfill the needs of the new black middle class suburbanites." She expands the definition of megachurches stating that they are "'this worldly' churches, are relevant to the 'here and now,' and generally participate in public life" (4) arguing that the participation itself is an area of great diversity among churches, even with a gendered division of labor.

Tucker-Worgs merges theology with political science, resulting in what she sees as Black religious thought. The aim of this exercise is to demonstrate her "politico-theological typology of black megachurches" in order to determine how they are publicly and politically engaged (97). But, research proves that Black American church structures are dynamic and typologies tend to harden categories and limit scholarship.

Considering the range of sources the author draws on, including extensive surveys of church leaders, interviews, site visits, sermonic analyses, and assorted church records, I am most convinced by the demographic data base she develops. Whether a map showing the location of these churches (29) or a table that breaks out "Black megachurch community development organizations (CDOs), black megachurch women-led CDOs and black megachurch men-led CDOs" (154), these hard-data gathering exercises are Tucker-Worgs's strength. If one wants to see the year Black megachurches reached two thousand average weekly attendance, she has got a figure for that (26); or to see the approval of women pastors by denomination, she has got a table for that (148). This constitutes a wonderful demography of the Black megachurch phenomenon.

The subtitle of the book, however, is "Theology, Gender and the Politics of Public Engagement." Though Tucker-Worgs cites approximately fifteen books by African Americans who write about religion, not all of them are contemporary theologians and few have deep commitments to gendered theology or Black womanist theology. Though she notes several sermons by Martin Luther King, Frederick Price, and Jeremiah Wright, none are authored by womanist theologians. Womanist ethics and theology is a significant development since the 1980s, and more sustained consideration of womanist theology would have added substantially to a book of this type. While the womanist designation does not flow into other disciplines, it has held a significant place among African American theologians and ethicists, and their academic and community audiences. Many Black communities continue to reject the term "feminist," and womanists have already developed a good deal of the analysis of gender and gender roles. African American women theologians and ethicists who emphasize gender, such as Emilie M. Townes, Katie Geneva Cannon, Barbara Holmes, and Stacey Floyd Thomas, have consistently addressed the politics of Black church leadership and their regimes of exclusion. They do not necessarily write about megachurches, but their analyses have important implications for the institutions that Tucker-Worgs studies. While Tucker-Worgs foregrounds the work of Cheryl Townsend Gilkes (a sociologist) and Kelly Brown Douglas (a theologian), a more comprehensive engagement with African American women theologians and ethicists helps us consider what is life giving and what is death dealing in this eminently political institution.

Many Black megachurches rewrite restricted, homophobic gender roles—but some do not, for example, Rev. Jeremiah Wright's old church, Trinity United Church of Churst. Dr. Tucker Worgs mentions these dynamics, but because she does not reference the writings by a wider range of Black theologians (including a growing number of gay/lesbian theologians), she misses the current state of this scholarship. Exploring the theological orientations of Black megachurches requires a firmer grasp on the state of this scholarship.

Such interdisciplinary work is a challenge to any scholar because we must be able to access that discipline's data, language, central debates, and have some clues about developments in that field. Even identifying some of the trends within the discipline can be significant. For instance, as Tucker-Worgs explains, Kenneth Hagin Sr. began the word of faith movement (82). Hagin, who was White, supported extremely conservative politics, including gender role constrictions for "real" women and men. He also supported a strict segregation of races. Rev. Frederick Price broke away from the word of faith groups because of this practice. Price's own writing after this could easily be compared to other forms of Black liberation theology. But there are other Black groups still tied to Hagin's approach, including the churches of Creflo Dollar, never mentioned by Tucker-Worgs.

Tucker Worgs discusses public engagement, but she funnels all this through community development organizations (113 ff.). She combines the sustaining activities of the megachurches with all public engagement. However, public engagement ventures, such as education, senior care, funeral homes, and housing, all take different directions in the churches discussed in the volume under review. Megachurches do not always engage communities in order to do good deeds; they do so to raise funds and retain members. How would one raise enough money to keep the doors open on churches the size of small college campuses? So the children and adults in the pay-as-you-go education programs have the churches' belief systems built in, whether it is about the holiness of becoming wealthy, healing your own illnesses, or the evils of listening to outsiders. Is this really to be understood as public engagement? That the churches spend so much time raising money from members, however they can, raises questions about one of Tucker Worgs's main contentions about these churches—they "fulfill the needs of the new black middle class suburbanites" (4). Many of the churches demand W-2s as part of the membership; if one does not tithe, the membership is revoked. But many who attend these churches have minimum and low incomes. Research on the economic breakdown of megachurches and the meanings of the idea that these churches are populated by the new Black middle class would be a good direction for further research.

In conclusion, *The Black Megachurch: Theology, Gender, and the Politics of Public Engagement* has some demographic strengths, raises some questions, and offers readers several directions for other research. It is very fine that this overall topic of the shape of Black churches is a component that attracts the attention of political scientists. However, scholars of color or scholars who research people of color (globally understood) need to have meaningful cross discipline conversations. By this, I mean rigorous interdisciplinary research that instigates work across multiple disciplines and which dispenses with the disciplinary "silo" model.

Stephanie Y. Mitchem
University of South Carolina

Harris-Perry, Melissa. *Sister Citizen: Shame, Stereotypes, and Black Women in America* (*For Colored Girls Who've Considered Politics When Being Strong Isn't Enough*) (New Haven, CT: Yale University Press, 2011), $28.00, 392 pp. ISBN: 978-0-3001-6541-8 (cloth).

Sister Citizen by Melissa Harris-Perry is an unconventional study of Black women's politics. This text is a must-read for students of political science, African American Studies, and women's studies. Her central argument that shame and stereotypes of African American women influence their participation as citizens within the polity illustrates that being a Black woman and an American citizen are often paradoxical and conflicting identities. The beauty of Harris-Perry's analysis is the reframing of the study of politics to include personal questions alongside political inquiry. She contends that "the internal, psychological, emotional, and personal experiences of Black women are inherently political" (5). Harris-Perry's thesis moves the study of Black women's politics from their policy choices, political representation, electoral choices, community organizing, and political protests to understand how shame and stereotypes impact Black women's personal lives and consequently their political lives. In this text, politics is defined beyond the traditional terrain of voting, elections, political parties, and policy outcomes. Instead, Harris-Perry is interested in uncovering the ways in which identity impacts politics. The lives of African American women provide insight into how citizens strive to gain recognition. In sum, Black women's politics is a struggle for recognition (from both others and of oneself).

The majority of the text centers on three prevailing stereotypes of African American women, which have caused society to incorrectly view Black women as well as caused Black women to "misrecognize" themselves. These stereotypes include the nurturing mammy who dotes on White children and families only to neglect her own; the lascivious Jezebel who has an insatiable sexual appetite and becomes an easy target for (unwanted) sexual advances from (White) men; and the obstinate matriarch who emasculates Black men. These stereotypes serve as archetypes and caricatures of Black womanhood. The enduring and powerful nature of these stereotypes has bound, constrained, and pigeon-holed Black women into typecasts that offer little room for negotiation or contestation. In turn, Black women have held onto the perceived strength of these archetypes and embraced the caricature of the Strong Black Woman. Harris-Perry notes that this is a default category for describing African American women. However, Black women may appear strong on the outside, but internally, this myth leaves Black women in a perilous position. Data from her multi-city, generation, and socioeconomic status focus groups of Black women found that Black women who attempted to live up to the Strong Black Woman myth were more likely to be sicker, less satisfied, and more burdened.

Drawing on focus group and survey data, Harris-Perry illustrates that not only are Black women "misrecognized" by society, but they often do not recognize themselves. How Black women see themselves, and fail to recognize themselves as citizens, influences their political involvement as well as their expectations from the state to treat them as full citizens. The strongest aspect of this text is Harris-Perry's willingness to investigate Black women's culture. Here she analyzes and exposes Black women's dirty laundry to demonstrate why self-misrecognition has disastrous effects for Black women's mental health, self-image and esteem, as well as their place in the American polity. The overcompensation of the strong Black woman does not allow Black women to be fully human—vulnerable, fallible, timid, soft, or fragile. Black women's misrecognition of themselves often leads to an awareness that they can never live up to the Strong Black Women myth. This misrecognition, turned failed expectation, produces shame. Shame is form of social control that harms Black women as individuals and society writ large. In a racist society, this shame is then identified with Blackness. Because African Americans are viewed as a malignant group within the American society, they are cast to the lowest rung of the social and political order. Indeed, shame inhibits every aspect of Black women's lives. As a result, Black women occupy a "crooked room" that makes it difficult to both stand and see straight. As occupants of a crooked room, some Black women may try to fight and struggle to assume an upright position or others may bend to fit within the crookedness of the room—a metaphor Harris-Perry uses to explain how stereotypes distort Black women's perceptions of themselves as citizens. Harris-Perry argues that Black women's political involvement is largely motivated by their quest to escape the shame associated with these controlling images and their internalization. Yet her larger point is that Black women have tremendous difficulty in challenging these stereotypes as well as gaining recognition for their authentic selves. These stereotypes and the crooked room limit the opportunities for Black women to engage in the public sphere.

Not only is the vantage point of this study unique, but Harris-Perry includes unique data to illustrate how Black women experience politics. This book is a hybrid of methodological approaches that is delightfully interdisciplinary. From literally analysis, focus groups, statistical analysis, and cultural critiques, this book provides readers with several vantage points to examine Black women's politics. This innovative approach compellingly centralizes how the intersecting identities of Black women impact both the public and private lives of this group of citizens. Indeed, the aftermath of Hurricane Katrina looms large in this study to illustrate how culture and Black women's misrecognition impact discussions of government's role to protect and provide for its citizens and what claims citizens can make to their government are viewed as legitimate. Taken together with the works of Zora Neale Hurston, Alice Walker, Ntozake Shange, and Sweet Honey in the Rock, Harris-Perry details how the personal is political for Black women by examining the intersection of race, gender, and class. Drawing from the Duke lacrosse scandal and stereotypical depictions of Michelle Obama as a jezebel, Harris-Perry points to how Black women have dealt with misrecognition to challenge media portrayal of themselves as sexually immoral, angry Black women, or reduced to only a physical body. Black women—from the First Lady of the United States of America to exotic dancers—are simultaneously hypervisible and invisible, are vulnerable citizens who must challenge the stereotypes that silence, marginalize, and constrain them within the American polity.

In sum, Harris-Perry weaves together a convincing explanation about how shame and Black women's stereotypes have real world consequences on Black women's politics.

Harris-Perry's work will certainly reach a broad audience with its multi-method, interdisciplinary, and easy to understand language. However, the book's main shortcoming is tied to its strength. The text takes on a tremendous task of speaking to many audiences and does not wholly speak to any of them. As a social scientist, the relegation of regression analysis, interview questions, and demographic information for the focus group participants to the appendices and endnotes left much to be desired. Readers are asked to take Harris-Perry's analysis on face value or spend the majority of the latter half of the book flipping between the written text and the appendices and endnotes. Next, while the literary analysis engages readers, Harris-Perry devotes too much time to painstakingly spelling out the novels rather than quickly identifying the main points that she would like readers to know about the text before moving into her analysis. Lastly, her cultural critique of how media have viewed Michelle Obama is overtly anecdotal. By attempting to speak in an interdisciplinary fashion to social scientists, humanities scholars, and the mass public, much of Harris-Perry's presentation of the myriad methodological approaches in this study undercut her meaningful theoretical contribution to the study of Black women's politics.

Sister Citizen is a path-breaking study of Black women's politics. By centering Black women's voices, Harris-Perry critically challenges political science to redefine politics to include personal and unique constructions of Black womanhood to better understand how citizens engage with government and how government responds to its citizens. By challenging public myths of Black womanhood, Harris-Perry moves the study of Black politics (and the subfield of Women and Politics) to acknowledge how the intersection of race, class, and gender lead to misrecognition and misunderstanding that impact Black women's self-definition. Moreover, Harris-Perry provides a stellar example of the type of political science research that engages scholarly and popular communities. While some may take exception with her attempt to reach such a broad audience, this text provides a model for how scholars may (or may not) elect to format their book to speak to diverse audiences. As a Black woman, Harris-Perry also includes her own narrative in the text, which adds to the richness of the story. This book is an exemplar for transformative political science research and feminist epistemology that centers on the voice of the research subjects as well as the researcher. Overall, Harris-Perry provides an engaging discussion of Black women's politics and groundbreaking interdisciplinary scholarship, and offers an innovative theoretical framework for future research in this growing body of scholarship.

Nadia E. Brown
St. Louis University

McKittrick, Katherine. *Demonic Grounds: Black Women and the Cartographies of Struggle* (Minneapolis, MN: University of Minnesota Press, 2006), $22.50, 240 pp. ISBN: 978-0-8166-4702-6 (paper).

In *Demonic Grounds: Black Women and the Cartographies of Struggle* (2006), Katherine McKittrick begins with two basic premises: (1) that geography is infused with sensations and distinct ways of knowing and (2) that humanness is always geographic. While this claim is not especially novel, McKittrick's sustained exploration and analysis of Black women's geographies is altogether revolutionary. In *Demonic Grounds*, geography is not confined to the material world. Instead, geography encompasses the full range of Black women's knowledge and experiences that have been concealed through histories of geographic domination. The author defines this domination primarily as the enslavement and racial-sexual displacement of Black bodies and subjectivities throughout the African diaspora. Her story begins with the slave castles off the Ivory Coast, then into the slave ships of the Middle Passage, journeying across the United States and Canada through the Underground Railroad, and ends up in a small northern California apartment in 1976. Through her vivid storytelling, McKittrick invites us into the "deep space" of Black female subjectivity. She creates an evocative conceptual arena that we can use to interpret fuller and nuanced intricacies of Black women's agency.

In basic terms, McKittrick's exploration of Black women's geographies takes place through literary analyses of essential readings in North American Black feminist fiction, which include Octavia Butler's *Kindred*, Toni Morrison's *Beloved*, and Harriet Jacob's *Incidents in the Life of a Slave Girl*. However, the theoretical framework that she uses to analyze the texts is entirely un-North American. Drawing from the dynamic and almost ecclesiastical writings of Afro-Caribbean writers Sylvia Wynters and Marlene Nourbese Phillips, McKittrick transports us into the dark, moist "in between places" of Black women's lives. She urges us into places and experiences of Black womanhood that have been exploited, denied, and often unrepresentable as result of physical, psychic, and epistemic violence. For McKittrick, the horrors of rape, containment, and commodification make up the real, remembered, and (re)imagined personhoods of Black women that have materialized within the global landscapes of White supremacy in the last four centuries.

McKittrick approaches Black women's geography through an (anti)epistemological framework that she calls "the demonic." She describes the demonic as a dark and unknowable conceptual terrain that has been denied within Eurocentric ways of mapping the world and charting epistemology. Untethered to the linear space-time of the present world human organization, the demonic enables her to confront the untold and forgotten struggles of Black womanhood. As (anti)epistemology, the demonic refuses firm knowing through sight, observation, and rationality. Being nonlinear, and essentially "unknowable," the demonic finds its expression through the texts that Black women create from memory (i.e., the testimonials of slaves sold on the auction block) and the remembrances of honest fiction (plays, poetry, and other forms of creative praxis). McKittrick clarifies, "The demonic then, is a non-deterministic schema. It is a process that is hinged on uncertainty and nonlinearity because the organizing schema cannot predict the future" (xxiv). The "demonic" that Enlightenment scholars have been trained vigilantly to fear and avoid is the very intellectual and psychic domain in which we can come to theorize how the horrors of rape, land theft, and human trafficking have structured Black women's ability to survive and negotiate human life in everyday life. The "everyday" for McKittrick includes the physical spaces of the auction block, the kitchen table, church, the streets, fields, and factories. It is within these spaces that Black people have imagined and re-imagined politics and human relationships, and most importantly have theorized and articulated our own unique expressions of justice and freedom.

Throughout *Demonic Grounds*, McKittrick embarks on a miasmic journey through literary and geographic social theory. In Chapter 1, "I Lost an Arm on My Way Home: Black Geographies," she introduces the reader to some of the precepts of the field of critical race theory and geography by way of a close reading of Octavia Butler's *Kindred*. By examining the existential time-place leaps of the novel's protagonist Dana through the writings of Eduard Glissant and Toni Morrison, McKittrick reveals how Blackness "becomes a site of radical possibility, supernatural travels, and difficult epistemological returns to the past and present" (1). For McKittrick, Black femininity is inevitably tied to the physical and psychic displacements, dismemberments, and dispossessions of slavery. Dana, a modern-day Black woman in Butler's novel, almost and without warning, is frequently sucked into the vortex of slavery. Dana, who returns from slavery to the present—minus an arm—is a reminder of the ever-present loss that structures Black femininity in time, place, and what she eventually ends up describing as s/place (space-place). In McKittrick's world of the demonic, Butler's retelling of Dana's traumatic episodes—is an important metaphor that illuminates the persistent ways that past continues to create and recreate life in the present. Whether it is through the erasure of familial histories, being forced to flee, hide, or simply suppress the tragic truths of Black personhood in order to survive, Black female subjectivity and agency rests in Black women's insistent negotiations and (dis)articulations of "truth"—a truth that insistently problematizes neat demarcations between past, present, and future realities.

In *Demonic Grounds*, place, like geography, is not perceived as simply a city, a home, and a neighborhood, or discretely defined or bounded geographic locale. Instead, place encompasses real and reconfigured histories that are materialized through the dismemberment and remembrances that unfold into what she calls the "geographies of the everyday" (12). For McKittrick, these geographies "are aptly expressed and re-expressed through black fiction, black theory, black music, and black imaginations" (21). McKittrick stretches the idea of geography to include reimagining of individual selfhood, family, community, and society writ large. To make her point, she invokes the works of Franz Fanon and Julie Dash, among others, to force us to consider how the psychic terrain of Blackness is informed by and unfolds through Black folks' spatial practices.

In Chapter 2, "The Last Place They Thought of: Black Women's Geographies," McKittrick further explores this thesis through a detailed examination of the spatial agency of Linda Brent. In order to avoid being sold off and likely forever separated from her children, Brent hid out in a garret—a tiny hidden room in the attic of her grandmother's house. After spending seven years in the garret, lacking light, adequate nourishment, and exercise, Brent was able to emerge and eventually bear witness to the terrors of slavery. McKittrick reads her confinement through the lens of resistance and political agency. "Garreting," as a verb, is translated as an important metaphor through which to understand Black female subjectivity. While confined and contained, like countless Black women today, McKittrick argues that Brent absorbed and recanted intimate knowledge about the ruthless machinations of power on the plantation. From the garret, McKittrick argues, Brent was able testify to the extreme risks her enslaved family was willing to assume to care for and protect the socially dead in order to maintain and fulfill a legacy of survival. The garret, while a dismal place of dehumanization, is alternatively read as an oppositional and agentic space through which the humanity of Black femininity can grasped, expressed, and represented. In subsequent chapters, including "The Authenticity of this Story: The Auction Block" and "Demonic Grounds: Sylvia Wynters," McKittrick continues to persuasively argue that Black political life can be most clearly grasped and articulated through the most horrific sites of Black subjugation. For McKittrick, it is within and through the darkness of the auction block, and the seemingly endless nights traversing the underground railroad—a necessarily invisible and denied geography—that Black people have miraculously charted an ongoing, and most likely never-ending path toward freedom. She finds in the demonic the very ways that Black women have asserted their humanness, and made more "humanly workable" geographies possible.

So what does all of this have to do with Black women's politics? Well, everything! First, McKittrick opens up an entirely new field of meaning through which to frame and interpret Black women's political agency. Within the schema of the demonic, Black women's politics must be understood as a means through which to assert their person-hood within a living history of racism-sexism that unfolds within the psychic landscape of White supremacy. The role of the Black woman scholar is to unearth, chart, and make sense of the cartographies of struggle that Black women have used to assert their humanness. The personal and political motivations behind Black women's participation within profoundly unjust political systems and regimes—which claim to be democratic yet persistently and systematically conceal and/or contain the full expression of Black femaleness—must be understood as not only ways to articulate a need for inclusion or fairness, but as the struggle for freedom.

Second, her framework insists that the realm of politics, as a central component of human life, necessarily unfolds in and across time, space, and place. As a result, our efforts to theorize Black women's politics must be conceived within and across multiple levels of scale, which include body, psyche, home, town, the community, the region, the national, and the global. McKittrick teaches us that if scale itself is also socially construct-ed, studies of Black women's politics must necessarily examine how Black womanhood (our bodies, spaces, and resistances) gets scaled as a result of ongoing processes of geo-graphic domination. Today, these processes include, but are not limited to, imprisonment, hypersegregation, containment, the hyperexploitation of Black female sexuality within neoliberalism, and the continued exposure to racial-sexual trauma as a result of police brutality, street violence, gentrification, disaster politics, hate, and the ongoing problem of intergenerational racialized poverty. Where we find geographic domination, we will also find important and dynamic sites of political resistance.

Another core lesson that students of Black women in politics should take from this book is that the realm of Black female political agency can never be fully confined to present behaviors, attitudes, responses, or circumstances. Rather, Black women's political agency should be contextualized within the field of their remembrances about self, family, community, and place. Such a perspective enables scholars, including political scientists, to locate Black women's modes and strategies of resistance within the resonances of their retold and re-narrated histories of simultaneous horrors and possibilities of migration, displacement, dispossession (i.e., rape, foreclosures, and eviction) and racial-sexual sub-jugation. McKittrick provides scholars with a new vantage point and (anti)disciplinary space through which to examine the diverse complexities of Black women's politics and activisms across multiple intellectual and geopolitical locales. Alongside other key Black feminists, including bell hooks, Hortense Spillers, Ruth Wilson Gilmore, and M. Jacqui Alexander, McKittrick urges us to make concrete and sustained linkages between the devaluation and sufferances of Black life within extant racial hierarchies that are made real in the violence of streets, neighborhoods, social institutions, and multiscalar political economies. Despite *Demonic Grounds* being a difficult read for social scientists, it is an essential read! It provides a unique interpretative framework for bold and theoretically rigorous interdisciplinary examinations of Black women and their resistances. Ultimately, McKittrick encourages us to learn from, rather than learn about, the unique ways that Black women have maintained our humanness in spite of consistent and ongoing (and rather demonic) efforts to render us subhuman.

Zenzele Isoke
University of Minnesota

Nealy, Lisa Nikol. *African American Women Voters: Racializing Religiosity, Political Consciousness, and Progressive Political Action in U.S. Presidential Elections from 1964 through 2008* (Lanham, MD: University Press of America, 2008), $47.50, 314 pp. ISBN: 978-0-7618-4457-0 (paper).

This is the first major book-length study that I have seen in my career devoted specifically to African American female voters, despite the fact that since the rise and evolution of political behavioralism in Political Science in the sixties, which uncovered in numerous scholarly and academic articles and book chapters, African American women simply out-protested, out-participated, out-organized, out-mobilized, out-registered, and out-voted African American males. These political differences among African American females and males have long been a political reality that no one, Black or White, was willing to research and write about, except in articles and book chapters. But these differences were far richer than the literature on the topic has ever been able to address until now. In addition, the promise of such a topical study was greater than most have conceived of until this magisterial work of Professor Lisa Nikol Nealy's.

Of course, what it took was a brilliant conceptualization, which Professor Nealy brought to the intellectual table in this volume. It also required careful definitional parameters as well as a theoretical skill and grounding that was immensely innovative and creative in giving this topical subject a foundation and rationality. But such a pioneering effort would also require the author to give the study a unique organizing structure and outline. Finally, this study would need to test a massive number of variables, so as to ferret out the causal mechanisms so that one could understand and grasp the most important variables and relationships inherent in, and accounting for, these differences between African American women and men in the American political process.

With the conceptualization, definitions, literature overviews, and theoretical matters that are presented and properly structurally organized, Professor Nealy moves to collecting data that allow her to test and analyze the relevant variables embedded in African American women's political behavior. Up until this book, most of the major data sets on African Americans combined the genders simply because of the high cost of generating a survey instrument that allowed greater focus and detail work on the female gender within the African American community. Hence, this led to book chapters and/or articles that provided limited empirical insights due to the limited data and questions that the datasets allowed to be asked.

For this pioneering study, the author has designed a first of its kind instrumentation, which includes forty-one focus group participants from four different religious communities in the African American communities in Washington, DC, and Meridian, Mississippi. Combined with this focus group data are the survey data collected by the

National Opinion Research Center (NORC) from 1972 to 2006 with the over samples of African Americans included. And with this bold type of data collection, the author has been able to cover some nine presidential elections and thereby provide a dynamic analysis and perspective of African American women voters over time. Single-year studies like the National Black Election Study of 1984, 1988, and 1993 do not have this built-in ability to tap into the ever-dynamic and moving African American electorate. Hence, this study offers a longitudinal perspective not found in the snapshot work of an earlier type of African American surveys. Thus, Professor Nealy, with this unique data collecting procedure, immediately distinguishes her work from that of others working on the same topic. This brings us to the nature and scope of her findings put forth in Chapter 5.

Presented in forty-six tables in Chapter 5 are the major findings based on the focus group data as well as empirical material generated from the NORC survey data presented in Tables 51–71. Also, several of these tables come directly from Census data instead of the NORC survey data; these data serve as background information for the NORC data and findings. What one sees from these two different datasets is a wholly new portrait of African American women voters in America.

Professor Nealy judiciously summarizes these two different data sets in the final chapter of her book. The result is an electoral portrait of gender in African American politics that exists nowhere else in the literature in a single study. To be sure, there are some similar but limited findings in a few scholarly and academic articles, but these are scattered, spotty, and fragmented in elusive and hard to find journals and/or book chapters and a few dissertations. The herculean task of pulling all of this work together and making it available for students and lay persons is no mean task and the end result would still come nowhere near the very rich set of findings that exist in this one of a kind scholarly book.

Also, the careful and nuanced empirical quantitative statistical methodologies as well as the qualitative ones found in the literature will not always approach the level of sophistication found in this volume. The statistical modeling in this volume is as impressive as one will find anywhere in disciplinary work. Some of it requires background training and usages that many in this subfield simply do not have, nor the talents to implement them. It is quite obvious that Professor Nealy has both the training and the talents to make these new methodologies in Political Science work splendidly in the area of African American politics and among its female political participants.

Finally, after reading this pioneering study, one must conclude that a bright young African American scholar of the first order has given the discipline, its literature, and a subfield a substantial contribution that others will find to be a path breaking study, which lays the groundwork for future scholars. Here is, simply put, the scholarly point of departure for all of the future work in the area. It will be a longtime before this work can be replaced. It has much to offer as well as to suggest for those who will work in gender politics in the area of race and politics in America. In addition, this is a thought-provoking book owing to its constant flow of insights and findings.

In conclusion, one cannot read this book with all of its creativity and innovations and vast arrays of new findings and not leave without understanding that the young scholar who produced this exceptional first book will surely continue to make major contributions to the discipline. One sees in this work a scholar with very big ideas, and the skills and talents to produce stunning books.

This is a book that I will highly recommend to my colleagues and the discipline.

Hanes Walton, Jr.
University of Michigan

Levi, Robin, and Ayelet Waldman, eds. *Inside This Place, Not of It: Narratives from Women's Prisons*. Foreword by Michelle Alexander (San Francisco, CA: Mc Sweeny's Books, 2011), $13.00, 300 pp. ISBN: 978-1-936-36550-0 (paper).

Richie, Beth E. *Arrested Justice: Black Women, Violence, and America's Prison Nation* (New York: New York University Press, 2012), $22.00, 244 pp. ISBN: 978-0-814-77623-0 (paper).

Shigematsu, Setsu, Cameron Granadino, and Jolie Chea. *Visions of Abolition: From Critical Resistance to a New Way of Life* (Oakland, CA: Critical Resistance/PM Press, 2011), $19.95, 92 minutes. ISBN: 978-1-60486-662-9 (DVD).

True stories and real lives are to be found everywhere in these works, which contain first-person narratives, life histories, and interviews, as well as a sustained attention to the data on public policy regarding convictions, sentencing, and judicial practice. First and foremost, the scholars of the works under review render an unrecognized population, imprisoned women, as human, alive, and central to the political issues surrounding policing, incarceration, and violence in the United States. Although men are incarcerated at a rate ten times higher, women are the fastest growing population in the imprisonment system. Female imprisonment has grown 757 percent since 1977 and exceeds men's prison growth in all fifty states.[1] Black women are incarcerated at three times the rate of White women (in the year 2000 it was almost six times), and considering the disparity in the incarceration rate, the effects of these numbers are devastating for Black communities and families. It is clear in these stories that Black women face abuse and violence before they enter the criminal justice system. Though such forms of violence exceed what is imaginable to mainstream society, as the editors explain, these stories "highlight human rights abuses in the U.S. prison system" that are prevalent, widespread, and constitutive in the US punishment system. The ubiquity of such forms of "state sexual assault" reminds us of the connection between Black womanhood and what can be done to Black women and what demarcates human from non-human.[2] Such normalized inhuman and anti-human state practices figure Black women as beyond the realm of the human and create safety, security, and fidelity concerns that legitimate state violence. There are stories here of women who have spent their lives being sexually violated, first by family members—husbands, fathers, brothers or community members, neighbors, landlords, pastors, and then by prison or jail officials for years on end. There are women who while giving birth are chained and shackled to gurneys only to have their babies immediately taken from them. And there are others who have been involuntarily sterilized at the whim of prison doctors or used as trade by prison guards and wardens.

Both books and the documentary provide a look at the conditions and the consequences of women's living relationship to the massive security structure in the form of the criminal justice system in the United States. Caught in what Ruth Gilmore refers to as the largest prison building project in the history of the world,[3] the experiences of these women not only reveal the abuses extensively documented by organizations such as Human Rights Watch, but they also demonstrate the limitations of the justice system that both cannot remedy these violent abuses and in fact produce and perpetuate them. Although justice is promised by law (and it is the possibility of that justice that keeps us waiting), violence is an irreducible component of law through its intimate connection with force. Although violence is already inherent in the law, what these difficult texts reveal is that imagining what the law does to Black women brings out something profound about the nature of the human and the possibility that ontologically Black women exist outside the parameters of what is considered "the human." If considered with these problematics in mind, the stories found in the works being reviewed may begin to render a humanity to this group of women.

In the collection of personal stories of the lives of people incarcerated in women's prisons, *Inside this Place, Not of It: Narratives From Women's Prisons*, editors Robin Levi and Ayelet Waldman gives readers a close look at the experience of mothers, daughters, and sisters either in prison or who have spent a significant number of years incarcerated. Thirteen stories (each a chapter titled with the storyteller's name—Francesca, Anna, Sheri, and Victoria) lay out for the readers the details of what Beth Ritchie calls the existence of systematic subordination. The stories give voice to the imprisoned population that is often overlooked. As Michelle Alexander explains in the foreword "Women in the criminal justice system are often mentioned as an afterthought, if at all" (3). The editors' main task is to have the voices heard in order to render a humanity to a population that has been completely disregarded and villanized.

This *Voice of Witness* imprint includes an extensive appendix that offers a glossary of important terms related to specific processing practices that identify jail and prison structures and a fairly comprehensive list of nonprofit organizations that work on issues of incarceration and women. It also includes a timeline that begins with the first prison built for women in 1835 and provides the dates of important cases such as the *State vs. Wanrow* (1977), which laid the groundwork for the battered woman syndrome defense. In addition, there are detailed descriptions of the legal framework of incarceration and the access to remedy and redress, an overview of pregnancy, abortion, sterilization, and shackling in prison as well as a mapping of post-prison consequences and barriers to communication from prison.

In *Arrested Justice*, Beth Ritchie also uses the lived experiences and stories of Black women who have borne the brunt of a double-edged public policy structure that has rendered Black women not only as marginalized individuals but also as a population that has been systematically subordinated in the system. Drawing on a brief and tragic story, Ritchie introduces us to the almost inexplicable experience of a young pregnant Black woman who decided she had no better option than to give birth in a south side Chicago High School bathroom stall, put her baby in a back pack and place it in a dumpster behind the school. Ritchie asks how it is that this young woman could not see another option for herself other than the one she chose. Ritchie goes on to describe to us the multiple layers of abuse, neglect, and disregard Black women face in personal relationships, in their communities, and within society at large.

Key in Ritchie's assessment of the present conditions of Black women in prison is the way in which they are caught between a White feminist anti-violence agenda that acknowledges the ongoing violence against women (and has garnered mainstream acceptance even among conservative policy makers and politicians) and Black community organizing efforts that do not pay sufficient attention to matters of gender-related inequality and violence committed against African Americans. Ritchie takes on the conventional analysis of the public policy of crime and victimization and its seeming lack of comprehension of the constraints Black women face would continue to foreclose all but the worst options for them. The intersection of these two forms of subjugation, gender, and inequality constitutes a "zero of the zero" calculus for these women. And in the process Black women in prisons, their babies, and their reproductive integrity are removed from the caring reach of the African American community and the ameliorative capacities of the state. While new laws may not change this situation, a different political vision might at least enable us to comprehend it.

In *Visions of Abolition*, Shigematsu, Granadino, and Chea present an overview of the politics of prison abolition as an alternative to the criminal justice system. It weaves together the voices of women caught in the criminal justice system alongside leading prison scholars Angela Davis and Ruth Gilmore who provide a structural, historical, and theoretical framework for the racial basis of incarceration and imprisonment in the United States. The stories of women in the Watts area of Los Angeles are as remarkable and quotidian as are the stories in the two previous texts, which show the experience of women whose lives do not exist on the map of what is understood as a humane society. These stories give way to the most important part of the documentary, the work of Susan Burton. Burton, who was awarded a CNN Heroes prize in 2010, is a formerly incarcerated woman who became dependent on drugs and spent more than ten years in and out of the prison system, all of which was triggered by the death of her five-year-old son after he was struck by a car driven by an off-duty police officer. Determined to make a change, she began the "A New Way of Life Reentry Project," which provided shelter and space for women in Los Angeles to avoid the vicious cycle of imprisonment.

Working with narrative and personal stories is challenging and it is important to think critically about the sensationalism that can emerge from graphic accounts of violent abuse. Black women's bodies have always been in danger of existing as sensationalized objects, even when involved in the context of abolitionist and anti-slavery movements. Critical Black feminist writers and critics have walked the fine line between trying to represent "scenes of subjection" and unspeakable horror that are central to the nature of US (and particularly as a prison nation) politics, and its perverse notions of justice.

Since Black women are always figured by the state as outside of the morality tales of state making, such inexplicable forms of violence tend to fall through the cracks even in work by prison abolitionists. However, what the stories accomplish is the capacity to address and be engulfed by the violence that exceeds the law. It is not unimaginable, inexplicable, gratuitous violence for its own sake. It is the kind of violence that Franz Fanon tells us goes into the interior life and undoes distinctions between interiors and exteriors, private and public, particularly for women of color. So, if attention is paid to the role of the state and the inherent violence in the law, a new form of political work may emerge in which the humanity of imprisoned Black women plays a central role.

Ofelia Cuevas
University of California, LA

Notes

1.   Women's Prison Association Report, *Hard Hit: The Growth in the Imprisonment of Women, 1977–2004*, http://www.wpaonline.org/institute/hardhit/
2.   Angela Davis, *Are Prisons Obsolete?* Seven Stories Press, Amanda George 211–12 cited on page 82.
3.   Ruth Wilson Gilmore, "Globalization and US Prison Growth: From Military Keynesianism to Post-Keynesian Militarism," *Race and Class* 40, nos. 2–3 (1998–1999).

Moore, Mignon R. *Invisible Families: Gay Identities, Relationships, and Motherhood among Black Women* (Berkeley, CA: University of California Press, 2011), $27.95, 318 pp. ISBN: 978-0-520-26952-1 (cloth).

The field of queer studies emerged in the late 1980s and early 1990s mostly in English departments, women's and gender studies, and other humanities-based disciplines. White gay men were the center of much of the research produced during the nascent years of the field with some attention given to White lesbians. Not until the intervention of Black queer studies in the last decade has there been a focus on queer communities of color. Mignon R. Moore's *Invisible Families* follows on the heels of important work in Black queer studies, but from within the discipline of sociology. This is an important distinction given the scant research on race and sexuality in the social sciences.

Moore's title is perhaps a misnomer, for it suggests that the book is about lesbian parents—which it is—but only partially. The title actually signifies in multiple ways: it is an indictment of the Black community's failure to "see" and affirm lesbian existence in the community; and it is a critique of social science research—including sociology—that has failed to conduct research on Black lesbian life. Throughout the book, however, Moore examines the resistance to this invisibility through the empirical and qualitative data gathered from a hundred Black and Latina lesbians in the New York metropolitan area, and by employing an intersectional approach to the experiences of the subjects in the study that "lie at the intersection of single dimensions of those and other categories" (4) and by theorizing race as a structuring paradigm in Black lesbian families. Focusing on how these women negotiate their identity within the context of Black communities where most of them reside is the framing logic of the text. The result is a thoroughly researched and nuanced study of Black lesbian life experiences within and outside the institutions of community, family, work, and religion.

Invisible Families is divided into an introduction, six chapters, and a conclusion. The introduction provides an overview of the extant literature in sexuality studies and studies of the family, pointing out the myopic focus on White, middle-class lesbian families, at the expense of working-class lesbian families of color. Moore also engages postmodern theorists who "understand identity categories to be so inconsistent, transient, and unstable that they are virtually meaningless" (5). Instead, Moore argues that identity—and particularly racial identity—"remains a relatively stable and slowly changing power system in the way it structures the life chances of Black Americans" (5). She also notes that while other studies have employed traditional methods for soliciting lesbian research subjects (e.g., flyers, posting at nightclubs, and public advertisements), these methods are ineffective among Black lesbian communities where social events, especially those held at people's homes, are much more effective spaces to recruit participants for research.

Chapters 1 to 3 focus on identity formation as it relates to lesbian sexuality, gender presentation, and self-understanding and group membership. The theorizations in these chapters analyze how Black women process their sexuality within various variables such as race, class, and gender as they *intersect*. The first chapter develops a typology of lesbian identity as women move from private to public expressions of their sexuality. The four types of lesbians that Moore describes on the basis of her subjects are "straight-up gays," or those who identified as gay at any early age; "conformists," or those who conformed to social norms and had heterosexual relationships before coming to terms with their sexuality; "hetero-identified," or those who never had same-sex attraction until adulthood and led heterosexual lives; and "sexually fluid," or those who disavow labels and believe that sexuality is what one does and not who one is. Moore uses these categories to discuss how the women so labeled negotiate their lesbian identity relative to race and class. Chapter 2 develops a second typology that characterizes gender presentation among the subjects—for example, "femme," "gender bender," "transgressive"—that become salient indicators of how, again, race and class are imbricated in lesbian identity. For example, Moore finds that middle-class women are more likely to embody a "femme" or "gender bender" gender presentation than working-class women, mostly due to their aspirations of Black respectability. Chapter 3 examines how Black lesbians' self-understandings of race, gender, and sexuality affect their sense of community and group belonging. The key finding here is that most women's sense of group belonging is situational, depending on a number of factors, such as whether the person was "the first" of her racial category to break a color barrier.

Chapters 4 to 6 draw on the findings and discussions in the first three on how Black women process lesbian identity to examine how it affects the institution of family. Chapter 4 actually draws on case studies of five families to provide a range of examples of how identity markers/intersections impact lesbian motherhood, while Chapter 5 discerns how couples embrace or disavow lesbian-feminists' promotion of egalitarianism within the household. The final chapter engages the way these women negotiate their Black and religious communities.

As Moore notes in the introduction and conclusion, *Invisible Families* is the first book of its kind to fully engage the complexity of lesbian identity with race as the critical lens of analysis. But perhaps more importantly, *Invisible Families* provides a multidimensional portrait of Black lesbian life by accounting for how these women *process* their own sexuality and how, in turn, that process informs the ways in which they move within the various social worlds that they traverse. While Moore is trained as a sociologist and certainly speaks to that audience in the text, her analysis also draws on Black queer studies, cultural studies, and other humanities-based theories to render an interdisciplinary perspective of Black lesbian identity. The payoff is that the book resonates far beyond the field of sociology, while also filling a void in social science research on sexual minorities and the institution of family.

Moore suggests that New York "is the best place to study gay populations of color" (14). Some might contest this statement as another example of a bi-coastal bias on research of queer people in general. For her part, Moore justifies the focus on New York based on the number of social events that cater to Black lesbians and, in an extended footnote, she notes that the 2000 Census lists New York as having the greatest number of Black same-sex unmarried partner households. Still, I wonder how the data would change for subjects living outside the Northeast and in rural areas. Recent Census Bureau information reveals, for example, that gay parenting is more prevalent in the South, particularly among queers of color in places like Jacksonville, Fl.[1] What might this new trend tell us about southern culture relative to acceptance and/or tolerance of non-traditional families? Moreover, since religion in general, and specifically the Black church in particular, plays such a significant role in the lives of Moore's subjects, I also wonder if the pressures to conform or repress one's sexual identity would be even greater in the Bible Belt where, unlike New York City, religious discourse and culture are woven into just about every aspect of Black culture? Would regional differences of gender roles alter Black lesbians' processing of their sexual identity? I also missed a sustained discussion of HIV/AIDS and its impact on these women. Although Black lesbians as a demographic have not been as disproportionately infected by the disease as their heterosexual-identified counterparts, I cannot imagine that it has not affected their social and sexual interactions, especially for those women who reside in the category, "sexually fluid."

Despite these questions, most of which reflect my own regional bias toward the South as an understudied region relative to (homo)sexuality, I believe that *Invisible Families* is a foundational text that will inevitably reframe the way sexuality studies in the social sciences and humanities thinks about race, class, and gender. Indeed, the text will be very useful as a way to introduce students to complex processes of sexual identity formation as it relates to other attendant identity markers such as race, gender expression, and social class. In turn, the book also affirms Black lesbians as not only worthy of scholarly research, but also as a group whose own agency resists the very invisibility their social world tries to impose upon them.

E. Patrick Johnson
Northwestern University

Note

1. See, for example, Sabrina Travernise's, "Parenting by Gays More Common in the South, Census Shows," *New York Times*.com, January 18, 2011, http://www.nytimes.com/2011/01/19/us/19gays.html?page-wanted=all.

Clay, Andreana. *The Hip-Hop Generation Fights Back: Youth, Activism, and Post-Civil Rights Politics* (New York: New York University Press, 2012), $23.00, 240 pp. ISBN: 978-0-814-71717-2 (paper).

It's Gonna Get Hard

To "incarnate the people," Franz Fanon, in *The Wretched of the Earth*, presciently warned us that

> We ought not to cultivate the exceptional or to seek for a hero, who is another form of leader. We ought to uplift the people; we must develop their brains, fill them with ideas, change them and make them into human beings . . . [for] each generation must out of relative obscurity discover its mission, fulfill it, or betray it.[1]

Andreana Clay in *The Hip-Hop Generation Fights Back: Youth, Activism, and Post-Civil Rights Politics* characterizes today's youth activism and the struggles by young people of color for social justice as a search not unlike what Fanon and Aimé Césaire called, "to invent souls."[2] The young people who Clay detailed in this important contribution to the study of contemporary social movements and protest politics live and work in Oakland, California, a place its Poet Laureate, Ishmael Reed calls, "an American wonder."[3] Oakland is a storied urban space graced with political activism and some of twentieth century's most potent campaigns against *unfreedom* and for justice in the United States. Indeed, from the resistance against the Klux Klux Klan in the 1920s and the Oakland general strike of 1946, to the Panthers and Black Power Movement of the 1960s, the welfare rights and anti-Apartheid struggles of the 1980s, and the anti-displacement and anti-prison protests of the 1990s, not to mention the Occupy Wall Street general strike and the Oscar Grant protests of the twenty-first century, Oakland assuredly has much to teach us about social protests and inventing souls in this era of financial entrapment, community dislocation, mass incarceration, and premature death.

Out of relative benign and not so benign federal, state, and municipal neglect for more than five decades and countering the perceived narcissistic apathy and cynicism that characterized their generational cohorts, the Oakland youth of color, as Clay tells us, have consciously forged an identity and a politics of their own. Framed as part of "the hip-hop generation," and within the context of "post-civil rights politics," the disenfranchised Oakland youth, Clay argues, influenced both by past social movements as well as hip-hop, are formulating their own identity as activists and as citizens, and in so doing, they fashion new strategies for youth activism, community mobilization, and social change. As stated in her first chapter, "Youth: Crisis, Rebellion and Identity," three central questions guided this ethnographic research: (1) "How do dominant representations of activism, which reflect previous social movements and struggles, inform how youth of color, members of the 'hip-hop generation' participate in social change processes?" (2) "How is youth activism affected by the activism of previous social movements as well as the current backlash against civil rights?" (3) "How does this participation, combined with dominant representations of activism, inform their political and activist identities" (4)?

Today, in Oakland, more than one in five residents lives in poverty,[4] and for children, this rate is much higher at nearly 30 percent[5]; the unemployment rate for the age group of sixteen to nineteen years (and those who are also not in school) stands at 86 percent[6], while the high school drop-out rate is nearly 28 percent.[7] It is against this backdrop that Clay's study of youth activism seems particularly cogent, and campaigns to empower and mobilize young people seem ever more urgent. Focusing on two Oakland-based, non-profit organizations, Teen Justice (TJ) and Multicultural Alliance (MA) and their activities, Clay attempted to "construct a genealogy and social history of the origins of youth activism in the post-civil rights era by providing an in-depth examination of the framing strategies, missions and influence, and assessment of the outcomes of the overall programs of Teen Justice and Multicultural Alliance" (19). TJ's campaigns for justice centers on "developing multiracial leadership and student organizing in their community and on high school campuses," while MA's "primary tool for creating this society free from oppression is teaching youth to facilitate anti-oppression workshops with other youth in Oakland" (17–18). Although Clay does not dwell on the specificities of the hip-hop generation or problematize that characterization, she echoes the argument that, "Hip-hop music often acts as a base for social protests among today's youth . . . [and it] can be a powerful tool in communicating to an outside audience what it means to be a youth of color in this particular historical moment" (93). The most important contribution of Clay's work, however, is her careful attention to the ways in which the young people of Oakland in general, and members of TJ and MA in particular, are deliberately and consciously active as citizens of their communities (especially in and around their schools), formulating and reformulating both what it means to be an activist, and demonstrating our own era's effervescent hope and sublime optimism in the process.

Apropos of the era in question, Clay paints broad strokes of the urban landscape to draw attention to the structural inequalities and the politics of backlash that activists must confront, namely concentrated poverty, housing segregation, police abuse, gentrification, educational divestment, not to mention the anti-immigrant and anti-affirmative action anxieties and their corresponding legislative campaigns. Clay argues that youth of color activists organize in light of the "burden" of the sixties, and "keeping it real" thus becomes an essential part of their activist toolkit (4–16). She found that "Drawing upon activist models of the past, contemporary youth are involved in traditional modes of protest and organizing . . . . In addition, youth take organizing tools into their everyday interactions at school, at work, with their families, and among their friends" (178–79). Among her many insights, Clay is convinced that this strategy is one of their most frequently employed tactics and also their most effective tool for interrupting racism and homophobia (179). Perhaps gifted by a more sophisticated reckoning of race/gender/sexual identities, TJ and MA members are more adept at forming multicultural alliances and organizing across race, gender, and sexual lines. Clay, thus, concludes that "By performing these acts of resistance and identifying as activists, the youth challenge the dominant understanding of activism by taking action to change their communities, however they define them" (179). She further suggests that these insights are critical to scholarly understanding of contemporary activism and social change.

Indeed, scholars of social movements as well as community activists of all ages would do well to heed Clay's insights so that we may better comprehend contemporary reper- toires of resistance, especially her careful attention to the salience of culture for political activism. This reader, however, laments the lack of greater attention paid to grassroots youth organizing (independent of the nonprofit structure or what Andrea Smith calls, "the non-profit industrial complex")[8] and the loosely affiliated mass youth protests such as those associated with the larger mobilization by communities of color against police abuse and prison construction including those against Propositions 184, 187, and 209.[9] Moreover, as racial capitalism and White supremacy have become increasingly more articulated and conceited in popular culture and the political process—characterized by the Supreme Court decision in *Citizens United*, the multi-billion dollar presidential campaign of 2012, and the concerted and aggressive attempt to roll back the voting rights of poor and people of color, coupled with the increasingly ever larger population who are either marked as criminal or heavily indebted persons or both—an emphasis on leadership training seems disappointing, however momentarily empowering it might be for a chronically disenfranchised group to think so. The work of social transformation, particularly one that may foment a feminist, socialist, and multicultural democracy as hip-hop-influenced Oakland youth activists intimately understand, would seem to include the work of inventing souls, not just inventing leadership. In "I Beg of You," Bambu, a Los Angeles based rapper (who from time to time collaborates with various Oakland based musicians), sums up well the pleasures, hard work, and acute consciousness of today's youth of color activism that extend what Clay suggests in the book:

Chorus:

. . . Will you please clap you hands.
Now get off on your feet
I beg of you to get up and dance
It's such a crazy, kick ass beat.

Very rarely do the poor gets opportunity like this,
to speak in front of thousands of kids and they listen and shit . . .

I just tell them I'm the same
my mama still rides the bus
my uncle's still smoking stuff
my credit's still fucked up.
That's the beginning of ground work
building on that face to face
and not just on that face book
organizing on the twitter page . . .

Hey I'm the same,
I speak that shit when I'm on stage
but if you knew me
you would know that I organize in L.A.

'cause I do recognize that music ain't no genuine change
merely your way to raise the way you thought the game got played
to get you to thinking about you critically . . . .

Not unlike many radical iterations of hip-hop, and as Clay keenly observes, the Oakland youths of color, queer and otherwise, are "not confused about their participation in the construction of history," nor are they naïve about the dispersed circuits of power (190). They know intimately their work is "gonna get hard." So, it is in Clay's sampling of Oakland youth of color activism that we glean that the very definition of activism gets (re)articulated to include the everyday life routines of young people of color and the ways in which they have creatively enlivened and embodied activism, something oddly but frequently marginalized in much of social movement literature, but a seemingly necessary task for any generation that seeks to author the content of its time.

H. L. T. Quan
Arizona State University

Notes

1. Franz Fanon, *The Wretched of the Earth* (New York: Grove Press, 1963), 197, 206.
2. Ibid., 197.
3. Ishmael Reed, *Blues City: A Walk in Oakland* (New York: Crown Journeys, 2003).
4. The 2010 U.S. Census records a rate of 22.3 percent among Oakland residents.
5. The National KIDS Counts also reports nearly 16 percent of Oakland's children are living in extreme poverty (American Community Survey's Census Data 2008–2011 series as compiled by the National KIDS Count).
6. American Community Survey's Census Data 2008–2011 series as compiled by the National KIDS Count.
7. California Department of Education's 2011 Oakland Unified School District data series.
8. INCITE! Women of Color against Violence, *The Revolution Will Not Be Funded: Beyond the Non Profit Industrial Complex* (Boston, MA: South End Press, 2009).
9. These California propositions sought to impose mandatory sentencing for "three strikes," limit social services to immigrants, and bar against affirmative action, respectively.

Cohen, Cathy. *Democracy Remixed: Black Youth and the Future of American Politics* (New York: Oxford University Press, 2010), $27.95, 304 pp. ISBN: 978-0-19537-800-9 (cloth).

In the wake of the killing of seventeen-year-old Trayvon Martin, the subsequent acquittal of his killer, the underlying messages about the value of young Black life, and the striking contrast with assertions by President Obama as evidence of "post-racialism," Cathy Cohen's 2010 work *Democracy Remixed: Black Youth and the Future of American Politics* provides a framework for distilling the complex space in which we now find ourselves. The text is about "the uncertain place of young Black people in our political communities," examining the ways in which the agency of Black youth interacts with the structures that stand, to a great degree, in opposition to them.

Cohen analyzes the contested and conflicted space occupied by Black youth, along with the political consequences of being young and Black. She asserts that there is a "politics of invisibility," which mutes the voices and needs of young Black people from the political milieu to such a degree that it creates a national crisis. Drawing quantitative data from the Black Youth Project, the Mobilization, Change and Political and Civic Engagement Study, as well as qualitative focus group data, *Democracy Remixed* works to amplify the voices of young Black people, to measure their positions on subjects that include, hip-hop, sexuality, government legitimacy, economic conditions, the criminal justice system, and their own sense of political buy-in and investment. Cohen's analysis examines the responses of Black youth to each phenomenon and then goes further, to unearth both the internal and external structural questions related to each subject area, or how the effects of individual agency vis-à-vis the institutional impacts compare with each other. She challenges the way democracy has been practiced in the United States by interrogating questions of marginalization, isolation, and exclusion.

The underlying premise of the book is that with the silencing of Black youth comes an erosion of democracy. By both seeking to shift existing structures and elevating the agency of Black youth themselves, we experience the "remix" that, as with hip-hop, builds on a classic base (the premise of democracy), and offers a reinterpretation that is fuller, more complex, more exciting, and carries greater resonance than the original. The remix serves as a rethinking of what it means to be young and Black in the context of a political system that stands as the antithesis of "the good" for that cohort, and most often seeks to pathologize Black youth, blaming them for their own oppression. Cohen breaks down the intragroup Black dynamic in which Civil Rights generation Black elites are often privileged as spokespersons for Blackness and, most often, parrot the deficit thinking of the White supremacist patriarchal capitalist establishment, creating a moral panic. While this generational and class divide is not new, "[w]hat is different today is the access some black elites have to the dominant media, where construction of black pathology by black elites is able to reach a broader public, including various white communities and public officials" (27–28). The result is a secondary marginalization of Black youth, the first coming from White-dominated society, and the second through the affirmation of older Black elites. What Cohen makes clear is that the moral panic that ensues is not simply a matter of rhetoric, but translates into public policy, as exemplified by over-policing that further entrenches the marginal status of Black youth. Remixing democracy requires the challenging of dominant rhetoric that places the responsibility for the success of Black youth on Black youth themselves (along with their parents), and examining the interaction between the agency of Black youth and the political structures that shape and frame their realities.

This is not to say that Black youth are absolved of all responsibility for their life choices. Cohen begins her work with a personal account of her nephew, Terry, and how the decisions that he made, along with the structures that have been erected to stand in the way of "success" for Black youth, shaped his reality. Instead, Cohen places the role of individual choice and decision making in context, arguing that while the choices made may be their own, it is more difficult for Black youth to recover from poor decisions. "[Y] oung black people—like other young people—make good decisions and bad decisions, but too often do not have the resources, buffers, and opportunities to recover from them" (79). Black youth acknowledge this interaction, recognizing the role that structural issues and personal responsibility play in outcomes.

One of the most striking findings of Cohen's work is the extremely high level of civic and political, engagement of Black youth despite a general feeling of political alienation. The election of Barack Obama has contributed notably to the increased political engagement of Black youth. Cohen notes that Black youth out-participate all other young people. "Being young and black is currently a positive predictor of civic engagement" despite the fact that "Black youth more than any other group of young people, hold negative views of government" (116, 117). Cohen explains, "These young people have not given up on the promise of our democracy, but they are sorting out the conflicting messages this country is sending—on the one hand the uplifting promise of equality witnessed in the election of Obama and on the other hand the renewed second-class citizenship of black people, witnessed in the country's and specifically the government's unwillingness to devote the resources needed to save and support the survivors of Hurricane Katrina" (150).

The final two chapters close with a discussion of Black youth and mass mobilization, underscoring how Black youth have shifted the dynamics of mobilization through their use of technology, their identification of nongovernmental (namely corporate) targets, and the ways in which they deploy the political history of Black politics. Cohen places us in a third wave that has moved from a highly racialized strategy in the first wave (1970s), and a technocratic approach in the second wave (1990s), to the deracialized strategy adopted by President Obama and others as the third wave. Third wavers sometimes engage in public reprimands of the Black poor in order to "demonstrate to white voters that they are willing to take on their own black community. They must prove that they are not *race* leaders but *raced* leaders, a title imposed, but not embraced" (210). Politicians of this hue have been able to capture the imaginations of constituents through the introduction of abstract ideals like "hope" and "change." While Black youth, especially middle- class

Black youth, have been excited by both the rhetoric and the Obama presidency, the study also reveals their skepticism about the President's ability to change their conditions. Instead, Black youth point to their own agency. "[T]he true empowerment of young people cannot be imposed on them. It is a process that must develop from their leadership, insight and experience" (235).

Cohen's work is a tremendous contribution to amplifying the voices of young Black people, elevating their conditions, and presenting the interactions between political structures and individual agency. Her work also points to how the notion of linked fate creates a sense of embarrassment, fear, and retreat on the part of some members of the Black elite, and how it compels action on the part of Black youth. The author's multivariate analysis, especially in teasing out the relationship between hip-hop and political engagement, is particularly interesting and opens the door for further research. With young hip-hop listeners being more skeptical of government and more civically engaged, the question is whether or not hip-hop might serve as a catalyst for mass mobilization. Three years after the volume's publication, Cohen's focus group findings that indicate the centrality of issue-based participation among Black youth has been clearly illustrated in the work of the Dream Defenders and youth who have organized around the Trayvon Martin killing. Additional questions that warrant research include how to grow these issue-based mobilizations into enduring movements, how to remedy the clear generational and class gaps within the Black community, and what strategies can be utilized to "remix" the institutions that lock out and target Black youth.

Melina Abdullah
California State University, Long Beach

The Editors: A Note on Passing:
William (Nick) Nelson and Hanes Walton, Jr.

A Note on Passing

Hanes Walton, Jr. (1941–2013)
William (Nick) Nelson (1941–2013)

The discipline of political science and the field of Black politics lost two giants during 2013. Hanes Walton, Jr. died on January 14. William (Nick) Nelson left us on May 13. Both were path breakers whose work was foundational for our field. Both mentored scholars who are conducting today's cutting-edge research. Both published in the *National Political Science Review* (*NPSR*) and cast their luster on the journal. Nick was a past president of National Conference of Black Political Scientists (NCOBPS). Until their last days, they continued to produce seminal work. Therefore, it is altogether fitting—even if serendipitous—that perhaps the last academic work penned by either person should appear in this issue of the *NPSR*. It is equally appropriate that the two are present in their prototypical roles of scholar and mentor. Nick co-authored, with Stefanie Chambers, the article, "Black Mayoral leadership in New Orleans: Minority Incorporation Revisited." Stefanie was able to tell him, before he passed, that their article had been accepted for publication. Hanes wrote an encouraging book review, filled with fulsome praise for Lisa Nikol Nealy's book, *African American Women Voters: Racializing Religiosity, Political Consciousness and Progressive Action in U.S. Presidential Elections from 1964 through 2008.* We are proud of the concrete manifestations, in these pages, of the blooming and flowering of their continuing legacies.

The Editors

The National Political Science Review (NPSR)
Invitation to the Scholarly Community

The editors of *The National Political Science Review* (NPSR) invite submissions from the scholarly community for review and possible publication.

The NPSR is a refereed journal of the National Conference of Black Political Scientists. Its editions appear annually and comprise the highest quality scholarship related to the experiences of African Americans in the American political community as well as in the wider reach of the African diaspora in the Western Hemisphere. It also focuses on the international links between African Americans and the larger community of nations, particularly with Africa.

Among the more common areas of research, which the NPSR considers for publication, are those typically associated with political behavior and attitudes, the performance of political institutions, the efficacy of public policy, interest groups and social movements, inter-ethnic coalition building, and theoretical reflections that offer insights on the minority political experience. On the basis of recent interest, the NPSR also considers work on the role of culture in politics.

Manuscripts should be submitted in the following format. Submissions should follow the style conventions of the *American Political Science Review* (APSR). Two copies of the submissions should be conveyed electronically to the editors at the email addresses listed below. One copy of the submission should include the author's or authors' information comprising the name that will appear in the published version along with the author's/authors' institutional affiliation and email addresses. The other copy should delete the author's/authors' information from the title page. Please indicate the lead author and his/her email address in cases of multiple authors. Manuscripts should not carry footnotes at the bottom of the page but should be inserted as endnotes. They should not exceed thirty typewritten pages, should be double spaced, inclusive of notes and references, and should be prepared and sent to the editors in the Microsoft Word format.

Manuscripts are reviewed on a rolling basis. However, submissions should be received no later than July 1 of the current year to be considered for publication in a forthcoming issue.

Further queries about the NPSR as well as submissions may be addressed (email only) to the editors at:

Michael Mitchell
Co-Editor of the NPSR
School of Politics and Global Studies
Arizona State University
Email: michael.mitchell@asu.edu

David Covin
Co-Editor of the NPSR
Government Department (Emeritus)
California State University-Sacramento
Email: covindl@csus.edu